2

SECRET
INGREDIENTS

■ ● ▲

MICHAEL ROBERTS
■●▲
SECRET INGREDIENTS

BANTAM BOOKS

TORONTO · NEW YORK · LONDON · SYDNEY · AUCKLAND

For Daniel Adams

SECRET INGREDIENTS
A Bantam Book / November 1988

LIBRARY OF CONGRESS

Library of Congress Cataloging-in-Publication Data

Roberts, Michael, 1949–
  Secret ingredients / Michael Roberts.
    p. cm.
  Includes index.
  ISBN 0-553-05320-5
  1. Cookery. I. Title.
TX715.R644 1988   88-14029
641.5—dc19   CIP

Published simultaneously in the United States and Canada

Bantam Books are published by Bantam Books, a division of Bantam Doubleday Dell
Publishing Group, Inc. Its trademark, consisting of the words "Bantam Books" and
the portrayal of a rooster, is Registered in U.S. Patent and Trademark Office and in
other countries. Marca Registrada. Bantam Books, 666 Fifth Avenue, New York,
New York 10103.

PRINTED IN THE UNITED STATES OF AMERICA
DH   0 9 8 7 6 5 4 3 2 1

ACKNOWLEDGMENTS

■ ● ▲

Maureen and Eric Lasher, my agents, approached me out of the blue one day and asked me if I had ever considered writing a cookbook. *Secret Ingredients* is the result—thank you both.

Charlene Castle, who tested all the recipes for this book, is never content with routine answers. Her irreverence for accepted kitchen mythology—she adores playing devil's advocate—always provoked me into improving a recipe or finding a better way of completing a kitchen task. Everyone, cook or not, should be lucky enough to have a Charlene Castle.

It is one thing to know what you want to say, and another to be able to communicate it. In writing this book I was very lucky to have had the help of Janet Spiegel, a woman who has eaten and understood my cooking for years, and who always knows what I mean to say about it. She mended everything I wrote so that my editors and readers could understand it better. I now call her "Doc."

A chef is, in a sense, an editor. He edits the marketplace looking for ingredients; he edits his own ideas, those of his second chefs, cooks, and even those of his customers. I am lucky to have a staff at Trumps who I can inspire and who, in turn, not only inspire me, but who force me to "keep up." I mention especially Don Dickman, Lil Miller, Jeanette Holley, and Raul Lujan . And I cannot forget my partners—Jerry Singer, Doug Delfeld, Waldo Fernandez, and the late Sheldon Andelson—who accepted my frequent absences from the kitchen because they believed I could write this book. And, of course, without the faith of my customers I would have no forum in which to explore new ideas.

Steve Rubin "acquired" me for Bantam, and for this I shall always be grateful, even when we play bridge. Coleen O'Shea put up with me while I tried to reinvent the cookbook, and Fran McCullough pulled the final drafts together into a coherent book. What a team!

I have always gotten somewhat blind encouragement from Lucille and Sidney Roberts, my parents. Though they couldn't fathom why I wanted to cook professionally, they believed that I could do it. And they are even happier that I have written about it.

CONTENTS

■●▲

A COOK'S PROGRESS

■●▲

Marc Chagall's painting and my mother's approach to food share something in common. Apparently unrelated objects are always strewn around his canvases, ungrounded and floating freely in space and time—but in the midst of the chaos you sense that these elements are there for an important reason. In our family eating had its own *raison d'être,* completely unrelated to anything practical, such as nourishment. Hungry or not, we were presented with food wherever and whenever—and in strange combinations, too. Steak could be followed by fruit and spaghetti, followed by chicken, followed by Jell-O mold, followed by potato salad and French fries. Eating wasn't confined to traditional mealtimes, although we had meals, too, in between eating. I don't know what food symbolizes to a mother, but as a child, of course, I didn't bother to wonder at it because I loved to eat.

When my mother made eggplant *parmigiana,* I insisted that she save a piece so I could have it cold for breakfast the next morning. Of course I was not a model child. It was okay not to like eggs, but no one could fathom why a child didn't like sweets. Even then, I liked butter best. (That should have told them everything.) The tastes, aromas, and textures of food have always had a strong effect on me, but I must confess that, for many years, eating itself was as important to me as food.

Recently a friend I hadn't seen in years reminded me of a dinner party I threw in high school. I don't even remember what was served except for an onion soup that somebody else made, but we both remembered how sophisticated we felt that evening. At that age dining without one's parents usually meant having a hamburger at a drive-in, so there was definitely something seductively mature about sitting down to a dinner no one's mother had prepared. It was decided that this had been a very cool thing to do. Often we don't realize what cultural totems the rituals of the table are. Being host, cook, and director of a successful social gathering made a powerful impression on me. Perhaps this was my first foray into the restaurant business, and perhaps right then I got hooked on cooking as theater. I was always a very good eater, but *dining* was a new experience, and I liked it.

I began to cook seriously when I was in college, living in a large apartment on New York's prefashionable Lower East Side. I was studying musical composition at New York University, but I didn't know yet that I had little talent in my chosen field. I would relieve my frustrations by cooking and soon learned that my kitchen compositions were far superior to my musical ones. I loved cooking—and because anyone who loves to cook also loves to please, I happily surrendered to the compliments. (Vanity is an established tradition among cooks.)

The next milestone came on my twenty-first birthday, when my college roommates bought me a copy of *Larousse Gastronomique.* Reading it through, I became obsessed with the possibilities of culinary improvisation. A musical scale has only 12 tones, but there are hundreds of vegetables in the world. There are no exact recipes in *Larousse* because it is more a dictionary than a cookbook; not knowing what most of the dishes were meant to be, I produced naive versions of classical French dishes. Fortunately it's harder to prepare really bad food than really good food, and I soon gained confidence in the kitchen. What I really enjoyed about cooking, though, was the immediate sense of accomplishment that preparing a meal provided. Because few in my circle cared to cook, I could always muster a full table of friends whenever I needed the creative gratification that eluded me in my musical pursuits. In my mind's eye I couldn't see myself as the obscure, struggling composer, my opus finally being performed posthumously. Rather, I began to see that I belonged in a creative discipline where I could see the results of my efforts before I lost interest in them. I wanted to be able, in the span of a few hours, to invent a dish, then cook and enjoy it.

The celebration of my parents' twenty-fifth wedding anniversary further charted the cook's progress. By myself I masterminded the large party and cooked the dinner. Although I was forced to serve the failed fish mousse as a chilled soup, I didn't apologize, and no one knew. I came closer to the mark with a *riz de veau à la financière,* and the *pâté de foie en croute* became standard in my repertoire for a couple of years. The party and the food were a great success. Having orchestrated the event, I got to direct what 50 people did for an evening and I loved the feeling. My parents and their friends were the actors and the food the props in this piece of living theater that I had just created. The fire kindled in me that night cooked the goose of my musical career.

My first cooking job after graduation was a disaster for the restaurant that hired me, one with an international hodgepodge menu. I relied on cookbooks for such things as Moroccan *couscous,* Thai *sate,* French *blanquette,* and who-remembers-what-else. I correctly followed recipes and found the preliminary preparations—the peeling, chopping, and mincing—hypnotic. Many of the ingredients and flavors intrigued me, and finally I gave up striving for culinary authenticity, put away the cookbooks, and began to improvise. Here at last was a peek at the self-expression I had not achieved through music, and I sensed that one day I would truly be able to express myself through food. However, the owner didn't change the restaurant's cuisine from international to improvisational, and I found myself seeking new work.

My second job, at Lady Astor's, across from the Public Theater in New York, was more successful than the first one, although hindsight tells me that the food must have been pretty strange. I was in my discovery period, and everything I discovered found its way onto the restaurant's small menu. Amazed that I could cook, I didn't bother to think about what it was that I was cooking. If one ingredient was good, then five ingredients had to be five times better, right? This was not great food thinking.

When new cooks are in their discovery period, they tend either to cook things in a pastry or stuff smaller ingredients such as quails into larger ingredients such as ducks. In the early seventies I discovered beef Wellington while working at Lady Astor's. As if fillet of beef, pâté stuffing, and pureed mushrooms in a pastry crust were not enough, I served mine with both Madeira and Béarnaise sauces and decorated them with a small nosegay of fresh flowers. The dish was a perfect example of beginners' mistakes, but fresh flowers on the plate gave it flair, and it must have tasted good, too, because a lot of people ordered it and seemed satisfied. It's nothing I would ever do now, but I was learning.

Not content to remain self-taught, I went to Paris in 1975. I was determined first to learn the language and then to get a more rigorous foundation in cooking than the one I had received in music. At the school I attended, l'Ecole Jean-Ferrandi, I learned basic principles of cooking and received a Certificat d'Aptitude Professionnel, the equivalent in this country of a vocational high school diploma. I was even certified English-speaking by the French Minister of Education. The course emphasized technique, and the most sophisticated discussions were about such things as the sizes of diced vegetables, the consistency of sauces, when to salt red meat, and when to stop whipping cream.

I felt like a downtrodden Dickens hero when we had to prepare diced vegetables with mayonnaise over and over. How cruel, I thought, to come to a country renowned for its food and be taught to prepare the kind of vegetables that I despised as a child. But gradually I realized that if the vegetables are not all cut to exactly the same size, some will overcook while others will be slightly raw. If the water is not salted, the vegetables will not fully develop their flavors. If the green vegetables are not plunged into an ice bath immediately after cooking, they will turn brown. If all the vegetables are not spread on an absorbent cloth to drain, the entire ensemble becomes soggy and the mayonnaise turns watery.

The mastery of basic skills was crucial to my development. The most successful cooking is a synthesis of technique (craft) and style (art). No amount of caviar garnish can moisten a poorly cooked fillet of sole. The finest lobe of *foie gras* is easily ruined by a cook who leaves it too long in the oven. One can design a brilliant combination of ingredients, but if they are not skillfully prepared, the dish is unworthy.

My sojourn in France was valuable for the strict formality it imposed on my cooking style, but on my return to New York I soon realized that a chef is different from a cook. I was confident, maybe even overconfident, in my cooking skills, but I needed to learn how to manage a large group of people. I quickly saw that if I wanted to cook food that reflected my tastes, I would have to be the boss.

I took a job at another New York restaurant called One Fifth Avenue. Here was a large, successful, stylish restaurant, professionally run, where I was second in command, a junior boss. The cuisine was "continental," so I was not confined to a single tradition. This left me philosophically unhampered and I was able to widen my culinary point of view. My solid technical background enabled me to expand my cooking style, add new foods to my cooking vocabulary, and enlarge my repertoire of dishes. My knowledge of beef Burgundy enabled me to create my own Irish stew because the same cooking method—transferring heat through a liquid to draw out flavor—is involved. I knew how the French roast a duck, so it didn't take me long to learn to do it Chinese-style; roasting is a universal technique that depends on a dry transfer of heat to produce a crust, sealing in moisture and flavor. And if one understands the principle of sauté, the concept of stir-fry is not far away; both depend on a quick transfer of heat through the medium of an oil so that moisture doesn't collect in the pan.

I began an informal mental survey of the different uses of certain ingredients. Throwing raw garlic into an aïoli mayonnaise gives a harsh, burning result, while using it cooked in a stir-fried eggplant dish adds a softer yet lingering aroma. If you like mint because it cuts the rich flavor of lamb, you won't necessarily like its taste in Southeast Asian cooking, where mint is used to refresh the palate and diminish the effects of salty soy and hot curries. Ingredients are to recipes as words are to sentences. We can combine and recombine them in many different ways, giving them very different tastes depending on their context.

When I moved to Los Angeles in 1979, I hadn't yet found a way of developing these disparate influences into a cohesive style of cooking. My artistic impulses led me toward combining elements of different cuisines to form something new, yet I felt like someone else's shopping list; all the ingredients were there, but I had no idea what the menu was. It took me a while to realize that I had the ability to take familiar ingredients and present them in a fresh light. I could please myself by putting my stamp on familiar classics. But of course any reinterpretation of a classic must be judged on its own merits. People are not necessarily interested in where the idea comes from. Must we have seen *The Wizard of Oz* to enjoy *The Wiz*? Does my chili taste better if you know that I conceived it as a *cassoulet*? Recipes succeed only because they taste good and they please people, not because they are merely clever or surprising.

I have learned, in my years in the restaurant business, that many people, even very worldly ones, are cautious about trying new foods. They want something familiar—French, Italian, or Chinese food, for example. As a cook I have the opposite interest—the availability of unusual ingredients tantalizes my creativity. My cooking style has evolved to encompass the hundreds of ingredients I've discovered and the many cooking styles I've encountered. I love to browse in ethnic grocery stores, asking questions about tamarind paste or lemon grass. I love to twist familiar things around, giving them a new look, maybe a new taste. This enables me to offer people something familiar, but with a surprise element. I can call a preparation fig *ratatouille* and people will be tempted to taste it because they've never imagined exchanging the eggplant in this traditional Provençal dish for figs.

By 1980, when we opened Trumps in Los Angeles, many of my creations reflected my new style. My renovated *tamale* recipe results in a dish that no Latin American would recognize except for the cornhusk wrapping because instead of stuffing them I feature the garnish on top. I make a *choucroute* that is not traditional in Alsace because it's made with seafood instead of pork. The notion of balancing hot, spicy flavors with sweet ones resulted in braised lamb shoulder with blue cheese, jalapeños, and port (page 158); pears poached in red wine with roquefort cream (page 250); and *brochettes* of peppered beef with sweet and sour peppercorns (page 157). These are theme and variations; they're not completely new because nothing can be, given our fixed repertoire of foods and techniques. Within that framework, though, there's a glorious wealth of possibilities.

Many of the recipes in this book are results of my improvisations at Trumps—and many of the dishes on the menu at Trumps are the result of working out ideas for this book. I have tried to bring my restaurant experiences home (like preparing cured salmon or braised *foie gras*) and sometimes I even bring home cooking into the restaurant (thus the chapter on quick stews). At Trumps I am the chef, but at home I am the cook. Home cooking is not restaurant cooking, yet we must be guided by the same rules of aesthetic and technique. Consider the difference between home and commercial equipment—your oven at home doesn't get as hot as my commercial range, and you can't sauté over the intense heat of a restaurant cooktop, so my recipes are adapted for the home. We all have less help at home than a chef does in a restaurant—there is no one to do the chopping and slicing or to wash up after you. I'm basically a lazy (although not a sloppy) home cook—the meals I prepare at home are less elaborate than the ones I prepare at Trumps because I know what I can do easily at home without becoming bored by a mass of little chores. The recipes in this book reflect this—as you will see, there are restaurant extravaganzas, but they've been streamlined. And there are home specialties, those wonderful dishes—One-Dish Meals, for example—that always taste more satisfying at home than they do in a restaurant. So this is a chef's book, yes, but you may be surprised to see that almost every recipe is easy—some dishes take longer than others to prepare, but my cooking doesn't depend on elaborate techniques beyond the range of the home cook. The heart of it is taste, the magical process of combining flavors.

ABOUT FLAVORS

■ ● ▲

A painter creates a painting by organizing colors and shapes in some coherent way, just as a musician organizes notes into melodies to form a musical composition. Cooking, likewise, is the act of taking basic ingredients and organizing them in a coherent way, using food as the medium and flavor as the message.

Ingredients can be organized into different *kinds* of dishes. Let's say we have chicken on hand. Whether we make a stew, a sauce, a casserole, or a sausage, flavors can be added to give the dish any taste we want. Suppose tarragon is our chosen flavoring. We can make chicken sautéed with tarragon or fried chicken with tarragon gravy. Imagine how different these dishes would be using chile peppers, or even rosemary, in place of tarragon.

Flavor is to food what hue is to color. It is what timbre is to music. Flavor is adjective, food is noun. "Stars and Stripes Forever" played on the banjo sounds different from the same music played on the tuba. Garlic on shrimps is quite unlike the flavor of garlic on steak. Each ingredient has its own particular character, which is altered by every other ingredient it encounters. It would be easy to master the use of flavors if we could simply put them into categories such as sweet, salty, sour, and bitter and assume that any one could be substituted for another flavor in the same category. But intelligent, good cooking is more complicated than that.

Most people who do not cook professionally think that those of us who do have secrets that we will never divulge. There are no such things as secrets in the kitchen, but there *are* secret ingredients, those ingredients that are not tasted but would be missed if they were omitted. A secret ingredient is one that mysteriously improves the flavor of a dish without calling attention to itself. It's either undetectable or extremely subtle. But its presence is crucial because the dish would not be nearly as good without it.

The word *flavor* comes from an Old French word meaning "odor." Taste and smell are irrevocably intertwined. Flavor is the quality of a substance that affects the sense of taste, and the nature of its aroma, whether pleasant, overpowering, or absent, will affect the way it tastes on our palate. For example, when I created chilled puree of beet and watermelon soup (page 26), I used watermelon for its lovely fragrance to make up for the lack of aroma in beets. The perfume of fresh dill in the dressing for pork and green cabbage salad with dill and caper dressing (page 64) makes up for the lack of aroma in capers. In other words, what we want to achieve is a combination of ingredients that pleases both senses. Our sense of smell excites our sense of taste, and when both our senses are excited, the food we eat tastes better. So secret ingredients add dimension to what we cook by making it possible for our tasting senses, taste and smell, to perceive more.

When we use more than one flavor ingredient in preparing a dish, not all of them will be perceived equally. Some will jump out at us and others will be lost. The flavors we taste can be broken down into two categories: primary and secondary flavors. Primary flavors are those that are obvious, such as the flavors of chicken and tarragon in a chicken tarragon, shrimps and garlic in a shrimp scampi, or beef and red wine in a beef *à la Bourguignon*.

Secret ingredients belong in the realm of secondary flavors. However obvious it is that you need tarragon to prepare a chicken tarragon, you would not achieve the most interesting result using *only* tarragon. Tarragon, in this case, needs secondary ingredients—a hint of celery seed and anise—to make it taste more *like* quintessential tarragon and at the same time more *than* tarragon. In this way, primary flavors often depend on secret ingredients to make them more interesting and complex. Using only one herb or spice to achieve a certain taste usually results in a lackluster dish—each mouthful tastes the same. For instance, when I prepare zucchini soup, I always finish it with a little walnut oil and a dash of Pernod. These two secondary flavors are the secret additions, not meant to overpower the zucchini but to keep it lively so that the first spoonful of soup does not taste exactly like the last. When I braise celery in mint jelly, I add tarragon vinegar to stress the celery flavor and make it more provocative. A pinch of curry powder will enhance the flavor of mussels, making their briny quality sweetly aromatic. And I wouldn't dream of letting a bean soup leave my kitchen without a final addition of lemon, the secret ingredient that adds piquancy, zest, and sparkle to the flavor combination.

Whether they function in a primary or secondary way, flavors combine in only three different ways: they marry, oppose, or juxtapose.

FLAVOR MARRIAGES

When flavors marry, they combine to form one taste—either something new or something superior to the original. Curry powder and chili powder are examples of flavor marriages. The combination of herbs and spices in each case creates a completely new flavor, very different from any of the single ingredients. And although curry and chili powder share several of the same ingredients, such as cumin, coriander, garlic, and cayenne, they taste a world apart.

Some secondary flavors marry with primary ones to create a new flavor greater than the sum of its parts, and often two flavors can do the job better than one. Instead of increasing the amount of sherry in a seafood bisque, I add a little brandy to make the sherry taste more prominent. The marriage of the two ingredients, sherry and brandy, creates one flavor, giving a more interesting sherry taste than if we merely added extra sherry. It may sound like an eccentric combination, but vanilla marries with the flavor of lobster, making it taste more like the essence of lobster than lobster does on its own. Sorrel marries with spinach to form a more perfect taste union, and when ginger and molasses marry, they create a flavor superior to either alone.

In another type of marriage, some secret ingredients act as a catalyst. Their function is not only to marry with a primary flavor but to spark a change in it. Garlic, when used as a background flavor, is my favorite catalyst. A hint of garlic will change the way lemon tastes by making it seem more than a merely tart flavor. A lemon/garlic combination is capable of adding a flavor interest that neither lemon nor garlic can accomplish alone. Cooked onions added to any vegetable soup help create a sweeter flavor. Salt is the most common of the catalysts. It marries with other flavors, making them brighter.

Acidic catalysts, such as vinegar, citrus juices, and wine, give backbone to the flavors of a dish; they keep the primary flavors from disappearing. That is why white wine is often used to embolden basil or other fresh herbs in a fish sauce; red wine keeps the flavors of a beef stew intact throughout the long cooking. Vinegar can be used as a catalyst to lift certain flavors out of the background and make them seem more prominent. Potato soup needs a hint of vinegar to make it more interesting, to lift the potato flavor out of the background. In certain parts of the country chili is always served with a cruet of vinegar to enhance the tomato flavor that would otherwise languish below its flavor potential. Lemon or lime juice is the important catalyst in dishes like *seviche* and other raw preparations because it marries all the flavors—and it also "cooks" the protein a bit.

FLAVOR OPPOSITIONS

The cliché "opposites attract" is particularly apt when applied to flavors. Opposite flavors can highlight or cancel each other; they can cut or balance each other.

Opposite flavors can highlight each other by their contrasting natures. Sweet/sour, sweet/salty, sweet/hot, salty/sour, and salty/tart are all opposites. Sometimes these opposites have a surprising effect on each other. You're probably familiar with the flavor transformation of vinegar and sugar to make the classic sweet and sour taste. But you may not realize that the sweetness of ice cream becomes even sweeter when contrasted with salted Spanish peanuts in a tin roof sundae or salted pecans in butter pecan ice cream. Salt and sugar are so opposed, in fact, that when used in equal amounts they cancel each other entirely. Sweet relish helps to cancel the salty flavor of hot dogs. Chinese sauces usually contain some sugar to help balance the saltiness of soy sauce.

Astringent ingredients such as mint, cucumbers, apples, and grapes oppose other flavors by cutting through them. Apples and grapes are popular with cheese because they cut the strong, rich cheese taste. Cucumbers will cut the taste of mustard in a sauce. Mint cuts the fatty sensation of lamb.

Opposite flavors can also be used to balance each other so that no single flavor stands out. A very salty ingredient can be highlighted or canceled with sugar, as we have seen, but it can also be balanced by the use of another flavor opposition, sour or tart. That is why smoked fish tastes better with the addition of lemon juice. And because sour or tart flavors balance salty ones, a lemon butter sauce will need more salt than a thyme butter sauce. Likewise, it is especially helpful to remember that the sourness of vinegar can diminish the taste of salt if we have been too liberal in its use.

Some flavor oppositions are quite familiar to us. Sugar cancels the bitterness of cocoa so that chocolate becomes delicious. Spicy flavors are balanced by sweet or fruity ones. You may not have tried it, but watermelon and Tabasco sauce is a pleasing combination. Sweet wine and black pepper make a delicious sauce. Other combinations that react together in this way are lime and capers or apples and tarragon. Sometimes a flavor is created when we use opposite flavors to balance each other. Fresh mint, dill and cilantro, when combined, form a new flavor. Combine them in equal parts and taste—you'll get the point instantly.

FLAVOR JUXTAPOSITIONS

Because different flavors are sensed on different parts of the tongue and palate and because they are tasted at different times, we can juxtapose them, using flavors side by side or in layers.

The taste buds on the tip of the tongue sense sweet flavors, the salty and sour receptors are along the sides, and the bitter sensors are at the back of the tongue. Although a first bite tasted with the tip of the tongue may not immediately reveal all the flavors of a dish, when flavors are juxtaposed we eventually taste all of them. In my recipe for mustard-fried shrimps (page 199) I flavor the batter with mustard seed and the sauce with tarragon. Putting mustard and tarragon together in both the batter and the sauce does not create as interesting an effect as separating them so that each flavor is tasted at different times. The layering of flavors makes the food we taste more interesting because each mouthful is different. A flavor may be tasted immediately or it may linger in the mouth. Cocktail sauce initially reveals tomato but finishes with horseradish (and lemon is the catalyst that marries them).

Secondary ingredients can be juxtaposed with primary ones to mask a certain aspect of flavor, making it less discernible but without canceling it entirely. Garlic masks the medicinal bitterness of rosemary, leaving mostly its herbaceous scent. This is how the juxtaposition of secret ingredients makes a single herb, such as rosemary, more intricate. I often add a pinch of ground cloves to mask the bitterness in a red-wine reduction without diminishing the presence of the red wine. And sometimes it is desirable to mask the bitter aspect of clove without negating its aromatic quality. Orange accomplishes this quite nicely; spice cakes are much better with orange zest in the recipe. Mulled cider can be sweetly redolent of clove because the apple flavor masks its bitterness.

Knowing how to combine many flavors and aromas to achieve a simple and pure result (and knowing when *not* to combine flavors) will make you a better, more confident cook. The most common mistake cooks make is flavoring a dish with too many herbs and spices. Tarragon and basil are too similar in their peppery flavor yet too contrasting in their aroma to be combined successfully. I would not combine vanilla and garlic, for instance, or oregano and mint because they would not help each other in any of the ways we've seen or combine in a pleasing way. I would not combine mace and nutmeg or allspice and cloves because in both cases the two flavors perform the same function. Arugula and watercress create a spicy muddle when used together in a salad—choose one or the other, combined with some bitter endive or radicchio.

All this may sound like alchemy—somewhat intellectual—when our very real interest in food is anything but; in fact, analyze all this too much and you can easily go right to the vanishing point. But there are the secrets I've learned in 15 years of cooking for thousands of people that I want to share in the hope of demystifying contemporary cooking. Good cooks over the centuries have known these things intuitively—but they've had neither the huge variety of ingredients nor the knowledge of world cuisines that we have today. You have already learned something about primary and secondary flavors, pleasing the nose as well as the taste buds, what secret ingredients can do, and how to use flavors that marry, oppose, and juxtapose each other. As you use the recipes in this book a practical knowledge of using flavors and secret ingredients will be yours.

PEP TALK TO
THE READER

■ ● ▲

Half of cooking is thinking about cooking. By understanding
how certain flavors combine, how certain cooking procedures
work, and why certain methods are appropriate to certain foods,
you can design a dish with a certain flavor. In creating a recipe,
for example, I first choose the ingredients and then choose a
vehicle for presenting them. Let's say I want chicken and baby
artichokes. I can poach them in enough chicken stock to serve in
a bowl as a main-course soup. I can reduce the stock and present
the chicken and artichokes in sauce. I can toss the chicken and
artichokes with pasta. I can flavor the dish *piccata* style with garlic
and lemon, or I can change the entire idea by adding blue cheese
and port to the stock. Ideally, with common sense and experience, a cook should be able to throw together ingredients in any
preferred way, adding something here, changing something there.
Recipes should guide you to produce a particular dish, but they

should not limit you. Rather, they should inspire creativity. As the cook develops confidence, suddenly everything becomes much easier, and the satisfaction becomes greater because self-expression has been achieved.

Few cooks exactly follow a recipe except perhaps the first couple of times they prepare a dish. After that we add something here, change something there. You might add a teaspoon of instant coffee to a pot roast, as my mother does to make its gravy richer, or cook a cream sauce with a half lemon to make it seem lighter. Improvisation is something that we all engage in each time we prepare food. It's impossible to re-create exactly, and we each interpret, bringing something of ourselves to a recipe. Do you prefer peeled or unpeeled potatoes in a potato salad? Do you want to add a large red or a small white onion to it? We each have favorite foods. Do you hate walnuts? Substitute pecans. If you find red meat difficult to digest, don't be afraid to substitute chicken or fish. All cookbooks are meant to help you achieve good results when you cook. Recipes are important, but not as important as the ideas they help to inspire. The ease with which you put ingredients together in a dish, especially flavor ingredients, frees you to experiment, to improvise, and ultimately to prepare a recipe that is appropriate to its setting and exactly to your taste. A recipe in this book may be my idea or even my version of someone else's idea (there's nothing new under the sun), but by preparing it you make that recipe your own. This is one of the most satisfying aspects of cooking. The thrill of creating a successful dish will make the job of preparing food more interesting, so don't be afraid to experiment beyond the recipes. Use the guidelines in the "About Flavors" section, fire up your imagination, and taste—above all, taste thoughtfully.

SOUPS
■●▲

MAKING SOUP

PUREED VEGETABLE SOUPS

Think of the difference in taste and texture between a boiled and a sautéed or roasted vegetable. Boiled or steamed vegetables taste most like the vegetables in their raw state. Sautéed or roasted vegetables develop both a softness and a richness of flavor. In most cases, cooking with a little fat brings out flavors that cannot be achieved by boiling or steaming.

Vegetable soups are prepared in two stages: First the vegetable is cooked slowly without liquid until soft. Then liquid is added to make the soup—but the actual flavor of the soup has already developed in the first step. The longest part of the cooking occurs with no liquid at all, so that most of the water can be eliminated from the vegetable. This is an essential step to ensure the success of all vegetable soups. Green vegetables and other nonroot vegetables need this preliminary cooking to break down the cellulose walls so that the flavor of the vegetables is released.

Root vegetables such as carrots, turnips, and beets contain a lot of sugar and must cook for a long time to release and even to caramelize the sugar. They need to cook longer than the green vegetables, most of which have little or no sugar.

THICKENED CREAM SOUPS

Thickened stock or broth is the basis for *veloutés,* chowders, and bisques. I prefer to use a *roux,* a mixture of butter and flour cooked together, to thicken because it gives a better texture than such thickeners as cornstarch and arrowroot. Always thicken the soup slightly, then let the liquid reduce to its proper consistency. This not only eliminates the floury taste of *roux;* it also concentrates the flavor of the original broth. Finishing the soup with a little cream adds richness and improves both color and texture.

BEAN SOUPS

Dried beans have already been completely deprived of their moisture and need to be rehydrated. They are starchy and not at all aromatic; they create a taste sensation rather than an aroma. So you need to fortify bean soups heavily with aromatic vegetables. The base of aromatics—onion, carrot, and celery—needs to cook slowly in butter or oil with no liquid until the vegetables are soft and sweet before you add the beans and liquid. The recipes for all the bean soups assume the use of dried beans. If you're using fresh beans, adjust the cooking time. I don't recommend that you use canned beans, but if you must, you can of course use the flavors introduced in my recipes to successfully "doctor" your canned vegetables.

VEGETARIAN SOUPS

PUREE OF TOMATO SOUP   SERVES 4 TO 5

Tomato soup is particularly easy to make because you don't need to use stock. Leftover tomato soup makes good tomato sauce; in fact, tomato soup becomes tomato sauce if you cook it long enough.

You'll notice that in the ingredient list below you have your choice of four herbs, balanced any way you'd like. Generally, you should avoid using several herbs or spices that all taste alike, but because of the acidic nature of tomatoes it is better here to use a combination of similar flavors. In this soup, four herbs—basil, oregano, thyme, and marjoram—create a single flavor, one that is more enticing to the palate than using the full amount of only one herb.

¼   cup virgin olive oil
1   medium onion, roughly diced (about ¾ cup)
1½ teaspoons minced garlic
2   pounds plum tomatoes, preferably overripe
1   cup dry white wine
3   tablespoons chopped fresh herbs, any combination of basil,
    oregano, thyme, and marjoram
    salt and freshly ground pepper to taste

Heat the olive oil in a 3-quart heavy stockpot over low heat. Add the onion and cook slowly, without coloring, for about 7 minutes.

Add the garlic, tomatoes, white wine, and herbs. Cover and cook over low heat about 30 minutes, breaking up the tomatoes with a wooden spoon as they soften.

Strain and reserve the liquid. Place the tomatoes in a blender or food processor and puree until very smooth. Add the reserved liquid to the tomato puree and pass the soup through a strainer to remove the tomato skins and seeds.

Taste for salt and pepper. This soup is excellent both hot and cold.

VEGETARIAN NOODLE SOUP

SERVES 6 TO 8

Don't feel confined to the list of vegetables I've suggested for this variation of minestrone; use any and as many different kinds of vegetables as you like. Let seasonal availability be your guide and remember that root vegetables (carrots, parsnips, rutabagas, turnips) take longer to cook than green vegetables (broccoli, zucchini, brussels sprouts, green beans, and peas). Cook the noodles in the vegetable broth just before serving to retain their texture.

2   quarts vegetable stock (page 257)
1   ripe plum tomato
1   tablespoon unsalted butter
½   small onion, finely diced (about ½ cup)
½   small carrot, finely diced (about ⅓ cup)
½   medium turnip, finely diced (about ¾ cup)
1   celery stalk, finely diced (about ½ cup)
1   small zucchini or yellow crookneck squash, finely diced (about ¾ cup)
4   tablespoons fresh or frozen (defrosted) peas
½   cup broccoli florets
½   cup sliced green beans, ¼ inch long
    salt to taste
2   ounces uncooked noodles or pasta, any shape
1   bunch Italian parsley, leaves only, chopped (about 4 tablespoons)
½   cup grated Parmesan or Romano cheese

In a 3-quart stockpot bring the vegetable stock to a boil over high heat and cook, uncovered, for 45 minutes or until reduced to 6 cups.

Meanwhile, using a small paring knife, cut off tip and stem of the tomato. Remove the seeds and core, leaving only firm, outer pulp. Slit one side of the tomato and lay the tomato flat on the work surface. Cut into ¼-inch strips, pile up strips, and cut into ¼-inch pieces. Reserve in a small bowl.

Melt the butter in a large skillet over low heat, add the onion, carrot, and turnip, and cook, covered, for 3 minutes. Add the remaining vegetables and continue to cook, covered, an additional 5 minutes. Add salt as desired.

Add the uncooked noodles to the boiling vegetable broth and cook until done (about 3 minutes for fresh pasta, 7 minutes for dry). Add the cooked vegetables to the soup and cook 1 minute.

Just before serving, add the chopped parsley to the soup. Pass the grated cheese at the table.

BRIE AND APPLE BISQUE

Beginning a meal with a cheese soup can be disastrous if the soup is not subtly flavored because it's difficult to choose an appropriate following course. This cheese soup is subtle; it depends on a delicate balance of sharp aroma, sweet flavor, and cleansing astringency for its success. Don't worry about the Brie being too strong—the white wine and apples mask its flavor and aroma. If you'd like to prepare the diced apple garnish ahead of time, toss it with the lemon juice to prevent discoloring; otherwise, cut the apple just before serving.

4   tablespoons unsalted butter
1   celery stalk, coarsely chopped (about ½ cup)
1   medium onion, coarsely chopped (about ¾ cup)
1   medium carrot, coarsely chopped (about ¾ cup)
3   tablespoons all-purpose flour
2½ quarts vegetable stock (page 257)
4   bay leaves
2   garlic cloves, peeled
1   teaspoon whole black peppercorns
2   sprigs fresh thyme or ½ teaspoon dried
2   ripe plum tomatoes (about ¼ pound), coarsely chopped
1   cup medium-dry white wine, such as muscat
2   pounds Brie, rind removed, cut into small pieces
1   cup whipping cream
1   medium Granny Smith or other green apple (for garnish)
2   tablespoons fresh lemon juice (optional)
    salt to taste

In a large stockpot, melt the butter over low heat and cook the celery, onion, and carrot 3 to 4 minutes, stirring, until softened. Sprinkle the flour over the vegetables and cook, stirring constantly, 1 minute.

Add stock, bay leaves, garlic, peppercorns, thyme, and tomatoes. Raise heat to high and bring to a boil. Reduce heat and simmer, uncovered, for 1½ hours. The soup should reduce to 6 cups, becoming slightly thick and more intense in flavor. Occasionally skim the soup as butter and flour particles form a scum on the surface.

Pass the liquid through a fine strainer to remove any lumps of flour that may have formed and discard them along with the cooked vegetables and spices. Now you have a vegetable *velouté*. Transfer it to a clean stockpot.★

Add the wine to the vegetable *velouté* and bring to a boil over medium heat. Reduce the heat and simmer, uncovered, for 5 minutes. Add the Brie to the soup and stir until melted. Add the cream. Peel and finely dice the apple and decorate each soup bowl with diced apple. Ladle the soup at the table.

★Can be prepared up to a day in advance to this point; refrigerate until ready to finish.

BASIL BISQUE   SERVES 6 TO 8

There are many ingredients in this bisque, but basil predominates. All the other ingredients are used to highlight its peppery flavor as well as its minty aroma. This is a velvety vegetable soup finished with a vivid, gutsy pesto sauce. To ensure a bright green color, add the basil puree to the soup just before serving.

Remember that raw garlic has a "kick" to it. This soup is not designed to be shocking to the palate, but to capitalize on the way raw garlic lingers on the palate and enhances the minty character of basil. Still, this soup is not for the fainthearted.

4   tablespoons unsalted butter
1   celery stalk, coarsely chopped (about ½ cup)
1   medium onion, coarsely chopped (about ¾ cup)
1   medium carrot, coarsely chopped (about ¾ cup)
3   tablespoons all-purpose flour

2½   quarts vegetable stock (page 257)
4   bay leaves
4   garlic cloves
I   teaspoon whole black peppercorns
2   ripe plum tomatoes, coarsely chopped (about ¼ pound)
I   cup whipping cream
4   tablespoons pine nuts
I   tablespoon olive oil
2   tablespoons finely minced garlic
3   bunches fresh basil (*not* dried; about 3 cups loosely packed)
¼   cup grated Parmesan or Romano cheese
       salt to taste

In a large stockpot melt the butter over low heat and cook the celery, onion, and carrot 3 to 4 minutes, stirring, until softened. Sprinkle the flour over the vegetables and cook, stirring constantly, 1 minute.

Add stock, bay leaves, peeled garlic cloves, peppercorns, and tomatoes. Raise heat to high and bring to a boil. Then reduce heat and simmer, uncovered, for 1½ hours. Occasionally skim the soup as butter and flour particles form a scum on the surface. The soup should reduce to about 6 cups, becoming slightly thickened and more intense in flavor.

Pass the liquid through a fine strainer to remove any lumps of flour that may have formed. Discard them along with the cooked vegetables and spices. Transfer the soup to a clean stockpot.★ Bring the soup to a boil over medium heat. Add the cream.

Meanwhile, combine the pine nuts and the olive oil in a skillet over medium heat and cook, stirring, until pine nuts turn a golden honey color, about 1 minute. Transfer the pine nuts and olive oil to a blender or food processor. Add the minced garlic, basil, cheese, and ¼ cup of heated soup. Blend until smooth. Return this concentrated puree to the remainder of the soup, taste for salt, and serve.

★Can be prepared to this point up to one day in advance and refrigerated.

SUMMER SOUPS

PUREE OF SWEET PEA
AND WATERCRESS SOUP   SERVES 6

I don't usually recommend frozen products, but frozen peas are usually better than fresh—unless they're just off the vine—because the sugar in them has not yet turned to starch. There is a sweetness but also an earthiness to peas that's reminiscent of digging a garden.

In this soup spicy watercress and sweet peas are complements, showing off each other's flavor. Spicy and sweet ingredients combine well when they're carefully balanced so that you don't overpower one with the other.

4   tablespoons unsalted butter
I   medium onion, roughly diced (about ¾ cup)
I   pound fresh peas or 2 10-ounce boxes frozen
I   teaspoon salt
I   quart chicken stock (page 258) or canned low-sodium chicken broth
3   bunches watercress (about 6 ounces)
I   cup whipping cream
    freshly ground pepper to taste

Melt the butter in a 2-quart pot over low heat, add the onion, and cook slowly, stirring, for about 7 minutes. Add the peas and salt and cook about 3 minutes. Add the stock, cover, and bring to a boil. Reduce the heat and simmer for 15 minutes.

Strain and reserve the liquid. Transfer peas to a blender or food processor. Add the watercress, reserving 12 to 16 of the nicest leaves for garnish. Puree until very smooth. Return the puree to the pot and add the liquid. The soup should be thick but not like a porridge. Add the cream, then the pepper to taste, and bring to a boil over medium heat.

Serve the soup in individual bowls or in a tureen and garnish with the reserved watercress leaves.

CREAM OF SPINACH AND SORREL SOUP   SERVES 6

You have the option of preparing two different soups from this recipe simply by exchanging the amounts of the two main ingredients. If you want to make a spinach soup, use the smaller amount of sorrel to give a tangier aspect to the spinach and sophisticate its flavor. Or if you prefer a sorrel soup, a little spinach will diminish the sourness of the sorrel. Our secret ingredient in both soups is the background taste of garlic. Garlic is oily and pungent; it smooths the sourness of the sorrel and sweetens the "grassiness" of the spinach.

I   tablespoon unsalted butter
I   medium onion, roughly diced (about ¾ cup)
2   pounds spinach and 3 bunches sorrel *or* 6 bunches sorrel and I
     pound spinach
1½   tablespoons finely minced garlic
I   teaspoon salt
1½   quarts chicken stock (page 258) or canned low-sodium chicken
     broth
I   cup whipping cream
     salt and freshly ground pepper to taste

Melt the butter in a stockpot over low heat, add the onion, and cook slowly, stirring, for about 7 minutes. Add the spinach, sorrel, garlic, and salt, cover, and continue to cook until very wilted, about 15 to 20 minutes. Add the stock, raise the heat, cover, and bring to a boil. Reduce heat and simmer for 15 minutes.

Strain and reserve the liquid. Transfer the spinach and sorrel to a blender or food processor and puree until very smooth. Return to the pot and add the liquid. Add the cream. Taste for salt and pepper. This soup may be served piping hot or well chilled.

CHILLED PUREE OF BEET
AND WATERMELON SOUP   SERVES 6

With their sweet and musty character, beets can be successfully combined with other vegetables, such as carrots, highlighting the beets' sweetness, or cabbage, highlighting an earthy mustiness. Adding watermelon to beet soup doesn't accentuate the sweetness of beets, as you might assume; it's a contrasting taste that brings out the musty character of the beets.

It's best to serve this soup cold because when heated, the presence of watermelon tends to dissipate—it's more aroma than flavor. Here the watermelon excites the nose and the beets excite the palate.

I	tablespoon salad oil
I	medium onion, sliced (about I cup)
½	pound beets, peeled and roughly diced (about 2 cups)
I	quart chicken stock (page 258) or canned low-sodium chicken broth
I	teaspoon salt
2½	cups diced watermelon (about I pound), rind and seeds removed
I	cup sweet and sour watermelon rind (for garnish; page 267)

Heat the oil in a stockpot over low heat, add the onion, and cook slowly, stirring, about 7 minutes. Add the beets and continue to cook slowly, covered, until most of their water has been released and they have fallen apart, about 35 minutes. Stir often to prevent sticking and burning. Add the stock and salt, cover, and bring to a boil. Reduce the heat and simmer, covered, for 15 minutes.

When the soup is finished cooking, strain and reserve the liquid. Transfer the beets to a blender or food processor and add the watermelon. Puree until very smooth. Return the puree to the pot and add the reserved liquid.

Chill the soup well, about 4 hours. Serve the soup from a tureen and decorate each bowl with sweet and sour watermelon rind.

CHILLED PUREE OF CARROT
AND CANTALOUPE SOUP

SERVES 6 TO 8

Cooked carrots become sweeter as the cellulose structure of the root breaks down, releasing the natural sugar in the vegetable. Cook them a long time to develop the best flavor, but don't cook melon too long or its aroma will dissipate. The result should be a carrot taste with a melon perfume.

The sweetness of the cooked carrots makes them a good foundation flavor for coriander, which is pungently aromatic and perfumy in an exotic way. When combined with cumin, it has a dry aroma. The two merge to form one taste, making the cumin a secret ingredient.

4	tablespoons salad oil
1	medium onion, roughly diced (about ¾ cup)
1	pound carrots, roughly chopped (about 4 cups)
1	quart chicken stock (page 258) or canned low-sodium chicken broth
1	cup diced cantaloupe (about ½ small cantaloupe)
1	teaspoon salt
2	tablespoons ground coriander
½	teaspoon ground cumin
3	tablespoons plain yogurt
2	tablespoons milk

Heat the oil in a stockpot over low heat, add the onion, and cook slowly, stirring, for about 7 minutes. Do not let the onion color. Add the carrots and continue cooking, stirring, until most of their water has been released and they fall apart, about 35 minutes. Add the stock, cover, bring to a boil, reduce the heat, and simmer about 15 minutes. Add the cantaloupe, salt, coriander, and cumin and cook 2 minutes.

Strain and reserve the liquid. Transfer the carrots and cantaloupe to a blender or food processor and puree until very smooth. Return the puree to the pot and add the reserved liquid. Chill in refrigerator for 4 hours.

Combine the yogurt and milk in a small bowl until smooth. Reserve until ready to serve.

Pour the soup into chilled soup bowls just before serving. Decorate the surface by spooning three simple lines of yogurt across the surface of each bowl of soup. Using the handle end of the spoon, lightly drag across the three stripes at a 90-degree angle to make a "feathered" decoration.

HEARTY SOUPS

CREAM OF ZUCCHINI SOUP   SERVES 6

Many vegetables that are delicious when lightly cooked lose their flavor entirely when made into soup. Zucchini, one of my favorite vegetables, does not make a very interesting soup by itself. Cooked for a long time, it loses all of its characteristic aroma and becomes merely a bitter taste. Pernod highlights zucchini by simulating its aroma. I add walnut oil to finish the soup, giving a toasted nuttiness—a flavor I particularly like. To maintain the strong zucchini flavor I use just a hint of Pernod and walnut oil—their flavors shouldn't be recognizable.

4   tablespoons unsalted butter
I   medium onion, diced (about ¾ cup)
2   pounds zucchini, diced (about 5 cups)
I   quart chicken stock (page 258) or canned low-sodium chicken broth
I   teaspoon salt
I   cup whipping cream
2   tablespoons walnut oil
I   capful Pernod
    freshly ground pepper to taste

In a stockpot melt the butter over low heat, add the onion, and cook, covered, for about 7 minutes without browning. Add the zucchini and continue to cook slowly until most of its water has been released, about 25 minutes. Stir frequently to prevent browning. Add the stock, then the salt. Cover and bring to a boil. Reduce the heat and simmer for 15 minutes.

Strain and reserve the liquid. Transfer the zucchini to a blender or food processor. Puree until very smooth. Return the puree to the pot and add the liquid until you have the desired consistency. (I like a heavy consistency, but not a porridge.) Add the cream.

To finish the soup, add the walnut oil and Pernod to the hot soup. Add pepper to taste. Serve piping hot.

PUREE OF ONION SOUP
WITH BEER AND CHEDDAR CHEESE   SERVES 4 TO 6

The longer they cook, the sweeter onions become. Their sugar browns, caramelizing in the same way that sugar heated to a certain temperature becomes caramel. Using a heavy copper or cast-iron pot will help you perform this task properly, caramelizing but not burning the onions.

Nutmeg is layered with onion flavor to enhance the sweetness with its aroma. I add both beer and cheddar cheese to this soup because I like a bitter, strongly contrasting element against the sweet onions.

4	tablespoons unsalted butter
4	medium onions, diced (about 6 cups)
I	quart veal stock (page 259) or low-sodium beef broth
1/8	teaspoon freshly grated nutmeg
I	12-ounce bottle dark beer
1/2	pound sharp cheddar cheese, crumbled
1/2	teaspoon salt
	freshly ground pepper to taste

In a heavy 3-quart pot, preferably cast iron or copper, melt the butter over low heat, add the onions, and cook, covered, for 15 minutes. Uncover and continue to cook, stirring frequently, until the onions turn a deep golden color, about 30 to 40 minutes, depending on your pot. Add the stock and the nutmeg, cover, and bring to a boil. Reduce heat and simmer for 15 minutes.

Meanwhile, in a small pot, bring the beer to a boil over medium heat and boil until the liquid is reduced by half. Remove from the heat and add the cheddar cheese, stirring until melted. Transfer this mixture to a blender. Add 1 cup of the onion soup and blend until smooth. Reserve.

Remove the onion mixture from the heat and strain. Reserve the liquid. Transfer the onions to a blender or food processor and puree until very smooth. Return the puree to the pot and add the reserved liquid and the cheddar cheese mixture. Add salt and taste for pepper. Serve piping hot in a tureen.

SPLIT PEA SOUP WITH SORREL SERVES 6 TO 8

Traditional split pea soup is made with a ham hock or bacon—something smoky and salty to keep the cooked beans from tasting like porridge. I don't think, however, that a little meat is enough. This soup, and any other bean soup, benefits from the addition of carrots, onions, and celery. These aromatics are better if cooked slowly for a long time, releasing their flavor. But there's another flavor here, too—sorrel and lemon give a nice sour spark to this soup.

2 tablespoons unsalted butter
2 medium onions, roughly diced (about 1½ cups)
1 medium carrot, roughly diced (about ¾ cup)
2 celery stalks, roughly diced (about 1 cup)
1 teaspoon finely minced garlic
1½ cups dried split peas
1½ quarts chicken stock (page 258) or canned low-sodium chicken broth or water (plus 1 cup if serving soup chilled)
1 small ham hock *or* about 6 ounces cooked ham or bacon
1 lemon, halved
3 bunches fresh sorrel (about 1 cup, tightly packed)
1 cup whipping cream
Salt and freshly ground pepper to taste

In a stockpot melt the butter over low heat and add the onions, carrot, celery, and garlic. Cook the vegetables, stirring, until limp, about 15 minutes, being careful not to brown. Add the split peas, stock, ham hock, and lemon and bring to a boil. Reduce the heat to low and simmer for 30 minutes or until the peas are completely soft.

Remove the ham hock (which makes a great snack while you are preparing the rest of your meal) and the lemon. Add the sorrel and cream. Transfer to a food processor or blender and puree until smooth. Strain through a fine sieve.

Taste for salt and pepper. Serve this soup piping hot or well chilled. If the soup is chilled, you will need to thin it with an additional cup of stock, canned low-sodium broth, or water.

CLAM AND OYSTER CHOWDER

SERVES 6 TO 8

When the ingredients of a soup are not pureed, you can use them as a garnish, straining them out of the soup before serving. When each soup bowl is decorated with the chunky ingredients—in this case, diced clams, oysters, and potatoes—and the smooth soup is ladled in front of your guests, they will be very impressed. I am always surprised at the effectiveness of this bit of table theatrics.

By using both clams and oysters in this chowder we juxtapose two contrasting ingredients. We combine salty clams and sweet oysters so that they each taste mild but not bland. Opposite tastes can cancel each other in an interesting way because each mouthful tastes different. There is nothing aromatic about oysters and clams, so some fresh thyme is necessary to complete the chowder.

6	tablespoons unsalted butter
1	medium onion, roughly diced (about ¾ cup)
1	medium carrot, roughly diced (about ¾ cup)
2	celery stalks, roughly diced (about 1 cup)
4	tablespoons all-purpose flour
1	quart bottled or canned clam juice
1½	quarts fish stock (page 260)
1	small baking potato
3	dozen shucked littleneck clams, chopped (about 1 cup)
3	dozen shucked oysters, chopped (about 1 cup)
1	cup heavy cream
	salt and freshly ground pepper to taste
2	sprigs fresh thyme, leaves only, or 1 teaspoon dried
4	tablespoons minced chives

In a large stockpot melt 4 tablespoons of butter over low heat, add the onion, carrot, and celery, and cook slowly 3 to 4 minutes or until softened. Sprinkle the flour over the vegetables and cook, stirring, 1 minute. Add the clam juice and fish stock, raise heat to high, and bring to a boil. Reduce heat and simmer, uncovered, for 1½ hours. The soup should reduce by half, becoming slightly thick and more intense in flavor. Occasionally skim as butter and flour particles form a scum on top of the soup.

Pass the liquid through a fine strainer to remove any lumps

of flour that may have formed and discard them along with the cooked vegetables. Transfer to a clean stockpot.★

Cut the unpeeled potato into ¼-inch dice and add it to the soup in the pot. Cover, bring to a boil over medium heat, and simmer 5 minutes. Add the clams and oysters to the soup and continue to simmer 5 minutes. Add the cream. If using dried thyme, add it now. Taste for salt and pepper. Simmer 5 minutes. Remove from heat and whisk in the remaining butter.

To serve, strain the chowder. Divide the strained clams, oysters, and potato among the soup bowls and sprinkle with fresh thyme and chives. Present the garnished bowls and ladle the chowder at the table in front of your guests.

★Can be prepared to this point up to a day in advance and refrigerated.

CORN AND LOBSTER CHOWDER   SERVES 6 TO 8

This soup tastes best in summer when corn is at its sweetest and least starchy. In winter you will do better with frozen corn kernels. The lobster needs to be undercooked so that it finishes cooking when you add it to the soup before serving—otherwise it becomes rubbery.

Like all shellfish, lobster has a lingering "iodine" aftertaste. Medicinal seafood flavors are softened by sweet ones, such as corn; they blend harmoniously without losing their individual personalities. Nutmeg and rosemary complete the flavors by adding highlights: the nutmeg allies itself with the corn, enhancing its sweetness, while rosemary and lobster become a stronger, medicinal contrast.

4   tablespoons unsalted butter
1   medium onion, roughly diced (about ¾ cup)
1   medium carrot, roughly diced (about ¾ cup)
1   celery stalk, roughly diced (about ½ cup)

4　tablespoons all-purpose flour
3　quarts fish stock (page 260)
I　cup dry white wine
I　3-pound live lobster
½　teaspoon freshly grated nutmeg
2　corn ears, shucked (about 2 cups kernels)
I　teaspoon chopped fresh rosemary or ½ teaspoon dried
　salt and freshly ground pepper to taste

In a large stockpot melt the butter over low heat, add the onion, carrot, and celery, and cook slowly 3 to 4 minutes or until softened.

Sprinkle the flour over the vegetables and cook, stirring, 1 minute. Add the cold stock and the wine, raise heat to high, and bring to a boil. Plunge the live lobster into the soup and cook, covered, for 15 minutes.

Remove the lobster and let cool until you can handle it comfortably. Remove tail and claws. Slice the lobster down the middle and scoop the "green meat" (tomalley) and roe from the body; reserve in a bowl. Add the body to the soup. Remove the tail and claw meat from the shell, roughly dice it, and reserve with the tomalley. Add the shells to the soup.

Meanwhile, reduce heat and simmer the soup, uncovered, for 1 hour. The soup should reduce by half, becoming slightly thick and more intense in flavor. Occasionally skim as butter and flour particles form a scum on the surface of the soup.

Pass the liquid through a fine strainer to remove any lumps of flour that may have formed and discard them along with the shells and cooked vegetables. Transfer the soup to a clean stockpot. If you're using dried rosemary, add it now. Add the nutmeg.

Place the corn and lobster meat in a processor and give it 15 quick pulses, until coarsely shredded. Meanwhile, bring the soup to a boil in the stockpot. Add the corn and lobster to the soup and simmer over low heat for 5 minutes.

Add the chopped fresh rosemary and salt and pepper to taste to the piping-hot soup just before serving and ladle the soup at the table.

MAIN-COURSE SOUPS

LENTIL SOUP WITH LAMB AND EGGPLANT   SERVES 6

Since nothing is pureed in this soup, the cutting of the ingredients is very important, both to the final appearance and to the cooking. Lentils, lamb, and eggplant make a musty combination that is heightened by the tart dilled yogurt.

¼	cup virgin olive oil
1	pound boneless lamb shoulder, cut into ¼-inch dice or finely minced
1	medium onion, finely diced (about ¾ cup)
2	celery stalks, finely diced (about 1 cup)
1	medium carrot, finely diced (about ¾ cup)
1	medium eggplant, cut into ½-inch dice (2 cups)
1	tablespoon finely minced garlic
2	quarts chicken stock (page 258) or canned low-sodium chicken broth
1	cup dried lentils
½	teaspoon salt
4	tablespoons chopped fresh dill
¾	cup plain yogurt
	freshly ground pepper to taste

In a large stockpot or Dutch oven heat the oil over high heat. Add the lamb in batches and brown well. Do not crowd the pan or the moisture from the meat will not escape quickly enough and the lamb will not brown. Remove the meat with a slotted spoon as it is done and reserve on a plate.

Pour off all but 1 tablespoon of the fat remaining in the pot. Add the onion, celery, carrot, eggplant, and garlic. Cook over low heat, stirring, until the vegetables are limp, about 15 minutes. Add the lamb, stock, lentils, and salt. Bring to a boil, lower heat, and simmer, covered, for 30 minutes. Meanwhile, combine the dill and yogurt.

When the lentils are soft but not mushy and the lamb is tender, pour the soup into a tureen and serve. Pass the dilled yogurt for your guests to spoon into their soup.

ALMOND CHICKEN BISQUE   SERVES 4

Although they come from the same nut, almond extract has a sharp perfume that is completely different from the flavor of toasted almonds. I use both almond flavors here to make an interesting, vibrantly flavored soup.

The sweetness of carrots and vegetarian stock help marry the two almond flavors. The spark of something tart, the lemon juice, finishes the soup.

5	tablespoons unsalted butter
I	medium onion, coarsely chopped (about ¾ cup)
2	medium carrots, coarsely chopped (about I ½ cups)
4	tablespoons all-purpose flour
2½	quarts vegetable stock (page 257)
4	bay leaves
2	garlic cloves, peeled
I	teaspoon whole black peppercorns
I	pound boneless, skinless chicken breasts
I	tablespoon unsalted butter
½	cup blanched and slivered almonds (2 ounces)
I	cup whipping cream
¼	cup fresh lemon juice
½	teaspoon almond extract
I	teaspoon salt

In a large stockpot melt 4 tablespoons butter over low heat, add the onion and carrots, and cook gently 4 to 5 minutes or until softened. Sprinkle the flour over the vegetables and cook, stirring, 1 minute. Add the stock, bay leaves, garlic, and peppercorns, raise heat to high, and bring to a boil. Reduce heat and simmer, uncovered, for 1½ hours. The soup should reduce by half, becoming slightly thick and more intense in flavor. Occasionally skim as butter and flour particles form a scum on top of the soup.

Pass the liquid through a fine strainer to remove any lumps of flour that may have formed and discard them along with the cooked vegetables and spices.★ Reserve liquid.

★Can be prepared to this point up to a day in advance and refrigerated.

Chop the chicken very finely by hand or pulse in a processor until very coarsely ground.

Melt the remaining tablespoon of butter in a clean stockpot over medium heat, add the almonds, and cook, stirring, until they turn golden, about 5 minutes. Add the chicken, then the soup, cream, lemon juice, almond extract, and salt. Cook, covered, 5 to 7 minutes. Ladle the piping-hot soup from a tureen.

MUSSEL AND BACON SOUP   SERVES 4

A good cook avoids one-dimensional flavors so that food never tastes flat before guests finish eating it. If you wonder why things taste different in a restaurant from the way they do at home, one reason is probably that a talented chef recognizes this flavor principle.

The impression of tarragon in this soup is intensified by the addition of other flavors, resulting in a stronger tarragon character than if you simply used tarragon. When a recipe calls for tarragon, it's often a good idea to add a pinch of celery seed, some fennel, and a capful of Pernod.

The kind of mussels you find will depend on the season and on where you live. Some varieties may be saltier or fishier than others. The addition of white wine diminishes the fish flavor of seafood, and its acidity helps to balance salt. Do not add any salt until the mussels have opened and you can determine how salty they are.

Garlic and shallots are foundation flavors, a backdrop to help the celery seed, fennel, and Pernod come together to be tasted as tarragon.

Clams or shrimps could replace mussels in this soup and either celeriac in ½-inch cubes or broccoli florets would be good substitutions for the fennel.

¼   pound slab bacon, cut into ¼-inch dice
1   medium fennel bulb, finely slivered tip to root (about 1½ cups loosely packed)
1   cup dry white wine
1   capful Pernod
8   dozen mussels, scrubbed and debearded
1½ quarts fish stock (page 260)
1   tablespoon finely minced garlic
2   teaspoons finely minced onion
1   teaspoon celery seed
1   teaspoon aniseed or fennel seed
¾   cup milk
    salt and freshly ground pepper to taste
2   tablespoons unsalted butter
3   sprigs fresh tarragon, leaves only, chopped, *or* 1 tablespoon dried

In a large, heavy pot or Dutch oven over low heat cook the bacon, stirring, for 2 minutes, without browning. Add the slivered fennel and continue to cook, uncovered, for 1 minute. Add the white wine, Pernod, and mussels. Cover, raise heat to high, bring to a boil, and cook 1 minute to burn off the alcohol. Add the fish stock, garlic, onion, celery seed, and aniseed. If using dried tarragon, add it now. Cover, bring back to the boil, and cook until all the mussels have opened, about 7 to 10 minutes.

When the mussels have opened, turn off the heat, add the milk, and taste for salt and pepper.

To serve, use a slotted spoon to transfer the mussels, bacon, and fennel to soup bowls. Return the broth to a boil and add the butter. Turn off heat and add the chopped fresh tarragon leaves. Serve the soup in a tureen and ladle it over the mussels at the table.

HOT AND SOUR BISQUE
SERVES 4 TO 5

The personality of this soup depends on the play between its spicy and sour ingredients, the combination of vinegar, cayenne pepper, sherry, and garlic. You can improvise, embellishing the soup with vegetable ingredients such as diced eggplant, red or green peppers, or bean sprouts, but try to add only those elements that are both flavorful and aromatic. Each ingredient must sparkle yet remain a coherent part of the ensemble.

5	tablespoons unsalted butter
1	medium onion, coarsely chopped (about ¾ cup)
4	tablespoons all-purpose flour
3	quarts chicken stock (page 258) or canned low-sodium chicken broth
½	cup rice wine vinegar
⅓	cup dry sherry
1	pound boneless, skinless chicken breasts, finely diced
12–16	small mushroom caps
2	tablespoons minced garlic
1	small white onion, finely slivered tip to root
1	small fennel bulb, finely slivered tip to root (1 cup loosely packed)
1	teaspoon cayenne pepper, or more to taste
1	teaspoon salt
8	snow peas, slivered lengthwise
4	sprigs watercress, leaves only

In a large stockpot melt 4 of the tablespoons butter over low heat, add the chopped onion, and cook gently until softened, about 3 to 4 minutes. Sprinkle the flour over the onion and cook, stirring, 1 minute. Add the stock, vinegar, and sherry, raise heat to high, and bring to a boil. Reduce heat and simmer, uncovered, for 1½ hours. The soup should reduce by half, becoming slightly thick and more intense in flavor. Occasionally skim as butter and flour particles form a scum on top of the soup.

Pass the soup through a fine strainer to remove any lumps of flour that may have formed and discard them along with the cooked onion.★ Reserve soup.

★Can be prepared to this point up to a day in advance and refrigerated.

In a clean 3-quart stockpot melt the remaining tablespoon butter over low heat and add the chicken, mushrooms, garlic, white onion, and fennel. Cook gently, stirring, for 5 minutes. Add the soup, cayenne pepper, and salt, raise the heat to high, and cook, covered, about 5 minutes.

To serve, garnish large soup bowls with the uncooked snow peas and watercress. Present the soup in a tureen and ladle it into the garnished bowls in front of your guests.

VANILLA SAFFRON LOBSTER SOUP   SERVES 4

Here is a recipe that sounds really eccentric—you probably won't believe that its flavors work until you've tasted it. Vanilla and lobster flavors combine to form one taste that is stronger than lobster alone. At the same time the vanilla is familiar yet surprising because of its unusual context. Your guests will suspect its presence but discard the thought because most of us stereotype vanilla in a sweet context, usually in a dessert. The secret here is to hint at the vanilla; the combination becomes vulgar if it ceases to be subtle. Saffron is a catalyst that insures a strong marriage between vanilla and lobster.

2	quarts fish stock (page 260)
1	teaspoon minced garlic
½	teaspoon saffron threads
¼	small vanilla bean, slit lengthwise, *or* 2 drops vanilla extract
2	3-pound live lobsters
3	ripe plum tomatoes
8	very small new potatoes
1	teaspoon salt, or to taste
	freshly ground pepper to taste

In a stockpot over high heat combine stock, garlic, saffron, and vanilla and bring to a boil. Add lobsters in batches if necessary so that they are completely submerged and cook 5 minutes. At this point they will be undercooked.

Separate the tail and claws of the lobsters from the body. Using a large knife, slice the body down the middle and add it to the pot. Remove the tail and claw meat from the shells, roughly dice it, and set aside on a plate. Add the shells to the soup. Boil the soup, uncovered, for 20 minutes, reducing the broth by one third and fortifying the flavor.

Meanwhile, using a small paring knife, cut off tip and stem of each tomato. Remove the seeds and core, leaving only the firm, outer pulp. Slit one side of the tomato and lay the tomato flat on work surface. Cut into ¼-inch strips, pile up strips, and cut into ¼-inch pieces. Reserve in a small bowl.

Remove the lobster bodies and vanilla bean from the fish stock. Add the unpeeled new potatoes and salt to taste. Cover and cook 5 minutes.★ Add the lobster tails and claws, cover, and cook another 2 minutes.

Using a slotted spoon, transfer the lobster and potatoes to four soup bowls and sprinkle with diced tomato. Pour the broth into a pitcher or soup tureen. Present the bowls to your guests, ladle the broth into bowls at the table, and offer freshly ground black pepper.

★Can be prepared to this point up to a day in advance and refrigerated.

SALADS

■ ● ▲

I think of salad as another way of presenting food. A salad can be a course, a meal in itself, or a side dish.

When creating a salad, you must first think it through. How will all the ingredients taste together? What size and shape should they be? What about the colors, the textures, the garnish, the dressing?

When ingredients are cut into varying shapes, the mixture you spear on your fork is quite different from a salad in which all the pieces are uniform cubes. How you cut ingredients determines not only how the salad will taste but also how it will look. Should the ingredients be slivered or cut into rounds? Do you prefer raw mushrooms thickly sliced or paper-thin? What about onion? A thin slice of onion combines with other flavors more easily than a thick slice. Should the salad be cut into bite-size pieces because the guests will be eating standing up?

Nowhere in the world of food is the idea of texture more important than in making salad. Should all the ingredients have the same texture, or do you want to combine limp ingredients with crispy ones, cooked ingredients with raw ones?

Temperature considerations are not as important with other kinds of dishes as they are with salads. Hot food should be hot, but in general cold food can succeed at room temperature, chilled, or juxtaposed with hot elements. Foods taste different at different temperatures, and you can design your salads to reflect this. A quickly sautéed apple will sweeten a salad while a cold raw one will be cleansingly astringent.

The dressing you choose to go with a salad is the important unifying element, the part of the composition that must go well with everything else. I think all salad dressings should have some vinegar or citrus juice—something tart or sour—to highlight the flavors of the salad components and to create the right background for them. Fortunately these highlighting ingredients come in a great variety—there are many types of vinegar as well as many choices of oil. It is essential to use the right vinegar and the right oil when making a salad dressing because these two ingredients can completely change the nuance of taste.

ABOUT VINEGARS

If you're confused about the many different flavored vinegars and kinds of oil, this chapter should help you understand why certain combinations are more successful than others.

- *Plain white vinegar* seems harsher than most other vinegars because it is a neutral, sour sensation, not really even a flavor; there is nothing else to disguise its acetic-acid quality. I generally avoid using it except in pickling, where there are enough added flavors to mask the harshness of this vinegar.

- *Wine vinegars* made from either red or white wine or Champagne are the most commonly used vinegars because they are the most versatile. Do use a vinegar that has been made from a decent wine. Although expensive, they are less harsh and still give an indication of the wine from which they were made. Red wine vinegar is the most appropriate highlight in mustard vinaigrettes.

- *Sherry vinegar* seems less strong than other wine vinegars. It has a smooth character that is greatly improved by long aging in wood casks. Because of its nutty background taste, it combines nicely with olive oil, yet a nut oil—hazelnut, walnut, or cold-pressed peanut oil—will emphasize the nuttiness of the vinegar even more. Grainy mustard, which is milder than Dijon mustard, marries well with sherry vinegar, while a Dijon can overpower its character if you are not careful.

- *Balsamic vinegar,* because of its long aging in oak casks, is dark, sweet, concentrated, and mild. It becomes nuttier with the addition of garlic and makes olive oil taste stronger. Walnut or hazelnut oil gives a mustiness that diminishes the sweet aspect of the vinegar. Dark sesame oil becomes less strong when used with balsamic vinegar. This vinegar is great with tomatoes. Especially successful with bitter lettuces such as Belgian endive, chicory, and radicchio, it's even nicer with spicy greens such as watercress or arugula. Sweet and spicy ingredients always complement each other because of their opposite natures. Grainy mustard would make this vinegar too sweet; I prefer to combine balsamic vinegar with the spiciness of a Dijon mustard.

- *Raspberry and other fruit vinegars* are made from fruit juices but can also be made at home by using fruit and a good white wine vinegar. These vinegars are not sweet, but they have a fruity aroma. Fruit vinegars don't combine well with olive oil. They make it seem almost rancid. I usually combine them with nut oils—walnut, hazelnut, cold-pressed peanut, or pine nut. Use them in fruit salads, where their aroma enhances the salad ingredients, or with poultry and white meats, where they add interest to the salad.

- *Tarragon and other herb-flavored vinegars* are most appropriately paired with the less tasty lettuces such as butter, red leaf, iceberg, and romaine. You must consider the flavor of each of these vinegars carefully before using them because each will add its own characteristic flavor to a dressing. I don't think tarragon vinegar and arugula would be good together, because arugula is aromatic in a way that interferes with tarragon. Tarragon vinegar is much better with the crispy bitterness of Belgian endive. Combine herb vinegars with any of the flavorless oils—safflower, soy, peanut—or with olive oil.

- *Rice wine vinegar* is sweet and mild. I use it when I don't want a pronounced vinegar character in a salad. It is also a secret ingredient for "doctoring" bland soups because it picks them up without adding much of its own personality. A shot of rice wine vinegar is especially good in potato soups and in any soups that are finished with sour cream or buttermilk.

- *Malt vinegar* is made from ale. It is a little sweet and seems less harsh than the wine vinegars. It can be used as a substitute for rice wine vinegar, but be careful; it does have its own personality and yeasty flavor. Combine it with a flavorless oil such as safflower or peanut, with a nut oil such as walnut or hazelnut, or with olive oil.

- *Cider vinegar,* made from apples, has a lemon tartness and an apple aroma. Used in salads featuring smoked fish or meats, it cuts the salty edge. This versatile vinegar combines with any oil. Its fruit flavor sweetens when cooked, and it is especially good when reduced in a dressing or sauce.

ABOUT OILS

- *Soy, safflower, corn, salad, vegetable, and ordinary peanut oils* are without flavor and should be used when you need no additional flavor or aroma in a dressing or when you want to dilute a strongly flavored oil. Vegetable and salad oils are usually a mixture of several flavorless oils. In the many recipes that call for salad oil, choose whichever of the above oils you prefer.

- *Olive oils* differ in their manner of production and from region to region. They must be chosen carefully as they range from green and bitter to light amber and sweet. They vary in aroma, too, from very light to very heavy. Spanish and Greek olive oils tend to be the harshest, while French oils are generally the most discreet. Italian oils range from green and harsh to amber and mild. There is a California olive oil from Mission olives that is very elegant and has a discreet character. There are others from Santa Barbara that are fruity and very strong.

There are two methods of obtaining olive oil: cold pressing and hot pressing. A cold-pressed oil has a pronounced olive flavor while a hot-pressed oil is merely bitter. The appellations "virgin" and "extra virgin" both refer to oil obtained by cold pressing. Extra virgin comes from the first cold pressing of the olive; virgin comes from a blend of subsequent cold pressings. If the oil is not labeled "100 percent," the oil usually contains only a small amount of cold-pressed oil, the remainder being composed of oil from both cold and hot pressings. Olive oils have a strong presence in any dressing in which they are used. For a less forward olive flavor, in a mayonnaise, for instance, combine olive oil with a flavorless oil.

- *Walnut and hazelnut oils* should also be cold pressed. Walnut oil is quite dark in color, hazelnut is dark amber, and both are nutty, smoky, and particularly successful when combined with fruit-infused vinegars. Use them as a substitute for toasted sesame oil in some Asian dishes. These nut oils are less stable than other oils. They should be used in dressings or as flavor additions to cooked food; never cook food in nut oils—except peanut oil—because they burn easily. Once opened, they should be refrigerated, as they quickly turn rancid.

- *Cold-pressed peanut oil* is somewhat difficult to find but worth the search because it gives the flavor of peanuts without the smoky flavor of the toasted nut oils. It is good with fruit vinegars in a fruit salad, with sweet vinegars such as malt or balsamic, or can be used as a substitute for sesame oil in an Asian-inspired dish. My source is Nuts D'Vine at 1–800–334–0492.

- *Dark sesame oil* is made from toasted sesame seeds; the flavor is very strong. It is associated with Asian cuisines, where it is used to perfume a dish rather than as a cooking element. In salad dressings it usually has too strong a presence and must be diluted with a flavorless oil. Rice wine vinegar is most successful with dark sesame oil because its mildness helps muffle the strength of the oil and its sweetness balances the distinctive taste.

ABOUT SALAD DRESSINGS

- *Unbound dressings* are basic vinegar and oil mixtures that are not emulsified in any way. Simple to make, they require only shaking before the salad ingredients are dressed. Because they have little texture and none of the dressing ingredients are reduced or fortified in any way, unbound dressings are light on the palate. I often like to fortify them with fresh herbs or infuse them with the flavor of dried spices.

- *Mustard vinaigrettes* are made from oil, vinegar, mustard, garlic, and shallots. Prepared mustard emulsifies oil and vinegar, binding them together into a different, thicker texture, one that will not separate into distinct layers of oil and vinegar, as with unbound dressings. The success of the simple vinaigrette depends on the quality and kind of mustard, oil, and vinegar used. Oil dilutes the strength of other flavors by coating the mouth. Vinegar provides acid, which diminishes the strength of the mustard. Finely minced garlic and shallots are very important to a vinaigrette—they marry the mustard and the vinegar but should not be added in such quantity that they can be noticed easily. Keep them secret.

- *Reduction dressings* are my favorites because they have an intensity of flavor produced by the concentration of a liquid. A liquid that has been reduced, or boiled down, becomes "thirsty" and will absorb a certain amount of oil to replace its lost liquid. Acidity is important for the emulsification of oil and water, and either a reduced citrus juice or a vinegar makes these dressings more stable and easier to make.

- *Puree-thickened dressings* depend on pastelike ingredients, such as yogurt, miso, peanut butter, or pureed green peppercorns for their texture. Thin these with a vinegar or a citrus juice, and add some oil to create a creamy-style dressing. The addition of a whole egg improves the texture enormously but is not necessary for success.

- *Mayonnaise dressings* depend on raw egg yolks to bind them, that is, to form an emulsion between the liquid ingredients and the oil. Think of these dressings as mayonnaises diluted with a flavored liquid (vinegar, lemon, etc.). In these dressings none of the ingredients are concentrated, or reduced, and therefore they are less intense in flavor than the reduction dressings. Egg yolks also coat the palate, making it harder to taste the flavors of the salad and the dressing.

- *Bacon vinaigrettes,* like most other salad dressings, are mixtures of oil and either vinegar or citrus juice, but in this case the fat rendered from cooked bacon substitutes for the oil. Bacon fat of course congeals when it is cool, so it follows that a bacon vinaigrette must be a hot or warm dressing. The saltiness of the bacon contrasts with the vinegar, and the bacon and vinegar combine to modify each other. Shallots are an important secret ingredient. Shallots give a slight sweetness, which also helps diminish the salt in the bacon and the acid in the vinegar. A hot vinegar is very strong to the nose; smelling this dressing, one would think there is too much vinegar, but on the taste buds the balance is just right.

FIRST-COURSE SALADS

BROCCOLI AND TOASTED PINE NUT SALAD   SERVES 4

Garlic sweetens the green, earthy taste of broccoli. Fresh garlic can be paired with it, but roasted garlic adds a nuttiness to broccoli and takes its taste into another realm. Here garlic is a catalyst that changes the way we taste the broccoli. The secret ingredient is tarragon, which highlights the licorice aspect of the broccoli taste.

Use cold-pressed peanut oil if you can; it reinforces the nutty roasted garlic flavor. Olive oil works well, too—the greener the better in this case. There is no mustard in this vinaigrette because it would interfere with the focus flavors: the nuttiness of the garlic and oil and the anise quality of the tarragon and broccoli. Red wine vinegar gives the balancing acetic edge without adding another strong flavor to the dressing.

1	bunch broccoli (about ¾ pound)
1	tablespoon salt
1	tablespoon cold-pressed peanut oil or olive oil, preferably Greek or Spanish
4	tablespoons pine nuts
12	garlic cloves, peeled
½	cup red wine vinegar
⅓	cup additional cold-pressed peanut oil or olive oil
1	tablespoon chopped fresh tarragon leaves *or* 1 teaspoon dried

Using a small knife, trim the tops (florets) from the broccoli and reserve on a plate. Fill a 2-quart pot with water, add the salt, and bring to a boil over high heat. Fill a large mixing bowl with water and ice cubes.

Meanwhile, using a knife or vegetable peeler, trim the woody outer skin from the broccoli stalks, exposing the light green, tender core. Your stalks should now look somewhat like squared-off logs. Slice the stalks lengthwise into ⅛-inch slices. Stack a few slices and cut them crosswise as finely as you can. You now have the matchstick shapes called *julienne*.

Submerge the broccoli florets in the rapidly boiling water and cook 1½ minutes. Remove with a slotted spoon and plunge into the ice water to stop the cooking process and to preserve the bright green color. Repeat the procedure with the julienned stalks, but cook only 30 seconds. Remove from water and plunge into ice water. When completely chilled, remove all the broccoli from the ice bath and drain completely on kitchen towels. (Wet broccoli will dilute the dressing and ruin all your work.) Preheat oven to 350°.

Heat 1 tablespoon oil in a small ovenproof skillet over medium heat. Add the pine nuts and cook, tossing, until they turn a light honey color. Remove with a slotted spoon and reserve on a small plate.

Add the garlic to the oil remaining in the skillet and toss briefly over medium heat, about 2 minutes. Add the vinegar, bring quickly to a boil, and place immediately in the oven. If you are using dried tarragon, add it now. Roast, covered, until garlic is tender, about 15 minutes. Remove from oven, let cool slightly, transfer to a blender, and puree until smooth. Place puree in a small mixing bowl and beat in the ⅓ cup oil until absorbed. If using fresh tarragon, chop the leaves and add them to the dressing now.

Toss the pine nuts and the julienned stalks of broccoli together with half the dressing and mound on plates. Toss the broccoli florets with the remaining dressing and place on the mound of julienne.

AVOCADO, TOMATO,
AND SHIITAKE MUSHROOM SALAD

SERVES 4

This salad is dressed with a hot vinaigrette made directly in the skillet with the juices of the sautéed mushrooms. It is fast and easy and should be made just before serving. In fact, the avocado and tomato may be arranged on plates up to half an hour before serving and left in the refrigerator. If you're preparing it longer in advance, squeeze a lemon over the avocado to keep it from discoloring.

Chosen for their textural contrast are the creamy avocado and the meaty mushroom. Garlic and shallots in this context are merely highlight flavors for the mushrooms, and the sweet but acid tomatoes contrast with the forest flavor of the mushrooms. Avocado is bland in comparison, diminishing the other flavors and highlighting the aroma of the warm vinaigrette.

If you can find other wild or exotic mushrooms such as *chanterelles,* morels, *cèpes,* or *matsutake,* it is always nice to make a mélange. Dried mushrooms found in Asian markets are stronger in flavor than fresh ones, and you might want to mix them with culti-vated mushrooms. You can also use only cultivated mushrooms, but the flavor focus will change from the mushrooms to the tomato and avocado. The salad will be less interesting but still delicious.

2	hothouse or beefsteak tomatoes *or* 4 plum tomatoes (about ½ pound)
2	avocados, halved, seed removed, peeled
⅓	cup virgin olive oil
12	medium shiitake mushroom caps (if using dried mushroom caps, soak to reconstitute)
1	tablespoon finely minced garlic
1	tablespoon finely minced shallots
¼	cup red wine vinegar
½	teaspoon salt
	freshly ground pepper to taste

Slice the tomato and avocado tip to stem and fan on plates.*

Just before serving, heat the olive oil in a medium skillet over medium heat, add the mushrooms, and cook, covered, for 5

*Tomato and avocado can be arranged on plates up to 1 hour in advance and refrigerated.

minutes. Add the garlic, shallots, vinegar, and salt. Cook, covered, 1 minute.

Remove the mushrooms and arrange over the avocado and tomato. Grind pepper over each salad as desired. Distribute the dressing equally on the salads and serve.

MÂCHE, APPLE, AND BACON SALAD SERVES 4

Mâche is a very delicate leaf, almost wilted, never crisp; the crunchiness of apples is an ideal textural contrast. The hot vinaigrette wilts the mâche even more, but the salad doesn't look flat because the apple slivers give it body. If mâche is unavailable, substitute Boston or baby red leaf lettuce.

The cleansing sensation of apples, their aroma and sweetness, contrasts with the saltiness of the bacon and bacon fat. Sautéed shallots always help mask the strength of hot vinegar by adding sweetness.

2   cups mâche (3 to 4 ounces)
½   Granny Smith or other tart, green apple
1   tablespoon fresh lemon juice
½   pound slab bacon, cut into ½-inch slivers or cubes
2   tablespoons salad oil
1   tablespoon finely minced shallots
⅓   cup sherry vinegar

Trim the bottom roots from the mâche and wash well to remove any sand. Core the apple but don't peel it. Cut into ¼-inch slices and cut each slice into pieces the size of matchsticks. Sprinkle with lemon juice to prevent darkening. Toss the mâche and apples together and divide among four salad plates.

Combine the bacon and oil in a medium skillet over medium heat and cook, rendering as much of the fat from the bacon as possible without burning. Add the shallots and cook another 30 seconds. Add the sherry vinegar and cook, tossing, for another 30 seconds. Using a slotted spoon, remove the bacon and divide among the salads. Drizzle the salads with the hot dressing and serve.

CHICORY, TOMATO, AND POACHED EGG SALAD
SERVES 4

To illustrate the principle of transposing ingredients and flavor combinations, this dish—basically a bacon, lettuce, and tomato sandwich—is prepared as a salad and garnished with a poached egg.

Chicory, a bitter lettuce, is successful in this salad because the salt and smoke of the dressing diminish its bitterness without overpowering its taste. We soften vinegar with sweetness; this time tomatoes are used for their sweetness, not their acidity. When the egg is broken, the runny yolk becomes part of the dressing.

4	tablespoons salad oil
½	pound slab bacon, cut into ½-inch slivers or cubes
8	¼-inch rounds French bread
I	small head chicory, curly endive, or *frisée*, trimmed of outer leaves and washed
4	poached eggs with runny yolks
2	hothouse or beefsteak tomatoes, cored and sliced tip to stem
I	tablespoon finely minced shallots
¼	cup sherry vinegar
	freshly ground pepper to taste

Combine the oil and bacon in a medium-size cold skillet and cook over medium heat to render the fat from the bacon. After 3 minutes add the rounds of bread and fry on both sides until golden. Remove the bread and reserve, but continue cooking the bacon.

Meanwhile, mound the chicory on salad plates and garnish each with a poached egg, 2 slices of fried bread, and some sliced tomato.

When the bacon is cooked, add the minced shallots to the skillet and stir. Immediately add the vinegar and cook another 30 seconds. Using a slotted spoon, remove the bacon and divide among the plates. Drizzle the salads with the hot dressing and grind the pepper mill over each one.

GREEN BEANS, APPLES, AND SMOKED TROUT   SERVES 4

Smoked foods have a fairly one-dimensional flavor that is basically salt and smoke. Tartness and acidity mask saltiness without diminishing flavor. For this salad I have chosen an acid-reduction dressing to highlight the trout taste. Reducing an acidic liquid not only concentrates its flavor but also transforms the acidity into a mellow tartness. Walnut oil is imperative here in making the smoke flavor taste nutty.

1	cup apple cider
½	cup cider vinegar
1	tablespoon salt
½	pound fresh green beans, preferably *haricots verts,* tips removed
1	medium Granny Smith apple
2	tablespoons fresh lemon juice
¼	cup walnut oil
2	smoked trout fillets, skinned, meat removed

In a small saucepan combine the apple cider and cider vinegar over medium heat and let the mixture cook until it is reduced by two thirds or until about 1 cup of viscous, shiny liquid remains. Scrape into a mixing bowl and cool to room temperature.

Meanwhile, fill a 2-quart pot with water, add the salt, and bring to a boil over high heat. Fill a large mixing bowl with ice water. Drop the green beans into the boiling water and cook 3 minutes. Drain and immediately plunge into ice water. When cool, drain again and pat completely dry on kitchen towels.

Core the apple, but don't peel it. Cut into ½-inch slices and cut slices into matchstick pieces. Sprinkle with lemon juice to prevent darkening.

When apple cider mixture has cooled to room temperature, slowly beat the oil into the apple cider mixture until absorbed. If the dressing separates, beat in a few drops of water or cider vinegar.

Toss the green beans and apples with half the dressing. Divide among salad plates, place half a fillet of trout on each, and lightly coat each piece of fish with the remaining dressing.

GLAZED HAM ON PAPAYA AND WATERCRESS   SERVES 4

This salad is based on combinations of sweet, salty, and peppery flavors. Remember that sugar and salt mask each other; both the ham and soy are salty, but the salad won't taste oversalty because of the honey.

Peppery flavors like watercress are also highlighted by sweet ones. Tabasco reinforces the peppery elements of the salad and will not overpower the sweet and the aromatic elements—papaya, coriander, cumin, and curry. The secret to this salad is a balance of ingredients that mask each other.

Corned beef, smoked chicken, or smoked turkey can be substituted for the ham without changing the flavor focus of the salad. Arugula, another spicy green, is a logical substitute for the watercress.

2	tablespoons honey
¼	cup soy sauce
I	tablespoon ground coriander
I	¾-pound boneless canned ham or leftover cooked ham
2	tablespoons rice wine vinegar
I½	teaspoons curry powder (page 264)
½	teaspoon ground cumin
¼	cup salad oil
I	tablespoon dark sesame oil
	Tabasco sauce to taste
I	papaya
2	bunches watercress, washed, heavy stems removed

Combine the honey, soy sauce, and coriander in a strong plastic bag or shallow container. Cut the ham into 4 slabs, cut each slab into 4 or 5 strips, and cut each strip into 1-inch cubes. Combine with the marinade and marinate for at least 1 hour, covered, at room temperature, or up to 2 hours in the refrigerator. Turn occasionally to marinate evenly.

Preheat oven to 375°. Transfer the ham and the marinade to an ovenproof container large enough to hold the meat in one layer and place, uncovered, in the oven. Baste with the marinade every 5 minutes until the ham begins to look shiny and is heated through, about 20 to 25 minutes. Scrape ham and basting syrup into a mixing bowl.

Meanwhile, make the dressing: In another mixing bowl combine the vinegar, curry, cumin, both oils, and the Tabasco and mix well.

Peel the papaya, discard the seeds, and cut into 1-inch chunks. Wash the watercress well, discarding any yellow leaves and long stems. Dry on towels. Add the papaya and watercress to the ham and add the dressing. Toss well and mound on plates.

CLAM, LEEK, AND GINGER SALAD   SERVES 4

There may seem to be many ingredients in this salad, but once you understand how they combine, you'll see that only three elements stand out. Leeks and tarragon combine to form a better leek flavor. The leeks would be lost without the tarragon pickup. Garlic and shallots combine with the clams, making them more briney. Ginger stands on its own and is the catalyst that harnesses and then directs the other flavors. Fresh ginger must be chopped finely by hand or it becomes stringy.

2	quarts cold water
16	baby leeks, *or* 8 medium
1	tablespoon salt
32	clams, preferably littlenecks or Manilas, scrubbed
1	teaspoon finely minced garlic
2	teaspoons minced shallots
2	cups fish stock (page 260) *or* 1 cup clam juice and 1 cup dry white wine
¼	cup red wine vinegar
3	tablespoons chopped fresh gingerroot
2	tablespoons chopped tarragon leaves *or* 1 teaspoon dried
½	cup salad oil

Fill a stockpot with 2 quarts water, add salt, and bring to a boil. Fill a large bowl with ice water. Depending on their size, trim 1 to 2 inches off the tops of the leeks, leaving about 1 inch of tender green. Slice baby leeks lengthwise from tip to root without cutting the root or separating into pieces. Wash in cold water. If you're using medium leeks, cut lengthwise into quarters and wash carefully. Blanch the leeks by placing them in the boiling water for 5 minutes. Drain immediately into ice water to stop the cooking process and to maintain the green color. When cooled, drain on towels and pat completely dry. Reserve.

In a 3-quart pot combine clams, garlic, shallots, and stock. Cover, bring to a boil, and cook over high heat until all clams have opened, about 5 to 10 minutes (depending on the type and size of the clams). Discard any clams that have not opened. Remove clams from the broth with a slotted spoon and chill. Add the vinegar to the clam broth and continue to boil until the cooking liquid is reduced by two thirds.

When the cooking liquid is thick and syrupy, transfer it to a bowl, add the ginger and tarragon, and cool to room temperature. Using a wire whisk, slowly beat in the salad oil, adding more as it is absorbed. If the dressing looks as though it's going to separate, add a few drops of water or, better yet, some fish stock, if it's available.

Place 4 leeks on each plate, garnish with 8 clams, and generously nap with dressing.

THIRD-COURSE SALADS

CHICORY, GRAPE, GOAT CHEESE, AND OLIVE SALAD   SERVES 4 TO 6

Between the cheese and the olives you may think that there is too much salt in this salad, but the sweetness in the vinegar and the cleansing effect of the grapes cancel it. Crisp, bitter chicory is the right background for these flavors. When composing a salad using strongly flavored ingredients, it's important to put them together so that their unharmonious natures fight in a balanced way, thereby modifying their strength and making them seem milder, better neighbors.

½ pound green seedless grapes
½ pound aged goat cheese, rind removed
12 Kalamata or large Greek olives, pitted and roughly chopped
¼ cup balsamic vinegar
1 cup chicken stock (page 258) or canned low-sodium chicken broth
⅓ cup Greek or Italian olive oil
1 small head chicory (about 5 ounces), trimmed, washed, and dried

Cut the grapes in half. Crumble the goat cheese. Mix together and reserve in a bowl.

In a small saucepan, combine the olives, vinegar, and chicken stock. Bring to a boil over medium heat and cook until the liquid is reduced by two thirds or until you have a little more than ¾ cup. Scrape into another mixing bowl and let cool to room temperature. When cool, beat in the olive oil.

Toss the chicory with half the dressing and mound on four plates. Toss the remaining dressing with the grapes and cheese and mound on the chicory.

CORN, ARUGULA, RED ONIONS, AND RED PEPPERS   SERVES 4 TO 6

Sweet things and spicy things go well together because they are tasted on different parts of the palate, so you can marry two strong flavors without compromising the taste of either. Although some spicy flavors, such as crushed black pepper, are tasted in the very back of the mouth, onions and arugula are tasted on the tongue, leaving plenty of room for the sweetness of the corn and red peppers to be sensed on the sides of the mouth. This separate tasting capacity makes it possible to layer flavors, which greatly increases the pleasure of eating. Make this salad only when fresh sweet corn is available.

2	tablespoons Dijon mustard
1	teaspoon finely minced garlic
4	tablespoons red wine vinegar
⅓	cup virgin olive oil
½	teaspoon salt
¼	teaspoon freshly ground black pepper
2	large fresh corn ears
½	small red onion
2	bunches arugula (3 to 4 ounces)
2	medium red peppers

In a small mixing bowl combine the mustard, garlic, and vinegar and mix until smooth. Using a fork or a small whisk, slowly beat in the oil, a few drops at a time, until incorporated. Season with salt and pepper.

Remove the kernels from the uncooked ears of corn and place in a mixing bowl. Peel the onion, finely slice from tip to stem, and add to mixing bowl. Wash the arugula, remove lower stem, and pat dry. Place in the mixing bowl. Remove stems and seeds from the peppers and thinly slice from tip to stem. Add to mixing bowl. Toss all ingredients in the mixing bowl with the vinaigrette and mound on plates.

SAUTÉED GRUYÈRE ON ARUGULA AND PEARS WITH GRAPES AND GREEN PEPPERCORNS   SERVES 4

Gruyère is a mildly robust cheese—earthy, but not in the "smelly" category. Don't use a commercial Swiss cheese in this recipe; it adds little interest to the salad. Any semihard cheese with good flavor, such as Emmenthaler, would make a good substitute, although raclette would be the best choice. Semihard cheeses are always more flavorful when melted.

Critical to the success of this salad is the spiciness of the green peppercorns and arugula contrasted with the earthiness of the cheese. The sweetness of the grapes is important to balance the spicy combination of peppercorns and arugula.

½   cup green seedless grapes
3   tablespoons green peppercorns packed in water, drained
⅓   cup olive oil
½   teaspoon salt
1   Bosc pear
1   tablespoon fresh lemon juice
2   bunches arugula (3 to 4 ounces)
½   pound Gruyère cheese, cut into 8 ¼-inch slabs
1   egg, lightly beaten
¼   cup fine fresh bread crumbs
3   tablespoons unsalted butter

In a blender or food processor combine the grapes, green peppercorns, and olive oil. Blend until chunky/smooth. Add the salt and reserve this dressing in a small bowl.

Peel and core the pear, cut into julienne strips, and sprinkle with lemon juice to prevent it from darkening.

Make a bed of arugula on each salad plate.

Dip the slices of Gruyère first in beaten egg, then in bread crumbs. Heat a large skillet over medium heat, add the butter, and when melted add the cheese and sauté until golden on the outside. (If the skillet is not large enough to hold cheese comfortably, perform this step in batches.) Flip and cook on the second side until golden and cheese is melted. Remove and place on the arugula. Garnish each plate with some of the julienne pear strips, drizzle with dressing, and serve.

SUMMER DINNER SALADS

SMOKED CHICKEN, SHRIMP, ENDIVE, AND WALNUT SALAD
SERVES 4

I once tried to take this salad off the menu at Trumps and nearly caused a riot in Beverly Hills. I attribute its success to a dressing that seems rich but isn't—a modern mock mayonnaise, light and refreshing.

Pairing unlikely ingredients can produce a pleasing effect and add interest to a salad. Endive and walnuts are classic together, the bitter and nutty flavors melding, but there is a personality conflict when we combine the flavors of smoked chicken and shrimp. A tart dressing highlights both the chicken and the shrimp and makes their flavors behave. It is particularly important that the endive and chicken be cut into a size and shape as similar as possible. The salad tastes better when guests spear the right ratio of different ingredients on their forks.

1	pound shrimps, cooked
1	pound smoked chicken meat
4	heads Belgian endive (about 1 pound)
½	cup coarsely chopped walnuts
⅓	cup plain yogurt
4	tablespoons fresh lemon juice
¼	cup walnut oil
4	tablespoons chopped chives

Peel and devein the shrimps, cut them into large dice, and place in mixing bowl. Cut the smoked chicken into ½-inch slivers about 2 inches long and add to shrimps. Wash the endive, reserve 8 large outer spears for decoration, and cut the rest into slivers the same size as the chicken, from tip to root. Combine with the shrimps and chicken. Add the walnuts.

In another mixing bowl, make the dressing by combining the yogurt and lemon juice. Slowly beat in the walnut oil, a few drops at a time, letting it become absorbed before adding more. Fold in the chives.

Toss the salad ingredients with the dressing, mound on plates, and decorate with the reserved endive spears.

ASIAN CHICKEN SALAD   SERVES 6

The amount of work that goes into this salad should not put you off—it's more than worth the effort. This is an Asian-inspired salad, although one would find nothing like it in the Orient. I have borrowed from one cuisine to satisfy another, combining ingredients in a new way. If you can make flavors work in new contexts, you've created something.

The many ingredients in this salad combine into groups. Mint, cilantro, and grapefruit form the acidic, aromatic, and tart group. Sesame and roasted garlic combine to form a nutty, musky group. Ginger is an accent that stands alone.

½   cup salad oil
24   garlic cloves, peeled
3   cups chicken stock (page 258) or canned low-sodium chicken broth
2   cups peanut oil, or enough to fill a medium pot to a depth of 2 inches
2   ounces fresh pasta or packaged egg roll skins, sliced into ¼-inch strips
3½   pounds cooked chicken, meat only (about 3½ cups shredded)
2   cups fresh grapefruit juice
¼   cup soy sauce
¼   cup dark sesame oil
½   pound snow peas, slivered and blanched
2   grapefruits, separated into sections, membrane removed
2   cups tightly packed finely slivered Napa or Chinese cabbage
3   tablespoons finely chopped fresh gingerroot
3   tablespoons chopped cilantro
2   tablespoons chopped mint leaves

To prepare the roasted garlic: Preheat the oven to 325°. In a small ovenproof skillet heat ¼ cup of the salad oil and sauté the garlic cloves over medium heat until they are golden, approximately 7 minutes. Add 1 cup of the chicken stock, bring to a boil, and place the skillet, uncovered, in the oven. Roast until the garlic is soft, about 15 minutes. Remove from oven, transfer the garlic to a plate, and reserve. Reserve the liquid for the dressing.

To prepare the pasta: In a wok or pot 5 to 6 inches deep heat the peanut oil to 325° and fry about 1 ounce of pasta at a time until golden and crisp, about 1 minute. Remove with a slotted spoon and drain on paper towels.

To prepare the chicken: Cut chicken into roughly ½-inch by 2-inch pieces and reserve in a large mixing bowl.

To prepare the dressing: Combine remaining 2 cups of stock, the grapefruit juice, and the liquid from the roasted garlic in a 2-quart pot, place over high heat, bring to a boil, and cook until reduced by three quarters. About 1 cup of thick, viscous liquid should remain. Add soy sauce, place in a medium bowl, and cool to room temperature. When cool, use a wire whisk to beat in sesame oil and remaining ¼ cup salad oil until incorporated.

To assemble the salad, toss together the fried pasta, chicken, snow peas, grapefruit sections, cabbage, ginger, cilantro, mint, and half the dressing. (The pasta will break.) Arrange on plates, garnish with roasted garlic, and spoon the rest of the dressing over the garlic.

CHICKEN, SPINACH, EGGPLANT, AND PEANUTS

SERVES 4

The chicken salads that are so popular, so much a part of American salad and sandwich culture, are perfect in conception, but they almost always disappoint me. This chicken salad will never become standard, and its flavors will excite even the most jaded palate.

Peanut butter, whose best friend is usually jelly, becomes a different ingredient in the presence of sour and salty companions. I use tart lemon juice and sweetly mild malt vinegar together to achieve a balanced contrast to the peanut flavor. Using a large amount of only one of these ingredients would overpower the others. Miso, the salty Japanese bean paste, mediates among all the elements of the salad.

1	medium eggplant (about 1 pound)
	salt
2½	pounds cooked chicken, meat only (about 2½ cups)
1	tablespoon dark miso paste
2	tablespoons unsweetened smooth peanut butter
¼	cup malt or rice vinegar
⅓	cup plus 4 tablespoons salad oil
1	bunch spinach, trimmed of stems and washed (4 to 5 ounces)
4	tablespoons fresh lemon juice

Cut the unpeeled eggplant diagonally into ¼-inch slices, sprinkle with salt, and layer in the bottom of a bowl. Place another bowl on top of the eggplant and weight it with a heavy jar or coffee can. Set aside for 1 hour.

Meanwhile, remove the meat from the chicken, shred it, and reserve on a plate.

To make the dressing, combine the miso and the peanut butter in a mixing bowl and dilute with the vinegar, then beat in ⅓ cup oil. The dressing will probably break at this point, but do not worry. Whisk in some water, a teaspoon at a time, until the dressing forms an emulsion.

Discard the liquid that has drained from the eggplant and pat the slices dry. Heat 1 tablespoon oil in a large skillet and lightly sauté 2 or 3 slices of eggplant. Remove and drain on paper towels. Repeat with more oil and the rest of the eggplant. Reserve on a plate.★

To assemble the salad, arrange the room-temperature slices of eggplant on plates. Toss the spinach with the lemon juice and arrange over the slices of eggplant. Toss the chicken with the peanut dressing and arrange on the spinach.

★Can be prepared up to 2 hours in advance to this point and kept covered at room temperature.

SEARED LAMB AND ENDIVE SALAD   SERVES 4

The combination of flavors in this dressing includes mint, a classic garnish for lamb that cuts the meat's fatty taste. Mint, dill, and cilantro together work even better than using mint alone. These three herbs are tasted as one, but they need garlic in the background—without it, the combination would not be as strong or as sensually pleasing.

2	tablespoons salad oil
1½	pounds lean lamb from the loin or leg (in one piece)
3	tablespoons chopped fresh mint
1	tablespoon chopped fresh dill
4	tablespoons chopped cilantro
2	tablespoons finely minced garlic
¼	cup salad oil
2	tablespoons red wine vinegar
2	medium heads Belgian endive (about 3 to 4 ounces each)
1	tablespoon fresh lemon juice

In a skillet heat the salad oil until smoking. Add the lamb and sear on all sides so that it's charred rare. Remove the meat and let it rest on a plate.

Combine the mint, dill, cilantro, garlic, ¼ cup oil, and the vinegar in a blender or processor. Blend until smooth and reserve in a small bowl.

Sliver the endive from tip to root. If not to be served immediately, toss with a little lemon juice diluted in water (acidulated water) to prevent discoloring.

Toss the endive with half the dressing and mound on plates. Cut the lamb into ½-inch slices. Place some of the seared lamb on each salad and dress with the remaining dressing.

PORK AND GREEN CABBAGE SALAD
WITH DILL AND CAPER DRESSING   SERVES 4

I like white meats—a category that includes pork—at room temperature. For this salad veal or chicken can be substituted. Meaty fish such as sturgeon or swordfish would also be delicious.

1	small head green cabbage, cored and finely slivered
1	tablespoon kosher salt
2	tablespoons salad oil
2	pork tenderloins (about 1¾ pounds)
2	tablespoons chopped fresh dill
4	tablespoons drained capers
2	tablespoons finely minced garlic
⅛	cup red wine vinegar
¼	cup olive oil

Toss the slivered cabbage with the salt and place in a colander to drain for 1 hour.

Meanwhile, in a skillet large enough to hold the meat, heat the oil to nearly smoking. Add the pork and sear on both sides. Lower flame and continue to cook for 5 minutes; it should be charred but not well done. Remove from heat and let stand 15 minutes before cutting into ½-inch slices. The pork continues to cook as it cools. (Don't worry about the pork being undercooked; it won't be.)

Combine the dill, capers, garlic, vinegar, and olive oil in a blender or processor. Blend until smooth.

Rinse the cabbage in cold water and pat dry. In a mixing bowl toss the cabbage with half the dressing and mound on salad plates. Place some of the sliced pork on each salad and drizzle with the remaining dressing.

WARM SCALLOP AND WATERCRESS
SALAD WITH BACON VINAIGRETTE

SERVES 4

Bacon is chewy and almost crisp when its fat is rendered. Undercook the scallops so they retain their creamy sweetness and don't become like little rubber bands. These textures should contrast with each other and with the texture of the apples.

Shellfish and bacon generally complement each other nicely because of the contrasting flavors of the sea and the smokehouse. Astringent and tart, apples make a good contrast to the spicy watercress.

2	bunches watercress (about 3 to 4 ounces)
½	medium Granny Smith or green pippin apple
1	tablespoon fresh lemon juice
¼	cup salad oil
¾	pound bacon, cut into ½-inch pieces
1	pound bay scallops, or horizontally halved sea scallops
2	tablespoons finely minced shallots
⅔	cup sherry vinegar

Wash watercress and trim away the bottom stems and any yellow leaves. Dry watercress on towels, then mound on four salad plates.

Core the apple without peeling. Cut into quarters, then cut each quarter into ⅛-inch slices. Toss with lemon juice to keep from turning brown and arrange around the watercress.

Combine the oil and bacon in a 9-inch cold skillet and sauté over medium heat 4 minutes. Increase the heat to high, add the scallops, and let cook for 2 minutes. Add the shallots and the vinegar and continue to cook 30 seconds.

Using a large slotted spoon, remove the bacon and the scallops and divide among the plates. Drizzle the salads with the dressing and serve immediately.

WARM SAUSAGE AND POTATO SALAD   SERVES 4

This recipe is a good exercise for developing confidence with a recipe. Do you want your potatoes peeled or not? What kind of sausage do you like—hot or sweet? Would you rather use a large onion or a small one? All these decisions will make this recipe your own.

This variation on a warm bacon dressing substitutes the fat of the sausages, which is full of flavor, for the oil of the vinaigrette. This salad makes a nice Sunday supper.

4   hothouse or beefsteak tomatoes
12   small new potatoes, cooked and quartered
1   medium red onion, peeled and finely slivered (about ¾ cup)
6   homemade sausages (any of the meat or poultry sausages from
      the Sausages chapter) or commercial Italian sausages
¼   cup olive oil
⅓   cup sherry vinegar

Slice the tomatoes tip to stem and toss with the cooked potatoes and raw onion. Divide among four salad plates.

Slice the raw sausages into 2-inch pieces and combine with olive oil in a cold skillet. Cook over medium heat until the sausages are no longer pink and have rendered their fat. Add the sherry vinegar and cook 30 seconds. Using a slotted spoon, remove the sausages and arrange on the salads. Ladle the vinegar and pan drippings over the top. Serve immediately.

RAW, MARINATED, AND CURED FIRST COURSES

■ ● ▲

Cooking without heat—or not cooking at all—is an intriguing way of preparing food. But you must follow these rules: Insist on the finest and freshest ingredients, assemble the dish immediately prior to serving, and serve well chilled. Whether raw, marinated, or cured, an uncooked dish depends for its success on the boldness of the cook—the confidence to combine flavors in an intense way. Choose the flavors of a dish—the herbs and spices—carefully, remembering that they do not mellow or change as they might when cooked by heat. A beginning course should leave your guests hungry for more food. These starters are spicy, tart, and aromatic introductions to a meal, stimulating the senses to crave what is to follow.

THE CLASSIC STEAK TARTARE SERVES 4

The saltiness and spiciness of this traditional tartare disguise the rawness of the meat, and that's probably why this dish has always been so popular. Horseradish, mustard, and Tabasco are spicy; they form the most immediate sensation yet linger longest on the palate. Because the capers and anchovies are salty, they highlight other aspects of the spicy elements so that the presence of the horseradish, mustard, and Tabasco is more than just a hot sensation. Lemon and parsley cut through both the saltiness and spiciness of the other ingredients. They cleanse the palate so that your mouth keeps asking for more. This tartare is also good with salmon and needs nothing other than good pumpernickel toast.

8	anchovy fillets
¼	cup drained capers
1	teaspoon grated horseradish, preferably fresh
2	tablespoons grainy mustard
2	tablespoons finely chopped parsley
2	tablespoons finely minced shallots
½	teaspoon Tabasco sauce, or to taste
1	egg yolk
¼	cup fresh lemon juice
2	tablespoons virgin olive oil
1	pound boneless fresh beef top round, trimmed and finely chopped by hand or put through the large holes of a meat grinder

Place four plates in the refrigerator to chill. Chop 4 anchovies together with the capers and place in mixing bowl. Add horseradish, mustard, parsley, shallots, and Tabasco sauce. Add the egg yolk and lemon juice and mix well. Slowly beat in the oil, mixing until absorbed.★ Add the meat to the mixing bowl and combine gently. Mound on cold plates and decorate with the remaining anchovies. Serve immediately with an accompaniment of warm toast or fresh dark bread.

★Can be prepared to this point up to 2 hours in advance and refrigerated.

LAMB CARPACCIO ON A
GRAPEFRUIT TARRAGON GLAZE

SERVES 4

Reduced grapefruit juice is both sweet and tart. Combine it with tarragon and a good amount of freshly ground pepper (I like this dish spicy, but you may not). Each flavor pops out, not unexpectedly, but surprising nonetheless.

2   cups fresh grapefruit juice
2   tablespoons finely chopped fresh tarragon *or* I tablespoon dried
¼   cup salad oil
8–12 boneless fresh lean lamb slices from the leg or loin (about 12–16 ounces total weight—see note below)
2   grapefruits, separated into sections, membrane removed
    freshly ground pepper to taste

Chill four plates. Combine the grapefruit juice and half the fresh tarragon in a small saucepan, bring to a boil over high heat, and continue boiling until mixture reduces and becomes thick and syrupy, about 10 to 15 minutes. Strain into a mixing bowl, discarding cooked tarragon, and cool to room temperature. When cool, beat in the oil until absorbed. If the mixture has a very shiny appearance and seems like it's going to separate, add a few drops of water or grapefruit juice.★

To serve, coat chilled plates with grapefruit glaze. Arrange lamb slices over the glaze and add pepper as desired. Garnish with grapefruit sections and the remaining fresh tarragon.

Note: You can have your butcher slice the meat for you, but with a little practice you should be able to perform this task yourself. The tricks are to have a very sharp slicing knife, one that is long and thin, and to partially freeze the meat for about 30 minutes to firm it before slicing. If not paper-thin, the slices may be very lightly flattened using the side of a large chef's knife, but do not flatten so much that you destroy the texture of the meat.

★Can be prepared to this point up to 1 hour in advance.

BRANDIED LAMB JERKY

SERVES 8 TO 10

(Allow 11 to 13 days advance preparation time)

In testing this recipe, I realized how easy jerky is to make and how charming it looks wrapped in cheesecloth and hanging in the refrigerator to dry. Once it's made, you can wrap the jerky in plastic wrap and keep it for several weeks in the refrigerator or even freeze it so you'll always be ready for an impromptu cocktail party.

The stronger aromatic herbs, the ones that seem to be oily—like sage, rosemary, oregano, marjoram, and thyme—are always good in marinated or cured preparations because they retain their flavor. The flavor of more delicate herbs such as tarragon, chervil, and parsley disappears over a period of time, so these should not be used.

This jerky is less salty than the commercial kind. The brandy gives it a dusky flavor that's enhanced by allspice—the secret ingredient.

½   cup brandy
2   tablespoons chopped fresh oregano *or* 1 tablespoon dried
1   1½- to 2-pound rack of lamb, bones removed
1   cup sugar
½   cup kosher salt
2   tablespoons freshly ground black pepper
¼   teaspoon ground allspice
1   loaf French bread
1   cup virgin olive oil
     lemon wedges

The first day, make a marinade by combining the brandy and oregano. Transfer to an airtight plastic bag or shallow covered container, add the lamb, and refrigerate overnight.

The second day, make the curing mixture by combining the sugar and kosher salt. Drain the lamb, discard the marinade, and cover lamb generously with the curing mixture. Place on a platter with edges to catch the liquid that will accumulate. Refrigerate overnight.

The third day, remove the lamb from the "cure" and pat dry. Discard the sugar/salt mixture and the liquids that have accumulated in it. Combine the pepper with the allspice and roll the lamb in this mixture. Tie the lamb loosely in two layers of cheesecloth, tie with a string, and hang in the refrigerator, allowing air to circulate around the meat. Leave to dry for 7 to 10 days. The lamb should be firm, almost hard, when you squeeze it.

To serve, cut French bread into ¼-inch slices. Preheat oven to 300°. Place rounds of bread on a baking sheet and generously brush with olive oil. Place in the oven for 5 minutes. Turn and continue to bake until edges turn golden. Transfer to a bread basket. Cut the lamb jerky into very thin slices. Place on a platter and surround with lemon wedges. Serve the toasted bread separately.

ORANGE AND PEPPER PROSCIUTTO   SERVES 12

(Allow 6½ weeks advance preparation time)

Home cooks seem to think they can't possibly prepare the processed meats that are found in delicatessens. And in fact you very seldom see recipes for these delicacies outside specialized charcuterie cookbooks. This recipe for a type of prosciutto, a cured Italian ham, is simple, safe to prepare, and should give you great satisfaction. The meat will need to be air-dried in the refrigerator for 6 weeks but, once done, will keep for several weeks or may be frozen. If you've never made anything remotely like this, be fearless; then it's a genuine adventure, and besides, it's both fun and easy.

¾	cup Cointreau or other orange liqueur
2	oranges, grated zest only
¼	cup sugar
1	2½- to 3-pound rack of veal *or* 2 pounds boneless pork loin
½	cup kosher salt
4	tablespoons freshly ground black pepper
2	oranges, separated into sections, membrane removed
	cheesecloth for wrapping meat

The first day, make the marinade by combining the Cointreau and grated zest of one orange. Transfer the marinade to an airtight plastic bag or shallow covered container, add the veal, cover, and refrigerate overnight.

The second day, make the curing mixture by combining the sugar and salt. Drain the veal and cover generously with the curing mixture. Place on a deep platter with edges to catch the liquid that will accumulate. Refrigerate, uncovered, overnight.

The third day, make a mixture of the pepper and grated zest of the remaining orange. Remove the veal from the "cure" and pat dry. Roll the meat in the pepper mixture, tie loosely in two layers of cheesecloth, secure with a string, and hang in the refrigerator, allowing air to circulate around the meat. Allow the meat to dry for 5 to 6 weeks. When the meat is dried, it should be firm and hard to squeeze.

To serve, unwrap the meat and cut into paper-thin slices using a long slicing knife. (If your knives are not sharp, or if your knife skills are not good, place the meat in the freezer and partially freeze to make slicing easier.) Arrange slices of meat on plates and garnish with orange sections. Offer freshly ground black pepper at the table.

SHERRY-MARINATED
CHICKEN AND MUSHROOMS
SERVES 4

(Allow 1 day advance preparation time)

The Chinese have a way of steeping chicken in hot liquid so that it cooks as it cools. The resulting texture is quite remarkable and cannot be attained by any other cooking method. The Spanish have a method of pickling called *escabeche* in which a hot pickling brine is poured over chicken, rabbit, or fish, which is then cooked and cooled before refrigerating. The method I use here for marinating chicken is akin to both these methods, but the flavors transcend any ethnic boundaries.

This dish combines several opposite flavors, layered in such a way that they highlight each other. Sherry is a fortified wine; its sweetness is balanced by the tart lemon juice. Rosemary stands out as a strong flavor in combination with sherry. But rosemary is not just aromatic; it's also slightly medicinal, although lemon juice and garlic cut through that quality.

2   cups dry sherry or Madeira
½   cup fresh lemon juice
I   tablespoon fresh rosemary *or* I teaspoon dried
½   medium onion, finely minced (about ½ cup)
I   tablespoon finely minced garlic
¼   cup virgin olive oil
½   teaspoon salt, or to taste
I   pound chicken tenderloins, or boneless, skinless chicken breasts
      cut into ½-inch strips
¼   pound whole button mushrooms, washed
      freshly ground pepper to taste

In a 2-quart lidded saucepan combine all ingredients except chicken, mushrooms, and pepper, bring to a boil over high heat, and cook 1 minute. Add the chicken and cook, stirring, for 30 seconds. Immediately remove from heat and pour into a container or large bowl. Allow to cool to room temperature, cover, and refrigerate overnight.

The next day, drain the marinade into a saucepan, bring to a boil, and cook until the liquid is reduced by half. Remove from heat, transfer to a bowl, and chill. To serve, combine chicken and mushrooms and marinade and mound on plates. Offer freshly ground pepper at the table.

SALMON TARTARE WITH
TOMATILLO AND MUSTARD

SERVES 4

Delicious as it is, the flavor of a classic tartare tends to over-power most fish. Sometimes you might want this effect (if your guests are not too adventurous), but if you prefer to taste salmon, this recipe makes an interesting departure from the original.

Tomatillo and mustard seed are the focus flavors here, with the other ingredients forming a foundation for them. Tart, cleans-ing lemon juice, parsley, and tomatillos are contrasted by the saltiness of the capers and mustard. When flavors are tart or sour, salt is essential to bring out the taste. Red onion is the only ingredient that excites the nose, and this helps us to taste all the other flavors. When you chew the mustard seeds, they pop, exploding with quick, short bursts of flavor. This textural con-trast is a lot of fun.

2	small tomatillos
¼	cup capers, drained
4	tablespoons chopped parsley
2	tablespoons mustard seed
l	tablespoon grainy mustard
2	tablespoons finely minced red onion plus 4 thin slices (for garnish)
¼	cup fresh lemon juice
2	tablespoons virgin olive oil
l	pound fresh salmon, skin and bones removed
4	lemon wedges
8	slices toast

Remove and discard the paperlike covering from the toma-tillos and finely chop. You should have ⅓ to ½ cup. Place in a mixing bowl. Chop the capers with the parsley and add to the tomatillos. Add the mustard seed, grainy mustard, minced on-ion, lemon juice, and oil and combine well.★

Just prior to serving, add the salmon to the mixture in the bowl and, using a fork, mash together well. Mound on plates. Decorate each mound with a slice of red onion and a wedge of lemon. Serve immediately with warm toast.

★Can be prepared to this point up to 6 hours in advance and refrigerated.

TUNA TARTARE WITH DRIED
TOMATOES AND GREEK OLIVES

SERVES 4 TO 5

Black olives, such as Kalamata or Niçoise, have a sultry personality. They are dark and rich, and no two bites ever taste the
same. Sun-dried tomatoes have a concentrated sweetness reminiscent of prunes. Because sweet is opposite salty, these two
elements complement each other nicely. The flavor of the dried
tomato highlights the flavor of the olive so that we taste something other than mere salt. Lemon juice is essential to cut through
these rich flavors, imparting a lightness, a cleansing astringency,
to the whole.

3	ounces sun-dried tomatoes in oil, drained and roughly chopped
16	black Greek olives, such as Kalamata, pitted and chopped
2	tablespoons chopped fresh oregano (not dried)
2	tablespoons minced shallots
3	tablespoons fresh lemon juice
2	tablespoons virgin olive oil
1	pound fresh raw tuna
4–5	lemon wedges (for garnish)
8–10	slices toast

Chill four or five plates. Combine the tomatoes, olives,
oregano, shallots, lemon juice, and oil in a mixing bowl. Finely
chop the tuna by hand.★

Just before serving, combine the tuna and the tomato/olive
mixture. Gently mix and mound on plates. Garnish each with a
lemon wedge and serve with toast.

★Can be prepared to this point up to 6 hours in advance and refrigerated.

TUNA SASHIMI ON AN ORANGE
AND GREEN PEPPERCORN GLAZE   SERVES 4

This versatile glaze makes a good sauce for grilled fish or poultry. It can also be used to dress salads. It's easy to prepare but tastes curiously difficult to prepare.

Reduced orange juice is sweet and contrasts with the peppery taste of green peppercorns, masking and diminishing their metallic quality. I find that when spicy tastes marry with sweet tastes, the sweet becomes a foundation flavor for the spicy one, pushing the hot quality off the tongue and back into the throat. Remember, when we taste flavors in different parts of the mouth we in effect layer them, so that the flavors of a dish change as we eat.

2   cups fresh orange juice
2   tablespoons green peppercorns in water, drained
½   teaspoon salt
2   ripe plum tomatoes
¼   cup salad oil
1   pound fresh tuna, sliced ¼ inch thick
2   oranges, separated into sections, membrane removed (for garnish)

Chill four plates. In a small saucepan over medium-high heat combine the orange juice, 1 tablespoon of the green peppercorns, and salt. Bring to a boil and reduce until only ⅔ cup remains. The mixture should be thick and syrupy.

Meanwhile, using a small paring knife, cut off tip and stem of the tomatoes. Remove the seeds and core, leaving only firm, outer pulp. Slit one side of the tomato and lay the tomato flat on the work surface. Cut lengthwise into ¼-inch strips, pile up strips, and cut horizontally into ¼-inch pieces. Reserve, covered, on a plate in the refrigerator.

When the orange juice mixture is reduced, transfer it to a bowl and cool to room temperature. When cool, beat in oil to make the "glaze." If the mixture has a very shiny appearance and seems like it's going to separate, add a few drops of water or unreduced orange juice. If not using immediately, reserve, covered, at room temperature.*

*Can be prepared to this point up to 2 hours in advance and refrigerated.

To serve, spoon the glaze onto plates. Arrange sliced tuna on top. Garnish with the orange sections, the remaining tablespoon of green peppercorns, and the chopped tomato.

TROUT ESCABECHE
SERVES 4 TO 6

(Allow 3 days advance preparation time)

Traditionally *escabeche*, a Spanish method of pickling fish, chicken, or rabbit, is first cooked and then marinated. My method takes a little longer, but the result is a delicately textured dish.

I like to pickle whole small fish, especially sardines or mackerel, but since these are not usually available, I have adapted this method for trout. This recipe also works well with fillets of any fish that is not too dense—especially halibut, tuna, salmon, cod, or snapper—either in whole fillets or 6-ounce pieces. To use the denser, more meaty fish such as swordfish, sea bass, or sturgeon, cut the fish into strips ½ inch thick.

I	cup fresh lemon juice
I	cup dry white wine
I	tablespoon whole coriander seeds
I	tablespoon finely minced garlic
½	medium onion, finely minced (about ½ cup)
¼	cup virgin olive oil
½	teaspoon salt
4	fresh trout, gutted and scaled, *or* I pound other fish, filleted
2	plum tomatoes, seeded and diced (about ½ cup)
2	tablespoons finely chopped parsley
	freshly ground pepper to taste
	crusty French bread

In a medium saucepan over high heat combine all ingredients except the trout, tomatoes, parsley, pepper, and bread, bring to a boil, and cook 1 minute. Place the fish in a glass dish in one layer, pour the boiling liquid over, and allow to cool to room temperature. Cover and refrigerate for 2 days.

After two days, remove the fish from the marinade. Decorate with parsley and spoon on some of the marinade, collecting the onions and tomatoes. Offer freshly ground pepper and some crusty bread at the table to soak up the marinade.

SPICY CINNAMON SHRIMP   SERVES 4

(Allow 1 day advance preparation time)

The result of combining cinnamon and orange is a new flavor—
reminiscent of both ingredients but resembling neither. This
combination has a fruity yet dusky flavor; it needs the spiciness
of cayenne pepper and the shrimp's metallic impression to make
cinnamon work in a savory context—I don't want this to taste
like mincemeat pie.

1	cup fresh orange juice
2	tablespoons fresh lemon juice
1	orange, grated zest only
2	cinnamon sticks
1	teaspoon cayenne pepper
1	teaspoon salt, or to taste
1	tablespoon dark sesame oil
16	jumbo shrimps, peeled and deveined with tails left intact
2	ripe vine-ripened or hothouse tomatoes, sliced from tip to stem
2	tablespoons chopped parsley

In a medium saucepan over high heat combine all ingredients
except the shrimps, tomatoes, and parsley. Bring to a boil,
cover, and cook 1 minute. Place the shrimps in a glass bowl and
pour the boiling marinade over them. Cover and allow to cool to
room temperature. Refrigerate overnight.

The next day, place sliced tomatoes on a platter, arrange the
shrimps on top, spoon the marinade over them and sprinkle with
chopped parsley.

LEMON AND GARLIC GRAVLAX   SERVES 16

(Allow 5 to 6 days advance preparation time)

When certain recipes take a long time to prepare, I always find it
rewarding to make a lot at one time. Preparing a large quantity
of food is also a good excuse to have a party. Gravlax, or cured
salmon, will keep for 10 days in the refrigerator after curing, or
it can be sliced and frozen for up to 1 month.

Gravlax makes elegant and unexpected picnic food and will make you the star of any summer potluck dinner. Of course it's possible to prepare a smaller quantity of gravlax, but you will have a problem getting nice slices from smaller fillets. Halibut, which can be lower-priced and is usually a better quality during the early summer months, is a good substitute for salmon.

Garlic and lemon is a favorite combination, but do we ever stop to think why it works so well? Garlic is an "oily" flavor, strong and sometimes overbearing; lemon is clean, astringent, and acidic. When combined, opposite sensations may either highlight or mask each other. Lemon is highlighted by garlic and becomes more than merely a tart sensation. Garlic has less bite in the presence of lemon, each softening the harshness of the other.

¼	cup salt
¼	cup sugar
2	1½- to 2-pound salmon fillets, skin on
½	cup fresh lemon juice
4	tablespoons finely minced garlic
	mayonnaise, lemon wedges, and toast (for garnish)

In a small container combine the salt and sugar, mixing well. Lay the salmon fillets flat and sprinkle them with lemon juice. Rub with garlic and evenly distribute the sugar/salt mixture on one fillet. Press the flat sides of the fillets together, flesh to flesh as if closing a book. Place between two platters or baking sheets with edges to collect the liquid that will run off. Place a 10-pound weight on top. Large juice cans or even a few bricks from the garden will do nicely. Refrigerate 5 to 6 days, draining off liquid as it accumulates in the bottom of the pan and turning the fillets once a day. When the flesh seems firm and no longer has a raw appearance, remove the weight and separate the two fillets.

To serve, slice thin diagonal strips from the fillet and arrange on chilled plates. Serve with mayonnaise, lemon wedges, and toast.

PLANTAINS AND CAVIAR   SERVES 4

Plantains are large, starchy bananalike fruits. When they're green, fry them like potato chips; when they're ripe—their skin mottled with black—they become as aromatic as overripe bananas so that when they're fried, their flesh is as smooth as buttery mashed potatoes.

I don't know why I ever thought of combining salty, crunchy caviar with sweet, creamy plantains; sometimes inspiration is a haphazard occurrence. For instance, a cook might be too busy to return something to its proper place in the refrigerator, and I might end up "discovering" a new pairing—like plantains and caviar.

1	cup salad oil, or enough to fill a medium skillet to a depth of 1 inch
3	medium-size ripe plantains, peeled and diagonally cut into ½-inch slices
4	heaped tablespoons sour cream or *crème fraîche*
4	heaped tablespoons black bean puree (recipe follows)
2	ounces black caviar
2	ounces golden caviar
¼	medium red onion, finely sliced tip to root

Heat a 1-inch depth of oil in a medium skillet over medium heat to 375°. Add the plantain slices, in batches if necessary, without crowding the skillet. Fry until lightly golden, about 2 minutes. Remove with a slotted spoon and repeat until all the slices are fried. Using the side of a cleaver or large chef's knife, gently flatten slices to a thickness of ⅜ inch.★ Refry slices until dark golden, another 2 to 3 minutes. Remove with a slotted spoon and drain on paper towels.

To serve, arrange 3 to 4 plantain slices on each plate. Spoon sour cream, black bean puree, and black and golden caviar over the slices. Garnish with slices of red onion.

★Can be prepared to this point up to 8 hours in advance and kept covered on a plate at room temperature.

BLACK BEAN PUREE
MAKES ½ CUP

I	large carrot, roughly diced (about I cup)
I	medium onion, roughly diced (about ¾ cup)
I	small ham hock (about 3 ounces)
½	cup dried black beans
I	sprig fresh thyme *or* ½ teaspoon dried
2	cups water

Combine carrot, onion, ham hock, black beans, thyme, and water in a small pot. Place over low heat and cook, covered, until beans are completely soft, 1 to 1½ hours. Discard ham hock, drain, and discard any remaining water.

Puree beans in food processor until smooth, with slight chunks. Beans may be prepared up to 1 day in advance. To reheat, place in the top of a double boiler for 20 minutes, stirring occasionally.

PANCAKES, FRITTERS, AND CROQUETTES

■ ● ▲

I think twice before attempting one of those sanctified recipes that have been "handed down from generation to generation." It's not that these recipes aren't valid or that the resulting dishes aren't delicious—often they are, but it's difficult to compete with a fond memory. Add something of yourself to an old favorite, update it, and create future memories. Listen to people talk and you'll hear that all grandmothers made pancakes or fritters or croquettes. Mine made pancakes out of all sorts of things, vegetables mostly, and I can taste them in my memory and I know how they were made. But my pancakes do not taste at all like hers because I am not her, I don't live in the same house, I don't cook with the same pots and pans. Which is not to say that I will never make good pancakes. Maybe I will and maybe I won't, but if I don't make *any* pancakes, I will provide no memories for anyone.

Pancakes are not only a sweet or a breakfast item. Think of them as simply another way of presenting food. Almost all cultures have dishes based on pancakes—French *crêpes,* Russian blinis, Chinese rice pancakes, and eastern European blintzes are just a few. Pancakes, fritters, and croquettes are opportunities for using odds and ends, even leftovers, in a creative way. The more often you cook, the greater your stock of miscellaneous trimmings in the refrigerator. Using these recipes as guides, you can make pancakes out of almost anything—leftover soups, cooked couscous, cooked vegetables, for example. You will have to fuss a little, adjusting the amount of milk, flour, and eggs for each individual kind of pancake. If your batter is too thin, add more flour. If it falls apart, add more egg. If it's too thick, add more milk. To "whip something up" is to be confident of your technique, sure of your idea, and capable of improvisation.

PANCAKES WITH FRUIT
AND SMOTHERED CHICKEN

SERVES 4

Few cultures are as fond of mixing savory and sweet ingredients as we Americans. Perhaps that is why Chinese food is so popular in America—the Chinese do a lot of that, too.

This recipe focuses on the contrast between sweet and hot. Sweet ingredients are sensed on the tongue and can balance peppery flavors by masking some of their heat. We enjoy hot sensations, such as black pepper, more when we taste them in the throat because then our tongue is free to experience other flavors.

I also tried the griddle cakes with the addition of chunky peanut butter and achieved a remarkable pancake. Try this variation; children particularly like them this way. Just add 2 tablespoons of chunky peanut butter with the diced fruit.

l   cup milk
4   tablespoons freshly ground black pepper
2   whole boneless chicken breasts, halved
l   cup all-purpose flour
½   teaspoon baking powder
¼   teaspoon salt
l   tablespoon sugar
l   egg, lightly beaten
l   cup buttermilk
4   tablespoons melted unsalted butter
4   tablespoons mixed diced fruits—such as banana, strawberries, blueberries, apple—and chopped nuts
½   cup bacon fat, salad oil, or shortening, or enough to fill a medium skillet to a depth of ½ inch

Topping:

maple syrup
butter
freshly ground pepper

In a medium bowl combine the milk with 2 tablespoons of the ground pepper. Add the chicken breasts and let stand while you prepare the pancake batter.

Meanwhile, make the pancakes: In a mixing bowl combine ½ cup of the flour, the baking powder, salt, and sugar.* Make a well in the center of the flour and add the egg and the buttermilk. Mix the flour into the liquid a little at a time, incorporating it as you go. The mixture should be smooth, but a few lumps won't hurt. Add 2 tablespoons melted butter. Add the fruit and nuts and mix.

Remove the chicken from the milk and lightly dredge in remaining flour, shaking off excess. Place back in the milk and dredge once more with the flour.

Fill a medium-size heavy skillet with fat to a depth of ½ inch and heat over medium heat to 325°. The fat is hot enough to cook in when a drop of water immediately splatters and dances on the surface or when a bit of food added to the fat immediately bubbles. Preheat oven to 200°.

*If using a processor or an electric mixer to prepare the batter, combine all dry ingredients, then slowly add the wet ones. Add the fruit and nuts after blending. Batter can be made up to 2 hours in advance.

Add the chicken to the hot oil and cook, turning once, until golden and crisp, about 5 to 6 minutes on each side. Drain on paper towels. Reserve in oven while cooking the griddle cakes.

Heat a medium skillet with ½ tablespoon butter over medium heat. When the skillet is hot, place small dollops of the batter in it and cook 2 to 3 minutes or until the pancake batter seems to dry out a bit and bubbles appear and begin to break on the surface. Flip and continue to cook another minute or two. Keep the griddle cakes warm in the oven while the other batches cook.

Arrange a stack of griddle cakes on each of four warm plates with the chicken next to it. Offer maple syrup and butter and encourage the liberal use of freshly ground pepper.

Note on frying oil: Strain your frying oil through a cloth or a coffee filter paper and refrigerate after using; it's wasteful to use it only once. Taste and smell the oil to make sure it's still good. Oil only gets tastier the more you fry in it—up to a point—but don't use the same oil for savories and sweets.

POTATO PANCAKES

MAKES 16 PANCAKES,
SERVES 4 AS A MAIN COURSE,
8 AS AN APPETIZER

Many different types of pancakes can be made from potatoes, from a smooth potato batter to thin slices of uncooked potatoes cooked into cakes. These are made of shredded, uncooked potatoes bound together with eggs, cream, and flour. With slight adjustments, you can use this recipe to make pancakes from any crisp, shredded vegetable such as carrot, zucchini, or turnip.

½   pound Idaho potatoes
1   teaspoon fresh lemon juice
4   tablespoons finely minced onion
3   tablespoons all-purpose flour
1   egg
¼   cup milk
¼   teaspoon salt
    freshly ground pepper to taste
4   tablespoons unsalted butter (for cooking pancakes)

Wash the potatoes and grate them, unpeeled, using the fine grating blade of a processor or with a hand grater. Place in a mixing bowl and toss with lemon juice to prevent discoloration. Add the onion, flour, egg, milk, salt, and pepper and mix well. Preheat oven to 200°.

Melt a scant teaspoon of butter in a large skillet over medium heat without letting it burn. Put heaped soupspoon dollops of batter into the hot skillet and cook several minutes, until golden. Flip the pancakes and continue to cook for 2 minutes or until golden. Remove and keep warm in the oven while you prepare the others, adding a pat of butter to the skillet each time.

Serve the pancakes with one of the following garnishes or use them as a side dish for meat or poultry.

POTATO PANCAKES WITH GOAT CHEESE AND APPLES

SERVES 4 AS A MAIN COURSE, 8 AS AN APPETIZER

I believe in supporting our cottage industries, especially when their products are good ones. Use a Laura Chenel or a Sadie Kendall California goat cheese. They are fresh, tasty, well-made cheeses. Or seek out a good cheesemaker in your region of the country and use its product.

Here I have layered an astringent, cleansing flavor with a strong, lingering flavor. The tartness of apples cuts the distinctive goat flavor of the cheese. Textures create an important dimension in this dish. Creamy goat cheese and crisp apples play against the almost crispy potato pancakes.

I	recipe potato pancakes (page 85)
½	pound goat cheese such as Montrachet or *chevrefeuille*
¼	cup sour cream or *crème fraîche*
I	tablespoon unsalted butter
2	Granny Smith apples, peeled, cored, and cut into 12 pieces each

Prepare the potato pancakes (see previous recipe) and reserve in a 200° oven.★ Preheat the broiler.

In a blender or processor combine the goat cheese and sour cream. Puree until smooth. Transfer to a bowl and reserve.

★Pancakes can be made up to 1 day in advance, kept, covered, in the refrigerator, and reheated at 250° before proceeding with the rest of the recipe.

In a medium skillet melt the butter over medium heat without burning, add the apples, and sauté until slightly soft but not falling apart, about 5 to 7 minutes. Place the potato pancakes on a heatproof platter, arrange the apples on the pancakes, and spread the goat cheese mixture over the apples. Place under the broiler until the cheese mixture melts, bubbles, and starts to turn lightly golden, about 3 to 4 minutes.

POTATO PANCAKES WITH OYSTERS AND CAVIAR

SERVES 4 AS A MAIN COURSE,
8 AS AN APPETIZER

Caviar purists will tell you that the only way to eat good caviar is by itself, spreading it with a mother-of-pearl spoon onto toast. I cannot say that I disagree; on the other hand, good eating depends partly on using the right ingredient in the right context. This recipe is more successful with a less expensive caviar, one that is saltier and fishier than Beluga—for example, whitefish roe, salmon roe, or an American sturgeon caviar.

The charm of this recipe is in its combination of flavors. When you marry flavors so that they harmonize, you must do so in a way that allows you to taste all the flavors, with none overpowering another. The seafood flavors here are muffled by the blandness of the potato, making the oysters less fishy and the caviar less salty. Sour cream is a pickup for the potato. The real secret ingredient is lemon juice, which not only strengthens the sourness of the cream but also gives an acidic backbone to this ensemble.

1	recipe potato pancakes (page 85)
1	tablespoon unsalted butter
16	shucked oysters
2	tablespoons fresh lemon juice
4	ounces caviar (let your pocketbook be the guide)
3	tablespoons sour cream or *crème fraîche*
4	tablespoons chopped chives

Prepare the potato pancakes (page 85) and keep warm in a 200° oven* while you prepare the oysters.

*Pancakes can be made up to 1 day in advance, kept, covered, in the refrigerator, and reheated at 250° before proceeding with the rest of the recipe.

Melt the butter in a small skillet over low heat and cook the oysters about 1 minute. Turn off the flame and add the lemon juice.

Garnish each pancake with a dollop of sour cream. Divide the oysters and their juices over the sour cream, top with a spoonful of caviar, and garnish with the chopped chives.

CORN PANCAKES

MAKES 12 TO 15 PANCAKES,
SERVES 3 TO 4 AS A MAIN COURSE,
8 TO 10 AS AN APPETIZER

If you decide to use canned corn in this recipe, which I do not recommend, drain the kernels well and be forewarned that they will sweeten the pancakes more than fresh or frozen corn will.

2   cups fresh or frozen (defrosted) corn kernels
4   tablespoons finely minced onion
1   cup cornmeal
½   cup all-purpose flour
1   teaspoon baking powder
1   teaspoon salt
4   eggs
1   cup buttermilk
    freshly ground pepper to taste
4   tablespoons unsalted butter (for cooking pancakes)

Place the corn in a food processor and pulse to break up the kernels into a coarse mixture, about 10 to 15 quick pulses, or chop by hand using a large chef's knife. Transfer to a mixing bowl and add onion, cornmeal, flour, baking powder, and salt. Mix well. Add eggs and buttermilk and mix well.* Preheat oven to 200°.

Melt a scant teaspoon butter in a large skillet over medium heat without letting it burn. Put large soupspoons of pancake batter into the hot skillet and cook until bubbles form in the pancake and the surface seems to dry. Flip the pancake and continue to cook for 2 minutes or until golden. As you finish batches of pancakes, keep them warm in the oven while making the rest. Serve as a side dish or prepare one of the following garnishes.

*Batter can be made up to 1 day in advance to this point, but do not add the baking powder more than 1 hour in advance of cooking.

CORN PANCAKES WITH MINCED LAMB AND RED PEPPERS

SERVES 4 TO 5 AS A MAIN COURSE,
8 TO 10 AS AN APPETIZER

We rely on secret ingredients here—garlic, coriander, lemon, and balsamic vinegar—to excite our senses by forming a background of flavor that is both perfumy and tart, thereby dressing up this dish, which would otherwise be uninteresting.

I	recipe corn pancakes
I	tablespoon olive oil
I	pound lamb loin or chop, trimmed of fat and minced, or cooked leftover lamb (about 1½ cups)
2	medium red peppers, seeded and thinly sliced tip to stem
I	teaspoon finely minced garlic
I	teaspoon finely minced onion
I	teaspoon ground coriander
I	tablespoon fresh lemon juice
2	tablespoons balsamic vinegar
2	tablespoons unsalted butter
½	teaspoon salt, or to taste

Prepare the corn pancakes (page 88) and keep warm in a 200° oven.*

Heat the olive oil in a medium skillet over high heat, add the lamb, and sauté briefly, about 1 minute. Add the sliced pepper and sauté another minute, tossing. Lower the heat to medium, add the garlic, onion, coriander, lemon juice, and vinegar and cook 1 minute. Turn off flame, swirl in the butter, and add the salt. Garnish the pancakes with the lamb and peppers and spoon the sauce over them.

*Pancakes can be made up to 1 day in advance and kept, covered, in the refrigerator. To reheat, place, uncovered, in a 250° oven until warm, about 20 minutes.

CORN PANCAKES WITH
CHICKEN LIVER AND BACON

SERVES 4 AS A MAIN COURSE,
8 AS AN APPETIZER

The combination of flavors in this recipe is designed to disguise the strong taste of liver. Sweet malt vinegar, grainy mustard, salty bacon, aromatic tarragon, shallots, and garlic are not obvious tastes; they mask the taste and aroma of liver.

I   recipe corn pancakes (page 88)
½   pound slab bacon, cut into ¼-inch cubes
I   pound chicken livers
I   teaspoon finely minced garlic
I   teaspoon finely minced shallots
2   tablespoons grainy mustard
I   tablespoon malt vinegar
2   tablespoons unsalted butter
2   tablespoons chopped fresh tarragon leaves or I teaspoon dried
     salt and freshly ground pepper to taste

Prepare the corn pancakes (page 88) and keep warm in a 200° oven.*

In a medium skillet cook the bacon over medium heat to render some of its fat. Raise the flame to high, add the chicken livers, and sauté until medium-rare, about 4 minutes. Pour off the bacon fat and add the garlic, shallots, mustard, and vinegar. If you are using dried tarragon, add it now. Lower flame and cook 2 minutes more. Remove from heat and swirl in the butter. Sprinkle with fresh tarragon leaves. Taste for salt and pepper. Arrange the pancakes on a platter, surround with the chicken livers, spoon the sauce over, and serve.

*Pancakes can be made up to 1 day in advance and kept, covered, in the refrigerator. To reheat, place, uncovered, in a 250° oven until warm, about 20 minutes.

CORN PANCAKES WITH MUSSELS AND TOMATO

SERVES 4 TO 5 AS A MAIN COURSE,
OR 8 TO 10 AS AN APPETIZER

When ingredients marry harmoniously, as mussels and curry do in this dish, some flavor electricity is needed to liven them up. A little curry blends so well with the flavor of mussels that you think you're tasting only mussels. Garlic helps the marriage, creating a strong background upon which we can layer sparks of dill and saffron.

1	recipe corn pancakes (page 88)
3	plum tomatoes
48	mussels, scrubbed clean and debearded
¼	cup dry white wine
1	tablespoon curry powder (page 264)
1	tablespoon finely minced garlic
½	cup whipping cream
½	tablespoon chopped fresh dill *or* ¼ teaspoon dried
	salt to taste

Prepare the corn pancakes (page 88) and keep warm in a 200° oven★ while preparing the garnish.

Using a small paring knife, cut off tip and stem of each tomato. Remove the seeds and core, leaving only firm, outer pulp. Slit one side of the tomato and lay the tomato flat on work surface. Cut into ¼-inch strips, pile up strips, and cut into ¼-inch pieces.

In a 3-quart pot combine the mussels, wine, curry, and garlic, cover, and bring to a boil over high heat. If using dried dill, add it now. Uncover, add the cream, and continue to boil until the mussels open, about 5 minutes or more, depending on the size of the mussels. When the mussels are opened, the liquid should have reduced to a sauce consistency that will nicely coat a spoon. Discard any unopened mussels. Add the chopped tomatoes. Add salt to taste.

To serve, arrange the opened mussels around the pancakes. If the sauce is too thin, let it boil another minute or until it thickens. Add fresh dill to the sauce and spoon the sauce over the mussels.

WILD RICE PANCAKES

When cooked wild rice is recooked into pancakes, the dark husks of rice become smoky and nutty in flavor. These cakes can be a wonderful accompaniment to a main course such as Game Hens, Roasted Garlic and Candied Anise (page 176) or in the Baked Salmon on Wild Rice Pancakes with Two Purees (page 202).

1½	cups slightly overcooked wild rice
1	tablespoon finely minced shallots
1	teaspoon finely minced garlic
1	egg
2	tablespoons all-purpose flour
6	tablespoons milk
¼	teaspoon salt
½	teaspoon baking powder
4	tablespoons unsalted butter, melted

Place all ingredients except for 3 tablespoons butter in a food processor and quickly pulse about 10 times to break the mixture into a very coarse batter consistency. Preheat oven to 200°.

Melt a scant tablespoon butter in a medium skillet over medium heat without letting it burn. Dollop soupspoons of batter into the hot skillet and cook until bubbles form on the surface and pancakes are firm. Flip pancakes and continue to cook for 2 minutes or until golden. Repeat until all batter is used, adding remaining butter to skillet as needed. Keep the pancakes warm in the oven while preparing the other batches. Serve with one of the following accompaniments or as a side dish.

WILD RICE PANCAKES WITH SHERRIED SMOKED TURKEY

SERVES 4 AS A MAIN COURSE,
8 AS AN APPETIZER

Smoked foods are always more interesting when there are ingredients to smooth the smoke, mask the salt, and emphasize their original, unsmoked flavor. The sweetness of sherry and other fortified wines, such as Madeira and marsala, cancels salt and masks the smoke flavor of these foods. Lemon, garlic, and shallots secretly help the sherry diminish the smoky flavor of the turkey.

If you prefer, use smoked eel, smoked chicken, or even ham to replace the smoked turkey.

I	recipe wild rice pancakes (see previous recipe)
4	tablespoons unsalted butter
I	pound smoked turkey meat, cut into ¼-inch slices
I	tablespoon finely minced garlic
I	tablespoon finely minced shallots
⅓	cup dry sherry
2	tablespoons fresh lemon juice
½	cup chicken stock (page 258) or canned low-sodium chicken broth
2	tablespoons chopped parsley
	salt and freshly ground pepper to taste

Prepare the wild rice pancakes and keep warm in a 200° oven.★

In a medium skillet melt 1 tablespoon butter over low heat, add the turkey, garlic, and shallots, cover, and cook gently, about 2 minutes. Add the sherry, raise the heat to high, bring to a boil, and cook, uncovered, until the liquid is reduced by half. Add the lemon juice and chicken stock and continue to boil until the liquid is thick enough to coat the back of a spoon. Remove from the heat and whisk in the remaining 3 tablespoons of butter. Add the chopped parsley and taste for salt and pepper.

Arrange the pancakes on a platter, top with diced turkey, and spoon the sauce over them.

★Pancakes can be made up to 1 day in advance and kept, covered, in the refrigerator. To reheat, place, uncovered, in a 250° oven until warm, about 20 minutes.

WILD RICE PANCAKES WITH
SHRIMPS AND LEMONGRASS

Seafood flavors are enhanced when they are combined with tartly aromatic lemongrass because both tastes are sensed fleetingly, here and gone in one swallow. Nothing lingers on the palate and each mouthful tastes new. I like to keep these fragile aromas pure, uncomplicated, and direct.

1	recipe wild rice pancakes (page 92)
4	tablespoons unsalted butter
16	large shrimps, peeled and deveined
1	teaspoon minced garlic
¼	cup rice wine vinegar
1	lemongrass stalk, cut into 1-inch lengths
½	teaspoon salt
2	tablespoons chopped chives

Prepare the wild rice pancakes (page 92) and keep warm in a 200° oven.*

In a medium skillet heat 1 tablespoon of the butter over medium heat, add the shrimps, and sauté lightly, about 2 minutes. Add the garlic, rice wine vinegar, and lemongrass and cook 1 minute. Remove from the heat and swirl in the remaining butter. Unless you are using the tenderest lemongrass leaves, remove the lemongrass from the sauce. Add the salt and chopped chives.

To serve, arrange the pancakes on a platter and surround them with the shrimps. Spoon the sauce over the pancakes and the shrimps.

Note: Lemongrass is available in Southeast Asian markets. It is often very woody, in which case you should peel off the outer layers, using only the centers. If these are also tough, cut them into large pieces so that they can be removed after cooking. If you're lucky enough to find—or grow—tender, young, lemongrass leaves, just chop them like any other fresh herb, leaving them in the dish for serving.

*Pancakes can be made up to 1 day in advance and kept, covered, in the refrigerator. To reheat, cover the pancakes and place them in a 250° oven for 20 minutes.

EGGPLANT PANCAKES   MAKES 8 PANCAKES, SERVES 4

1	medium eggplant (about 1¼ pounds)
1	tablespoon finely minced garlic
1	tablespoon finely minced shallots
2	tablespoons olive oil
⅓	cup plus 4 tablespoons all-purpose flour
½	teaspoon baking powder
2	eggs
½	cup chicken stock (page 258) or canned low-sodium chicken broth
2	tablespoons chopped parsley
1	teaspoon salt
½	teaspoon freshly ground pepper
2	tablespoons unsalted butter

Preheat oven to 350°, place the eggplant on a baking sheet, and bake 30 to 35 minutes, turning every 10 minutes. When the eggplant is desiccated and wrinkled, remove from oven. Scoop the flesh into a mixing bowl and mash with a fork until smooth.

In a small saucepan cook the garlic and shallots lightly in olive oil over low heat for 1 minute and add to the eggplant puree. Add the flour and baking powder, then the eggs, stock, parsley, salt, and pepper. Mix well.

Melt ½ tablespoon of the butter in a medium skillet over medium heat without letting it burn. Dollop soupspoons of batter into the hot skillet and cook until the pancake surfaces begin to dry out, about 3 minutes. Flip the pancakes and continue to cook for about 2 minutes more or until golden. Repeat until all batter is used, adding the remaining butter as needed. Serve with one of the following accompaniments or as a vegetable side dish.

EGGPLANT PANCAKES WITH SAFFRON, CHICKEN, AND BELGIAN ENDIVE

SERVES 4 AS A MAIN COURSE,
8 AS AN APPETIZER

What we smell and taste depends not only on how we combine ingredients but also on their texture and temperature. Crisp foods explode with flavor when we bite into them, while the flavor of creamy foods blends more easily with other ingredients. Cold foods are less perfumed than hot ones. The textural and temperature contrast between cooked and uncooked ingredients is essential to this dish. Smooth, creamy pancakes and chicken blend with saffron, cumin, and garlic to contrast with crisp endive and red pepper.

I	recipe eggplant pancakes (see previous recipe)
½	cup dry white wine
I	tablespoon finely minced garlic
2	pinches saffron threads *or* ¼ teaspoon powdered
I	teaspoon ground cumin
I	pound boneless, skinless chicken breasts, cut into 4 strips each
½	cup whipping cream
3	tablespoons unsalted butter
I	medium red pepper, diced into ¼-inch pieces
½	teaspoon salt
	freshly ground pepper to taste
12–16	Belgian endive leaves

Prepare the eggplant pancakes and keep warm in a 200° oven.★

Combine the white wine, garlic, saffron, cumin, and chicken in a medium saucepan, bring to a boil over high heat, and cook 2 minutes. Add the cream and reduce until the liquids thicken enough to coat the back of a spoon. Remove from the heat, whisk in the butter, and add the red pepper and salt. Taste for pepper.

To serve, arrange the pancakes on a warm platter. Place the endive leaves under the pancakes on one side of the platter. Arrange the chicken on the other side of the platter. Pour the sauce on top so that it is evenly distributed over the endive and the pancakes.

★Pancakes can be made up to 1 day in advance and kept, covered, in the refrigerator. To reheat, place, covered, in 250° oven for 15 minutes.

EGGPLANT PANCAKES WITH QUAIL AND SAGE

SERVES 4 AS A MAIN COURSE,
8 AS AN APPETIZER

Boneless quail are becoming more readily available, but if you cannot find them, a dark-meated fowl such as squab will do. Sliced breast of duck or grilled duck legs would all make delicious substitutes for quail.

With their slight bitter edge and their garlic background, these pancakes are tasty and require a garnish that will complement their bold flavors. The flavors of sage and garlic do not blend, but they are complements, showing each other off nicely. Garlic sweetens the bitterness of sage, while sage takes the edge off garlic. Both these flavors make the quail seem gamier.

I	recipe eggplant pancakes (page 95)
I	tablespoon olive oil
4	boneless quail
I	tablespoon finely minced garlic
½	cup dry white wine
½	cup chicken stock (page 258) or canned low-sodium chicken broth
I	tablespoon chopped fresh sage *or* I teaspoon dried
2	tablespoons unsalted butter
½	teaspoon salt, or to taste
	freshly ground pepper to taste

Prepare the eggplant pancakes and keep warm in a 200° oven.★

Heat the olive oil in a medium skillet over medium heat. Add the quail, breast side down, and cook 3 minutes on each side. Remove the quail, discard the fat in the pan, and return quail to the pan along with garlic and wine. If using dried sage, add it now. When the wine comes to a boil, add the chicken stock and continue to cook over medium heat until the liquid reduces, thickens, and becomes saucelike, about 7 minutes. Remove from heat, add the fresh sage, and swirl in the butter. Taste for salt and pepper.

Arrange the pancakes on a platter. Arrange quail on the pancakes and pour the sauce on top.

★Pancakes can be made up to 1 day in advance and kept, covered, in the refrigerator. To reheat, place, covered, in 250° oven for 15 minutes.

CRAB CAKES

MAKES 8 CRAB CAKES, SERVES 4

Providing recipes for favorite dishes like crab cakes is a little like trying to put oral history to paper: it loses something in the transcription. Everyone seems to have a favorite crab cake or to know the "only authentic recipe." The following is my contribution.

The background of carrot, onion, and celery gives the crab an aromatic character. The secret ingredients of curry, nutmeg, and Tabasco add aroma to the crab but need to be kept discreet.

6	tablespoons unsalted butter
½	small onion, finely diced (about ⅛ cup)
½	celery stalk, finely diced (about ¼ cup)
½	small carrot, finely diced (about ⅓ cup)
2	tablespoons all-purpose flour
¼	cup milk
¼	teaspoon curry powder
⅛	teaspoon freshly grated nutmeg
¼	teaspoon Tabasco sauce
l	egg
l	pound fresh crabmeat
l	teaspoon salt

In a medium skillet melt 3 tablespoons of the butter over medium heat. Add the onion, celery, and carrot and cook, covered, until wilted, about 3 minutes. Sprinkle with flour and cook, stirring, another minute. Add the milk, curry, nutmeg, and Tabasco. Stir until the mixture thickens, almost immediately. Scrape the mixture into a mixing bowl. Add the egg and mix. Add the crabmeat and salt and mix. Form the mixture into 8 patties.★

Heat remaining butter in a large skillet over medium heat, add the crab cakes, and cook until golden, about 5 to 7 minutes on each side. Pile the crab cakes on a warm platter. Serve them with asparagus in their own juices (page 218), in season, or with braised endive.

★Can be prepared to this point up to 1 day in advance and kept, covered, in the refrigerator.

SALMON AND MUSHROOM FRITTERS WITH CREAM SAUCE

Oil coats the palate and makes it harder to taste flavors accurately. A good well-fried fritter, though, has aromatic elements that excite the nose, making it easier for the tongue to taste flavors. Fried foods benefit from an aromatic garnish of carrots, onions, and celery because their strong aroma seems to cut the palate-dulling oil. Nutmeg is our secret ingredient; it not only adds aroma, but also sweetens the salmon.

½   pound mushrooms, cleaned
3   tablespoons unsalted butter
½   small onion, finely diced (about ¼ cup)
½   celery stalk, finely diced (about ¼ cup)
½   small carrot, finely diced (about ⅓ cup)
2   tablespoons all-purpose flour
¼   cup milk
1   egg
¼   teaspoon freshly grated nutmeg
1   pound fresh salmon, chopped
½   teaspoon salt
     freshly ground pepper to taste
1   cup dry white wine
2   tablespoons finely minced shallots
2   sprigs fresh thyme *or* ¼ teaspoon dried
2   cups fish stock (page 260)
½   cup whipping cream
3   cups salad oil, or enough to fill a 10-inch skillet to a 3-inch depth
2   tablespoons finely chopped parsley

Place half the mushrooms in a processor, puree, and reserve on a plate. Slice the remainder very finely by hand and reserve on another plate.

In a medium skillet melt the butter over medium heat. Add the onion, celery, and carrot, cover, and cook very gently until wilted, about 2 minutes. Add the pureed mushrooms and cook, uncovered, until the mixture looks dry, about 5 minutes. Add the flour and stir. Add the milk and stir until the mixture thickens, almost immediately. Remove to a mixing bowl, add the egg and nutmeg, and mix well. Add the salmon, salt, and pepper and mix. Cover and reserve in the refrigerator.

In a medium-size heavy saucepan, preferably copper, combine the white wine, shallots, thyme, and sliced mushrooms. Bring to a boil over high heat and cook 5 minutes. Add the fish stock and continue to boil until the liquid reduces, becoming almost dry. Add the cream, lower heat to medium, and cook until liquid thickens enough to coat a spoon.

Remove from heat, cover, and set aside while you fry the fritters.* Preheat the oven to 200°.

In a deep heavy 10-inch skillet, heat a 3-inch depth of oil to 375°. A small amount of fritter mixture dropped into the oil should immediately bubble when the oil is hot enough for frying. Drop tablespoon-size balls of the mixture into the oil and fry until golden, about 6 to 8 minutes. Do not crowd the oil. Keep the first fritters warm in the oven while you prepare the others.

Pour the sauce into a sauceboat. Arrange a cloth napkin on a platter and pile the fritters on top. Sprinkle with chopped parsley and serve immediately.

*Can be prepared to this point a few hours in advance.

ONION, ARTICHOKE, AND
GRUYÈRE CROQUETTES   MAKES 16 TO 18 SMALL CROQUETTES,
SERVES 3

These croquettes can be a course by themselves or a vegetable side dish, but I think they are best as cocktail food.

1	lemon
4	large artichokes
1	tablespoon unsalted butter
2	medium onions, finely diced (about 1½ cups)
¼	pound Gruyère or Emmenthaler cheese, grated
3	tablespoons all-purpose flour
8	tablespoons bread crumbs
1	teaspoon baking powder
2	eggs
½	teaspoon salt
2–3	cups salad oil

Combine water and the juice of 1 lemon to fill a 2-quart pot. Keep the lemon for rubbing the cut surfaces of the artichokes as you work. Cut the stems off the artichokes. Trim the tops, leaving a base about 1½ inches deep and exposing the center choke. Trim all around the sides and bottom to remove the dark green exterior. Place bottoms in the water as they are done. When the artichokes are trimmed, bring the water to a boil, covered, over high heat and cook for 20 minutes, or until bottoms are tender. Remove from heat and remove artichokes from the liquid. When cool enough to handle, scoop out center chokes and discard.★

Melt the butter in a small skillet over medium heat, add the onion, cover, and cook 3 minutes, until softened. Remove from heat and reserve in a mixing bowl.

Place the cooked artichoke bottoms in a food processor and pulse until coarsely chopped. Add to the onion in the mixing

---

★Cooked artichokes can be re-placed in cooking liquid and kept, covered, in the refrigerator for up to 2 days.

bowl. Add the cheese, flour, 6 tablespoons of the bread crumbs, the baking powder, and 1 egg. Mix well.★

In a small bowl lightly beat the remaining egg. Place the remaining 2 tablespoons bread crumbs in another bowl. Drop small soupspoons of batter into the egg and then roll to coat in the bread crumbs. Preheat oven to 200°.

Heat a 2-inch depth of oil to 375° in a medium-size heavy skillet. A small amount of croquette mixture dropped into the oil should immediately bubble when the oil is hot enough for frying. Fry croquettes in batches until golden, about 6 minutes. Keep the first ones warm in the oven while finishing the rest. Place a cloth napkin on a platter and pile the croquettes on top. Serve immediately.

★Can be prepared to this point up to 1 day in advance and kept, covered, in the refrigerator, but do not add the baking powder more than 1 hour before frying the croquettes.

SAUSAGES

■ ● ▲

Although everyone loves them, sausages have earned a reputation for being bad guys—greasy, full of preservatives, and generally unhealthy. The simplest way to overcome your mistrust of sausages is to make your own. Making sausages is not at all difficult, and the results are not only much healthier than commercial sausage but particularly delicious as well. There are lots of options—you can get very modern and form the sausages with heat-resistant plastic wrap, or you can use chicken breast skins. Or you can forget about making sausages altogether and use these savory mixtures to fill ravioli, make lasagna, or stuff a bird. But you should attempt, at least once, to make sausages. At Trumps I can put almost anything tasty into a sausage casing and people will order as much of it as I can prepare.

ON MAKING SAUSAGES

A note on stuffing sausages: If you don't have a meat grinder with a sausage attachment, fill a large pastry bag with the sausage mixture. Secure one end of the casings over the metal pastry tip to form one long sausage. Tie the other end of the casings in a knot. Stuff the sausage mixture into the casings. If air pockets form in the casing when you are stuffing it, prick with a pin.

An alternate method: Any of the following sausage mixtures that require preliminary poaching in water can be spooned onto an 8-inch piece of plastic wrap and tightly rolled into the shape of a long sausage.

Sausage casings: Most butchers don't stock sausage casings but will special-order them for you. They sometimes come dry and salted but are most commonly packed in salted water. Soak the dried casings for 1 hour before using. Rinse the wet ones in cold water before using. Both kinds, when wet, may be kept in the refrigerator for up to 1 week or frozen for up to 3 months.

SALMON AND DRIED-TOMATO SAUSAGES WITH ORANGE SAUCE

MAKES 8 SAUSAGES,
SERVES 4

I use salmon in this sausage for its color. You can substitute any filleted fish except those with "silvermeat," such as tuna and swordfish, because they become stringy when ground. (Silvermeat is the white covering that is found in the muscle separations of the meat.) This smooth sausage stuffing, called a *mousseline,* can also be made with chicken.

By using fresh tomatoes and a reduction of orange juice in this dish, we juxtapose the fresh flavors of the sauce ingredients to highlight the cooked and dried flavors of the same ingredients in the sausages. Sauces should not have exactly the same flavor as what's being sauced; when all the elements of a dish taste the same, it's very boring. Dried tomato has a sweet aftertaste of prune, which marries well with the orange flavor.

½ cup dried tomatoes in olive oil, drained and loosely packed
1 pound boneless, skinless salmon
½ teaspoon salt
¼ teaspoon cayenne pepper
4 tablespoons grated orange zest
2 tablespoons minced shallots
1 tablespoon minced garlic
6 large egg whites (¾ cup)
4 feet sausage casing
2 ripe plum tomatoes
2 cups fresh orange juice
1 cup fish stock (page 260)
½ cup whipping cream
3 tablespoons unsalted butter
3 oranges, separated into sections, membrane removed

Combine dried tomatoes, salmon, salt, cayenne pepper, orange zest, shallots, garlic, and egg whites in the bowl of a food processor or blender and blend until smooth. Stuff the mixture into casings or form 2 long sausages in plastic wrap (see page 104). Fill a 3-quart pot with water, bring to a boil, reduce heat to low, add the sausage, and poach in barely simmering water for 7 minutes.

While the sausages are poaching, prepare the plum tomatoes for the sauce. Using a small paring knife, cut off tip and stem of each tomato. Remove the seeds and core, leaving only firm, outer pulp. Slit one side of the tomato and lay the tomato flat on work surface. Cut into ¼-inch lengthwise strips, pile up strips, and cut across into ¼-inch pieces. Reserve on a plate.

Remove sausages from water and let cool while making the sauce. If you have used plastic wrap to form the sausage, remove it when sausages are cool. Cut sausage into 6-inch pieces.*

To make the sauce, place the orange juice in a small saucepan and cook over medium heat until reduced by two thirds or until it starts to become thick and syrupy, about 12 to 15 minutes. Add the fish stock and reduce by half, 5 to 7 minutes. Add the cream and reduce by one third or until the reduction has a consistency that coats the back of a spoon. Remove from heat, add the chopped tomatoes, and whisk in the butter.

*Sausages can be made up to 3 days in advance, poached, and kept in the refrigerator. These sausages freeze well for up to 1 month.

To serve, grill the sausage pieces or place under a preheated broiler. Since the sausages are already cooked, we want only to reheat them and crisp their skins. Arrange the sausage pieces on a platter. Pour the orange sauce over and garnish with orange sections.

MIXED SEAFOOD SAUSAGES   MAKES 8 SAUSAGES, SERVES 4

This coarsely ground sausage is good made with almost any mixture of fish and seafood, except swordfish or tuna. If you want to add scallops, cook them first or they will release too much moisture into the mixture and make it crumbly.

½   pound boneless, skinless bass, snapper, halibut, or whitefish
¼   pound shrimps, peeled
¼   pound cooked crabmeat or lobster meat
2   tablespoons finely diced onion
I   bunch parsley, long stems removed
½   teaspoon salt
½   cup egg whites
4   feet sausage casings

Combine all ingredients except sausage casings. If you're using a meat grinder, grind the fish though a die that has large holes. If you're using a food processor, first cut fish and seafood into 1-inch pieces and then pulse until coarsely chopped. Transfer to a mixing bowl.

Stuff the mixture into sausage casings or form 2 long sausages in plastic wrap (see page 104). Fill a 3-quart pot with water, bring to a boil, and reduce heat to low. Add the sausages and poach in barely simmering water for 7 minutes. Remove sausages from water when done and let cool. If you have used plastic wrap to form the sausages, remove it when sausages are cool. Cut sausage into 6-inch pieces.*

To serve, grill the sausage pieces or place under a preheated broiler. Since the sausages are already cooked, we only want to reheat them and crisp their skins.

*Sausages can be made up to 3 days in advance, poached, and kept in the refrigerator. Frozen, they will keep for up to 1 month.

CHICKEN AND VEAL SAUSAGES

MAKES 8 SAUSAGES, SERVES 4

I like to use bacon in meat sausages because of its smoky flavor. Most of us cannot smoke foods at home, but adding bacon to certain dishes approximates the smoky taste. These sausages are best eaten like hot dogs, with mustard and sauerkraut.

6	ounces slab bacon, cut into 1-inch cubes
14	ounces boneless, skinless chicken, preferably dark meat, diced
14	ounces lean veal, diced
1	teaspoon ground coriander
¼	teaspoon freshly grated nutmeg
2	tablespoons minced garlic
½	teaspoon salt
¼	teaspoon cayenne or ground white pepper
2	feet sausage casings
2	cups sour cabbage (page 265)
	mustard, preferably several kinds

If you're using a food processor, puree the bacon until smooth. Add the chicken, veal, coriander, nutmeg, garlic, salt, and pepper and pulse until smooth. If you're using a meat grinder, combine the chicken, veal, and bacon in a mixing bowl with the coriander, nutmeg, garlic, salt, and pepper. Fit the meat grinder with a die that has large holes and grind the mixture through twice.

Stuff this mixture into a sausage casing (see page 104), forming 1 long sausage, or form into 8 patties.*

To serve, place the sausage on a hot grill and cook for 5 to 6 minutes on each side. The sausage is cooked when it is firm to the touch and completely opaque at the center. While the sausages are cooking, heat the sour cabbage in a small covered pot.

If you have made a long sausage, cut it into 8 pieces. Arrange sausage pieces or patties on a bed of sour cabbage. Put mustards on the table for your guests. Your favorite mashed potatoes would be the perfect accompaniment to these sausages.

*Sausage can be made up to 2 days in advance to this point and refrigerated. These sausages freeze well for up to 3 months.

CHOCOLATE LAMB SAUSAGES   MAKES 8 SAUSAGES, SERVES 4

The idea of combining meat and chocolate seems a little outrageous, but of course it's been done for centuries in the Mexican *molé* sauce, which people seem either to love or to hate. I'm fascinated by using ingredients out of their usual context, so I developed this savory chocolate concoction, a perfect example of how flavors can merge to form something new. In this combination the flavors combine into groups. Red wine, chocolate, clove, and cinnamon form a tannic, rich ensemble. Garlic and onion help to sweeten this almost bitter flavor. If one sensation stands out in this confusion, it's the spiciness of the cayenne pepper. By layering this hot sensation over the other flavors, we change the focus and bring all these elements into balance.

1	cup red wine
4	tablespoons unsweetened cocoa powder
¼	teaspoon ground cloves
½	teaspoon cinnamon
½	teaspoon cayenne pepper
1	tablespoon minced garlic
1	small onion, finely diced (about ¼ cup)
1	teaspoon salt
2	ounces slab bacon, coarsely diced
1½	pounds ground lamb
2	large egg whites (about ¼ cup)
2	feet sausage casings

In a small saucepan combine the wine, cocoa, cloves, cinnamon, cayenne, garlic, onion, and salt. Bring to a boil and continue to cook over high heat until the wine is reduced by half, about 5 to 7 minutes. Transfer to a food processor. Add the bacon and puree until smooth. Transfer to a mixing bowl, add the ground lamb, and mix well. Stuff this mixture into a sausage casing to make 1 long sausage or form into 8 patties (see page 104).*

To cook, place the sausage on a hot grill or under a preheated broiler and grill 5 to 6 minutes on each side. The sausages are cooked when they are firm to the touch and completely

*The sausages can be prepared to this point up to 2 days in advance and refrigerated. They can be frozen for up to 3 months.

opaque in the center. If you have made a long sausage, cut it into 8 pieces. Arrange sausage pieces or patties on a platter and accompany with new potatoes in white wine (page 228).

CHICKEN LIVER AND SAGE SAUSAGES
WITH SAUTÉED APPLES   MAKES 8 SAUSAGES, SERVES 4

These sausages aren't at all like liverwurst. They aren't creamy, and they don't have a pronounced liver flavor. Since the sage marinates for several hours in white wine, you can successfully use dried.

½ pound veal or pork stew meat, cut into 1-inch cubes
½ pound chicken livers
4 tablespoons chopped fresh sage *or* 2 tablespoons dried
2 tablespoons minced garlic
4 tablespoons drained capers
¼ teaspoon freshly ground black pepper
¼ cup dry white wine
½ pound slab bacon, coarsely diced
3 green pippin apples
1 tablespoon fresh lemon juice
3 tablespoons unsalted butter

In a mixing bowl combine the veal or pork and the chicken livers with the sage, garlic, capers, pepper, and white wine. Cover and marinate in the refrigerator for at least 4 hours, preferably overnight.

Add the bacon to the marinated ingredients. Fit a meat grinder with a die that has large holes and grind twice. Or place in food processor and pulse until well combined but not quite smooth.

Stuff the mixture into a sausage casing (see page 104), forming one long sausage, or form by hand into 8 patties.★

Peel and core the apples. Cut each of them into 8 sections tip to stem and toss in lemon juice to keep from discoloring.

To cook, place the sausage on a hot grill or under a pre-

★Sausages can be prepared up to 2 days in advance to this point and refrigerated. These sausages freeze well for up to 3 months.

heated broiler and grill 4 to 5 minutes on each side. The sausages are cooked when they are firm to the touch and completely opaque at the center.

While the sausage is cooking, melt the butter in a large skillet over medium heat and add the apples. Cover and cook for 5 to 7 minutes or until apples soften and begin to fall apart. Arrange apples on a serving platter. If you have made a long sausage, cut it into 8 pieces. Arrange sausage pieces or patties on the bed of apples and serve.

BREAKFAST SAUSAGE

MAKES 12 TO 16 SAUSAGES,
SERVES 6 TO 8

Although I am partial to spicy flavors, I don't want to eat them in the morning—but I do like food that will open my eyes. Eggs and cereals alone are too bland; they put my taste buds back to sleep. I much prefer them accompanied by something salty and aromatic like these sausages.

Pork and bacon don't have a strong flavor when they are ground together; despite the smoked flavor of bacon they are particularly unaromatic. Orange zest sparks these sausages nicely, surprising the palate. The background of garlic, mace, and coriander complements the orange and highlights it. These sausages have great flavor without being spicy. They seem almost fruity without being sweet. You will of course want to spread your morning toast with a bitter orange marmalade.

1	pound pork butt, cut into 1-inch pieces
4	ounces slab bacon, cut into 1-inch pieces
1	small onion, finely diced (about ¼ cup)
1	tablespoon chopped fresh sage *or* 1½ teaspoons dried sage
1	teaspoon minced garlic
½	teaspoon salt
½	teaspoon ground white pepper
¾	teaspoon mace
¾	teaspoon ground coriander
2	oranges, grated zest only
2	tablespoons unsalted butter

Combine all ingredients except butter. If you're using a meat grinder, fit it with a die that has large holes and grind the mixture through twice. If you're using a food processor, put only a small quantity in the work bowl at a time and pulse carefully so that the mixture doesn't turn into a paste. Repeat until all the mixture is ground; then mix the separate batches together well. Form the ground meat into small patties.*

To cook the sausages, first preheat the oven to 200°. Melt 1½ teaspoons of the butter in a skillet over medium heat and cook the sausage patties 2 to 3 minutes on each side. Keep the first patties warm in the oven while you cook the rest, adding the remaining butter as needed.

*Sausage can be prepared up to 2 days in advance to this point and refrigerated. These sausages freeze well for up to 3 months.

TURKEY SAUSAGES   MAKES 14 SAUSAGES, SERVES 7

Ground turkey from the supermarket makes a great sausage. If you prefer to grind your own, use two parts dark meat to one part white meat. The sausages will have better texture and more flavor.

A hint of clove makes beef and lamb richer in flavor; it can also be an important flavoring with game or tasty fowl. But clove is a difficult spice to use because it can so easily overpower everything it meets. The mistake most people make when adding clove to a dish is the notion that there should be a distinct clove flavor. In this recipe there is at most only a suspicion of clove. It blends with the brandy and should be hidden.

¼   cup brandy
1   tablespoon chopped fresh thyme *or* 1 teaspoon dried
½   teaspoon ground cloves
1   small onion, finely diced (about ¼ cup)
½   teaspoon ground white pepper
½   teaspoon salt
4   ounces bacon
1½ pounds ground turkey
6   egg whites (about ¾ cup)
2   feet sausage casings

In a small saucepan over high heat combine the brandy, thyme, cloves, onion, pepper, and salt. Bring to a boil and cook until most of the brandy has evaporated, about 3 minutes. Transfer to a food processor, add the bacon, and puree until smooth. Or grind twice in a meat grinder fitted with a large-holed die. Place in a mixing bowl, add the turkey and the egg whites, and mix well. Stuff the mixture into a sausage casing to form 1 long sausage or form into 14 patties (see page 104).

Poach sausage gently in barely simmering salted water until done, about 7 minutes. The sausages are done when they are firm to the touch. Drain and let cool. If you've made 1 long sausage, cut the sausage into 14 pieces when cool enough to handle.★

To serve, place on a hot grill or under a preheated broiler for 5 to 6 minutes on each side. Accompany with warm potato salad.

★Sausages can be made up to 5 days in advance to this point and refrigerated. They can be frozen for up to 3 months.

ONE-DISH MEALS

■ ● ▲

A typically good meal is one in which you, the cook, take control and create a provocative and pleasing progression of ingredients, flavors, and aromas, each course following in a coherent and logical way. But even when you're making a one-dish meal, it's possible to maintain the same level of interest that different courses—or a main course and its side dishes—provide.

Meals that cook in one pot must be designed so that the various ingredients don't compete; however, you don't want them to blend too completely or they become boring. The charm of a casserole, for example, is lost if all the ingredients look and taste alike. You can add a spark of flavor, a fresh herb for instance, just before serving, superimposing this taste over the long-cooked flavors of the dish. Meals that cook in one pot usually need careful attention at the beginning, but once begun they more or less cook by themselves. These deceptively "homey" dishes are associated with family cooking. When you serve your guests a meal from one pot, you establish an immediate sense of camaraderie and belonging. This kind of cooking puts people at their ease and also frees the cook to enjoy the guests. Such unpretentious food is not designed to impress, but when thoughtfully prepared, these dishes are, in fact, elegant.

CHILI

Chili is a brilliantly complex combination of interesting flavors and can be the theme of many variations. A successful chili must have a good variety of chile peppers and a strong foundation of flavor—onion, garlic, cumin, cinnamon, and tomato. I have developed a chili base, a backdrop upon which you can base many different chilies. The four chili recipes that follow are only some of the possibilities.

I'm always amazed at how certain combinations of herbs and spices combine to form an entirely new flavor, which is what happens with cinnamon and cumin here. The mixture must be in the right proportion for this magic to occur or the cinnamon will be too forward and out of balance. Garlic, onions, and dried chile peppers finish the chili foundation, helping the marriage of cumin and cinnamon. Tomatoes give a general sweetness to this ensemble, muffling the disparate flavors.

In order for the cumin and cinnamon to merge, it's essential that the cinnamon remain subtle. You don't want to taste it, but you would miss it if it were omitted. The sweetness of the peppers and tomatoes makes the hot jalapeño and cayenne different—you don't taste them at first; they sneak up on you. This is an important concept with hot peppers. Different hot peppers are tasted in different places. For these dishes we want a pepper that is tasted in the throat, not on the tongue. That way guests can continue to taste the other flavors at the same time. Of course we all have different sensitivities to hotness, so you will want to adjust the amount of cayenne according to your own taste and that of your guests.

CHILI BASE   MAKES BASE FOR 6 TO 8 SERVINGS

Make a large quantity of chili base and keep it in the freezer. Making chili this way can solve the problem of what to do with leftovers such as steak, ham, turkey, or fish.

2   fresh pasilla chile peppers
2   fresh Anaheim chile peppers
2   red peppers
2   dried ancho chile peppers, stems removed and seeds discarded
2   tablespoons salad oil
1   medium onion, diced (about ¾ cup)
4   fresh jalapeño chile peppers, seeded and finely minced
2   tablespoons minced garlic
8   plum tomatoes, seeded and diced (about 1 pound)
1½ teaspoons ground cumin
1   teaspoon ground cinnamon
     salt and cayenne pepper to taste

Roast, peel, and seed the pasilla, Anaheim, and red peppers, then dice them.* Dice the dried ancho chiles.

Preheat oven to 325°. Heat the oil in a medium ovenproof skillet over medium heat, add the onions and jalapeño peppers, and cook, uncovered, until the onions are translucent, about 5 minutes. Add the garlic, tomatoes, roasted peppers, dried chiles, cumin, cinnamon, salt, and cayenne pepper. Cover and place in the oven for 20 minutes.

Remove the chili base from the oven and scrape into a bowl. Proceed with any of the following chili recipes. This base will keep for a week in the refrigerator or may be frozen for up to 4 months.

*Wear rubber gloves when handling raw chile peppers, or wash your hands well after handling. Be careful not to rub your eyes. The capsicum—that's what makes the peppers hot—is volatile and will irritate the skin and eyes.

CHILI BEANS   SERVES 6 TO 8

Dried beans cook best in a slow oven. They develop a wonderful texture and become creamy without being mushy. My chili beans are prepared like Boston-style baked beans, but with chili flavorings. When cooking dried beans, avoid salting them until they begin to soften or they might remain tough.

1   recipe chili base, uncooked (see previous recipe)
3   cups dry red kidney beans
4–5 cups chicken stock (page 258), canned low-sodium chicken broth, or water to cover
1   small ham hock
    salt to taste

Prepare all ingredients for chili base, but do not cook them.

Preheat oven to 275°. In a heavy 3-quart ovenproof pot over medium heat combine the oil, onion, jalapeño peppers, and garlic and cook over medium heat, uncovered, until wilted, about 3 minutes. Add tomatoes, roasted peppers, dried peppers, cumin, cinnamon, and beans. Cover with 3½ cups of the stock or water, bring to a boil, cover, and place in the oven for 30 minutes.

Add the ham hock and another ½ cup of the stock. Cook slowly until beans are tender but not mushy, another 2 to 2½ hours. Check the beans every 30 minutes and add ½ cup more stock each time if all the liquid has been absorbed. Taste for salt. These beans may be served with rice or as a side dish.

GREEN CHILI WITH
LAMB AND ARTICHOKE

SERVES 6 TO 8

When we combine opposite flavors and sensations—in this case sweet but spicy chili base juxtaposed with acidic, astringent tomatillo and artichoke—we create a tense balance of flavor. Garlic plays the "go-between" here, marrying the sweet and mellow with the tart and acidic.

1	recipe chili base, cooked (page 116)
1	lemon
6	large artichokes
3	tablespoons olive oil
2	pounds boneless lamb shoulder, cut into ½-inch strips
6	tomatillos, papery skins removed, diced
3	tablespoons finely minced garlic
¼	cup fresh lime juice
1	cup chicken stock (page 258) or canned low-sodium broth
½	teaspoon salt, or to taste
1	bunch cilantro, leaves only, chopped (about ¾ cup)
24	corn tortillas
2	cups sour cream

Fill a 2-quart pot with water and the juice of 1 lemon. Keep the lemon for rubbing the cut surfaces of the artichokes as you work. Cut the stems off the artichokes. Trim the tops, leaving a base about 1½ inches deep and exposing the center choke. Trim all around the sides and bottom to remove the dark green exterior. Place bottoms in the water as they are done. When the artichokes are trimmed, bring the water to a boil, covered, over high heat and cook for 20 minutes or until bottoms are tender. Remove from heat and remove artichokes from the liquid. When cool enough to handle, scoop out center chokes and discard.*

Meanwhile, heat the oil in a Dutch oven or deep oven-proof skillet over high heat, add the lamb, and sauté, stirring, 5 to 7 minutes. Reduce the heat, add the artichokes, tomatillos, and garlic, and cook another 5 minutes. Add the

*Artichokes may be prepared to this point, re-placed in cooking liquid, and kept covered, in the refrigerator for up to 2 days.

chili base, lime juice, and stock. Cover and place in oven for 1 hour.

Remove from oven and taste for salt.★ Arrange the chili in a covered dish or serve individually in bowls and sprinkle with chopped cilantro. Serve warm tortillas instead of bread and pass sour cream on the side.

★This chili may be prepared entirely in advance and reheated. It will keep for up to 1 week in the refrigerator or may be frozen for up to 3 months.

TURKEY AND CRANBERRY CHILI SERVES 6 TO 8

Sweet flavors and hot flavors, when combined, fight for predominance and ultimately obliterate each other as the tongue tires of the battle. In this recipe sweet and sour cranberries combine with the chili base to create a sensory overload that is very pleasing. The sugar cancels the tartness of the cranberries so that their fruitiness can marry with the sweetness of the roasted peppers in the chili base. Vinegar not only cancels the sweetness of sugar but also gives backbone to the chili and brings these opposite elements into balance.

1	tablespoon sugar
2	tablespoons white vinegar
1	cup fresh or frozen cranberries
1½	pounds boneless turkey breast, cut into 2-inch cubes
1	recipe chili base, cooked (page 116)
½	cup chicken stock (page 258) or canned low-sodium chicken broth
	salt to taste
24	tortillas
1½	cups sour cream

Combine the sugar and vinegar in a deep ovenproof skillet or Dutch oven, bring to a boil, and continue to boil until the liquid has a syrupy consistency. Add the cranberries and cook 1 minute. Add the turkey, chili base, and chicken stock. Cover and place in oven for 1½ hours or until turkey falls apart. Taste for salt. Remove from oven and, using a fork, mash or shred the turkey with the other chili ingredients.* Serve with warm tortillas instead of bread and pass sour cream on the side.

*This chili may be prepared entirely in advance and reheated. It will keep for up to 1 week in the refrigerator or may be frozen for up to 3 months.

SURF AND TURF CHILI   SERVES 6 TO 8

Ingredients that cook for a long time and develop subtle flavors combine nicely with foods that cook briefly and retain their original flavor and aroma. Garlic and allspice merge into the background, catalysts bringing richness to both the steak and the chili base. All this is foundation for the forward shrimp flavor.

1	recipe chili base, cooked (page 116)
1	tablespoon salad oil
¾	pound skirt or flank steak
6	garlic cloves, finely minced
½	teaspoon ground allspice
1	cup veal stock (page 259) or canned low-sodium beef broth
12	jumbo shrimps, peeled and deveined
	salt to taste
1	bunch cilantro, chopped (about 1 ounce)
24	corn tortillas
1½	cups sour cream

While the chili base is cooking or defrosting, heat the oil in a Dutch oven over high heat, add the steak, and brown well on both sides. Pour off the fat. Add the chili base, garlic, allspice, and stock to the steak. Bring to a boil, cover, and place in the oven for 1 to 1½ hours or until the steak is falling apart.* Add the shrimps, return to the oven, and cook, uncovered, another 10 to 12 minutes. Taste for salt.

Using a fork, shred the steak with the other chili ingredients. Arrange the chili on a serving platter or in individual bowls and sprinkle with chopped cilantro. Serve with warm tortillas instead of bread and pass sour cream on the side.

*Can be prepared to this point up to 2 days in advance and refrigerated.

GUMBO

The secret to a good gumbo is not burnt *roux,* as most southern cooks will tell you, but rather an overpowering combination of flavors, both complex and confusing, that causes each bite to taste new. Dark *roux* is only one ingredient of this gumbo background, imparting a nutty taste upon which the other flavors are superimposed. Gumbos always contain rice and okra. Gumbo filé powder—ground sassafras leaves—helps thicken the gumbo and has its own distinctive flavor. If you don't have any, leave it out—there is no substitute. Other than that, I'm sure that all southerners make their own version, so why shouldn't you?

I've developed a base that can be used for making countless gumbos. It may be frozen for up to 3 months and will enable you to improvise many variations by adding other ingredients to it—any meat, poultry, or seafood.

GUMBO BASE

MAKES 6 CUPS, ENOUGH BASE
FOR 4 TO 5 GUMBO SERVINGS

½   cup all-purpose flour
2   quarts any mixture of poultry stock (page 258), fish stock (page 260), and meat stock (page 259)
1   tablespoon tomato paste
1   medium onion, roughly chopped (about ¾ cup)
1   celery stalk, roughly diced (about ½ cup)
2   sprigs fresh thyme *or* ½ teaspoon dried
1   teaspoon cayenne pepper
2   bay leaves
     salt to taste
½   cup melted unsalted butter
2   tablespoons gumbo filé powder

Preheat oven to 350°. Place flour on a pie plate or medium ovenproof skillet and place in oven. Toast until it is a deep golden color, about 45 minutes. Check the flour every 10 minutes and stir so it browns evenly.

Combine the stocks in a heavy 3-quart pot over high heat and add the tomato paste, onion, celery, thyme, cayenne pepper, bay leaves, and salt. Bring to a boil, reduce heat to low, and simmer gently, uncovered, ½ hour.

When the flour is a dark golden color, remove from oven and whisk in the melted butter until completely blended. It will dramatically darken in color. Place over very low heat and let cook 5 minutes more. Transfer the flour mixture (called *roux*) to a heavy pot or Dutch oven and pour the hot stock over it, stirring. Raise heat to medium and simmer, uncovered, for 1 hour. Skim frequently as the liquid reduces. The liquid should be slightly thickened. Add the gumbo filé powder.

Pour through a strainer into a clean saucepan if you plan to use the gumbo base immediately or into a storage container. You are now ready to make gumbo.

Note: The gumbo base is quicker and easier to prepare if you keep a store of toasted flour on hand. Combined with an equal amount of butter, it makes a superior dark *roux* and can be used in other sauces, gravies, and stews.

GUMBO RICE   SERVES 6 TO 8 AS PART OF A GUMBO

All gumbos contain rice. This gumbo rice has the same flavor as the preceding gumbo base.

¾ cup chicken stock (page 258) or canned low-sodium chicken broth
I   tablespoon unsalted butter
2   tablespoons finely minced onion
½ cup uncooked long-grain rice
I   teaspoon gumbo filé powder
I   teaspoon cayenne pepper

Preheat oven to 350°. Place the chicken stock in a small pot over high heat and bring to a boil.

In a small ovenproof pot melt the butter over low heat, add the onion, and cook about 2 minutes. Add the rice and toss to coat with the butter. Add the stock, gumbo filé powder, and cayenne pepper. Cover and place in oven for 15 to 20 minutes. The rice is now ready to go into one of the following gumbos.

DUCK AND CRAB GUMBO   SERVES 4 TO 5

This may seem like an eccentric pairing, but the duck and the crab wear each other's flavor well. The strong taste of dark *roux* helps counsel this surprising marriage. If you prefer, you can use lobster in place of crab, in which case you boil the lobster in fish stock and use this stock along with the lobster shells to make the gumbo base.

1	4- to 5-pound duck
2	cups salad oil
1	recipe gumbo base (page 121)
1	recipe cooked gumbo rice (see previous recipe)
16	okra
¾	pound crabmeat
	gumbo filé powder
	Tabasco sauce

Preheat oven to 350°. Cut up the duck according to method one (page 175). Combine the duck and oil in a medium ovenproof pot, heat over medium heat, cover, and place in the oven for 1½ hours or until meat is falling apart. Meanwhile, prepare the gumbo base. While the gumbo base is reducing, make the gumbo rice and reserve in a covered bowl.

Remove the duck from the oven and remove from the fat. Strain fat and reserve for another use. When duck is cool enough to handle, remove meat from the carcass, discarding skin and bones.*

Cut the stems from the okra and discard. Cut the okra into ¼-inch rounds. In a large pot combine duck meat, crabmeat, okra, and the gumbo base. Bring to a boil, reduce the heat, and simmer, covered, 15 minutes. Meanwhile, preheat the oven to 200°. Heat the gumbo rice by placing, covered, in the oven for 10 to 15 minutes.

Just before serving, pour the gumbo through a strainer into a large tureen. Garnish individual bowls with the gumbo rice and top with duck, crab, and okra. Ladle the gumbo "soup" in front of your guests. Pass extra gumbo filé powder and a bottle of Tabasco sauce.

*Can be prepared to this point up to 2 days in advance and refrigerated.

TURKEY AND SAUSAGE GUMBO   SERVES 4 TO 5

1½   pounds turkey, either breast, thigh, or drumstick
1   recipe gumbo base (page 121)
1   recipe gumbo rice (page 122)
4   turkey sausages (page 112) or spicy pork sausage such as Cajun
     andouille
16   okra
     gumbo filé powder
     Tabasco sauce

Preheat oven to 375°. Place the turkey in a medium roasting pan in oven for 1½ hours or more, depending on the cut of turkey used. Thighs will take longer to cook than breasts. The turkey should be very well done.

While the turkey is roasting, prepare gumbo base. While the gumbo base is cooking, prepare gumbo rice and reserve in an ovenproof dish.

Cut each sausage into 4 pieces and place in a medium skillet over medium heat. Cook 5 minutes to render some of the fat. Drain sausages and reserve on a plate.

When the turkey is done, remove from oven and, when cool enough to handle, remove skin and bones and discard. Dice the meat into 1-inch pieces.★

Cut the stems from the okra and discard. Cut okra into ¼-inch rounds. In a large pot combine the turkey, sausages, okra, and gumbo base. Bring to a boil, reduce heat, and simmer, covered, 15 minutes.

Meanwhile, preheat oven to 200°. Heat the gumbo rice by placing, covered, in oven for 10 to 15 minutes.

Just before serving, pour the gumbo through a strainer into a large tureen. Garnish bowls with the gumbo rice and top with turkey, sausage, and okra. Ladle the gumbo "soup" in front of your guests. Offer extra gumbo filé powder and a bottle of Tabasco sauce.

★Can be prepared to this point up to 2 days in advance and refrigerated.

RICE AND BEAN CASSEROLES

Spanish *paella* and French *cassoulet* inspired these variations on simple, hearty themes. The casserole ingredients blend flavors by imparting them to rice or beans; other flavors can be added at the end of the cooking for zesty contrast to the long-cooked flavors. When dishes cook for a long time, I often like to layer the quickly cooked flavors over the mellow background of the long-cooked flavors.

PORK AND SUCCOTASH STEW   SERVES 6 TO 8

Although long cooking diminishes its strength and we use only a hint of it, the surprise here is caraway seed—I like the aroma it imparts to the stew. Finishing the sauce with yogurt sparks all the mellow flavors of the stew, keeping everything, especially the beans, lighter.

1	tablespoon salad oil
2	pounds pork butt, cut into 2-inch cubes
1	small onion, finely diced (about ¼ cup)
5	cups chicken stock (page 258) or canned low-sodium chicken broth
¾	cup dried lima beans
1	teaspoon caraway seeds
1	teaspoon salt, or to taste
1	cup corn kernels
3	medium red peppers, seeded and diced
½	cup plain yogurt
	freshly ground pepper to taste

In a Dutch oven or heavy 3-quart pot heat the oil over high heat, add the pork in batches, and brown very well. Do not crowd or the meat will not brown. Remove and reserve the meat on a plate as it is browned. Preheat the oven to 325°. Discard the fat in the pot. Lower heat, add the onion, and cook, stirring, 5 minutes to dissolve the browned bits that have stuck to the bottom of the pot. Return the meat to the pot and add the stock, beans, and caraway. Cover and place in oven for 1½ hours or until pork is tender and the beans are cooked.★

★Can be prepared to this point up to 2 days in advance and refrigerated. It may be frozen for up to 3 months.

Transfer pot to the top of the stove. Add ½ teaspoon of the salt, the corn, and the peppers. Cook, uncovered, over high heat for 5 minutes to thicken the liquid in the pot. Stir constantly. Remove from heat and stir in the yogurt. Add remaining salt and freshly ground pepper to taste. Serve directly from the pot and accompany with a tossed green salad.

LAMB AND COLLARD CASSOULET   SERVES 6 TO 8

Both lamb and sausages are always more distinctive when accompanied by something that makes your mouth pucker—sorrel plays that role here, although tamarind or pomegranate could fill in for it.

Some ingredients—fresh dill, tarragon, basil, or chives, to name just a few—need little or no cooking to impart their flavor to a dish; indeed they do not tolerate long cooking. Other ingredients need to develop, mellow, or otherwise change their flavor through long cooking. Garlic and sorrel are the important flavors in this version of a *cassoulet*. Garlic mellows as it cooks, but sorrel doesn't and must be added just before serving.

Dishes such as this one that taste better the second or third day are usually flavored with herbs such as thyme, oregano, or rosemary, roots such as ginger or horseradish, or tubers and bulbs such as garlic, shallot, or onion. The flavors of these ingredients do not dissipate, but rather mellow during long cooking and even develop additional smoothness during the two or three days the dish may rest in the refrigerator.

2   tablespoons salad oil
24   garlic cloves
4   chicken liver and sage sausages (page 109) or Italian-style pork sausage, cut into 3 pieces each
1½   pounds boneless lamb shoulder, cut into 2-inch pieces
1   medium onion, finely diced (about ¾ cup)
4–5   cups lamb or veal stock (page 259) or chicken stock (page 258) or canned low-sodium chicken broth
¾   cup dried *flageolet* beans or small white navy beans
1   lemon, halved
12   collard leaves, roughly chopped
16   sorrel leaves, stems removed, leaves roughly chopped

1   teaspoon salt, or to taste
     freshly ground pepper to taste
½   cup fresh bread crumbs

In a Dutch oven or heavy 3-quart pot heat the oil over medium-high heat, add the whole peeled garlic cloves, and sauté until golden, about 7 to 10 minutes. Using a slotted spoon, remove to a plate and reserve. Add the sausages and cook, stirring, for 5 minutes. Remove and reserve with the garlic.

Raise heat to high. Add the lamb in batches and brown well on all sides. Do not crowd the pot or the meat will steam rather than brown. Remove the meat as it browns and reserve on a plate. Preheat oven to 325°.

Reduce heat to low, pour off the fat from the pot, add the onion, and cook, stirring, for 3 minutes. Return the meat to the pot and add the stock, beans, and lemon. Cover and bake for 45 minutes, checking occasionally to see that the beans do not dry out. If the beans have absorbed all the liquid, add stock or water to moisten, ½ cup at a time as necessary.*

Add the sausages, the browned garlic, and the collard greens to the pot. Cover and continue to cook in oven until the lamb and beans are tender, about 20 minutes. You may need to add more stock or water if the beans have again absorbed all the liquid. The finished dish should be moist but not soupy.

Remove the *cassoulet* from the oven. Remove the lemon and mix in the sorrel. Add salt and pepper to taste. Sprinkle the top of the *cassoulet* with the bread crumbs, return to oven, and bake 15 minutes to brown the top. Serve the *cassoulet* directly from the pot or place in a covered serving dish.

*Can be made to this point up to 2 days in advance and refrigerated, but if preparing in advance or reheating this dish, add a little lemon juice to restore a spark of tartness.

ARROZ CON POLLO

Half the restaurants in southern California serve this dish, it seems, but I no longer order it because for me this is home cooking. There are certain preparations, usually stews and roasts, that do not translate well to a restaurant context, and you risk having a bad meal by ordering them. In a restaurant these dishes usually become what we refer to as "steamtable food."

It's no surprise to anyone familiar with the cuisines of Mexico that the focal flavors of this dish are cilantro and cumin. Cilantro is a soapy-tasting herb that becomes astringent in combination with tart tomatillo and should not be cooked at all. Cumin has a somewhat dry perfume. It is sweetened by garlic and becomes darkly rich in the presence of clove and cinnamon. The flavor of cumin develops best through long cooking.

2½   cups chicken stock (page 258) or canned low-sodium chicken broth
¼   cup salad oil
1   3- to 3½-pound frying chicken, cut into pieces using method one (page 175)
3–4 red peppers, coarsely diced (about 2 cups)
2   medium onions, finely minced (about 1½ cups)
1½ teaspoons finely minced garlic
1½ cups uncooked long-grain rice
1½ teaspoons salt
1   tablespoon ground cumin
½   teaspoon ground cinnamon
¼   teaspoon ground cloves
4   ripe plum tomatoes (about ½ pound)
4   tomatillos, papery covering removed, finely diced
2   jalapeño peppers, seeded and diced
1   bunch cilantro, bottom stems removed, leaves chopped
1   recipe sweet pea guacamole (page 261, optional)

In a 1-quart pot bring chicken stock to a boil, covered, over high heat.

In a large ovenproof skillet or 11-inch roasting pan heat the oil over high heat. Place the chicken skin side down and sauté 5 minutes on each side or until golden. Remove chicken to a plate.

Lower the heat to medium and add the red peppers, onions, and garlic. Cook, stirring, 5 minutes or until wilted. Preheat oven to 350°.

Reduce heat under the skillet to low, add the rice, salt, cumin, cinnamon, and cloves, and toss to coat the rice with the cooking oil. Replace the chicken thighs and drumsticks on top.* Add the boiling chicken stock, cover, and place in oven for 10 minutes.

Meanwhile, using a small paring knife, cut off tip and stem of the tomatoes. Remove the seeds and core, leaving only firm, outer pulp. Slit one side of each tomato and lay the tomato flat on work surface. Cut lengthwise into ¼-inch strips, pile up strips, and cut across into ¼-inch pieces.

Remove casserole from oven and add the tomatoes, tomatillos, jalapeño peppers, and chicken breasts. Return the casserole, covered, to the oven and cook another 20 to 25 minutes or until the chicken is cooked and the rice is tender.

Arrange on a warm platter or serve directly from the pot, sprinkling with cilantro just before serving. Sweet pea guacamole (page 261) is a lovely accompaniment. A tossed green salad and well-chilled beer complete the meal.

*Can be prepared up to 1 hour in advance to this point and kept, covered, at room temperature.

SEAFOOD AND CHICKEN CURRY   SERVES 6

This *paella* variation has Indian and Thai flavors. It is certainly
not an authentic ethnic recipe, but this is new American cooking:
we take ingredients and ideas from anywhere and recombine
them in new ways to suit our taste. A large repertoire of ideas,
techniques, and influences and a greater availability of products
result in more interesting dishes. A larger vocabulary is the secret
of creative freedom. Let your intuition be your guide with this
sort of cooking—and taste constantly.

The primary flavor here is curry—an aromatic, spicy
combination of herbs and spices that's pleasantly confusing to the
palate. Coriander, saffron, fennel, and cumin, although they're
already present in the curry powder, emphasize a certain "medicinal" aspect of curry. I don't want to reinforce its sweetness; I
want to feature a more aromatic aspect. Dill merges with curry,
becoming part of it, and I nearly always add fresh dill whenever
I'm using commercial curry powder.

1	cup chicken stock (page 258) or canned low-sodium chicken broth
1	cup clam juice
1	tablespoon salad oil
3	Chicken and Veal Sausages (page 107), cut into 1-inch slices, or Italian-style sausages
1	medium onion, finely diced (about ¾ cup)
1½	cups uncooked long-grain rice
2	jalapeño peppers, seeded and finely minced
4	tablespoons curry powder (page 264)
½	teaspoon saffron threads
½	teaspoon ground coriander
¼	teaspoon fennel seed
¼	teaspoon ground cumin
2	pounds boneless, skinless chicken breasts, cut into 6 pieces
1	cup canned or fresh unsweetened coconut milk (if unavailable, use all stock)
6	jumbo shrimps, peeled and deveined
12	clams
12	mussels
2	tablespoons chopped fresh dill *or* 1 tablespoon dried lemon pickle, garlic pickle, or mustard seed and papaya chutney (page 263)

Combine chicken stock and clam juice in a small pot and bring to a boil, covered, over high heat.

In a Dutch oven or *paella* pan heat the oil over medium heat, add the sausages, and sauté to render some of their fat, about 5 minutes. Pour off all but 2 tablespoons of the fat and return pan to stove. Add the diced onion to the sausages and sauté, without coloring, until translucent, about 5 minutes. Add the rice and toss to coat with the fat.* Preheat the oven to 375°. Add the stock, jalapeño peppers, curry, saffron, coriander, fennel, and cumin. If using dried dill, add it now. Place the chicken, skin side up, on top of the rice.

Cover the casserole and place in oven. After 15 minutes, add the coconut milk or extra stock, the shrimps, clams, and mussels, and return to oven, covered, for another 15 minutes or until the rice is tender and the shells have opened. Sprinkle with the fresh dill. Arrange on a platter or serve from the pan. Offer Indian condiments such as lemon pickle, garlic pickle, or mustard seed and papaya chutney (page 263).

*Can be prepared up to 1 hour in advance to this point and kept, covered, at room temperature.

ORANGE DUCK AND BAKED BEANS   SERVES 6

This is a hybrid dish of Boston baked beans and French *canard à l'orange.*

2   oranges
2   ducks, cut up using method one (page 175), excess skin and fat
       removed
1   medium onion, finely minced (about ¾ cup)
1   tablespoon dark brown sugar
1   tablespoon dry mustard
3   tablespoons molasses
¾   cup white navy beans
4–5   cups chicken stock (page 258) or canned low-sodium chicken broth
       salt and freshly ground pepper to taste

Preheat oven to 400°. Grate the zest of one orange and reserve on a small plate. Juice both oranges and reserve juice in a glass.

Place the duck pieces, skin side up, on a rack in a roasting pan and roast for 30 minutes to render some of the fat. Remove from the oven, pour off fat, and reserve it for another use. Reduce the oven temperature to 325°.

In a Dutch oven or 4-quart casserole combine the onion, sugar, mustard, molasses, orange juice, beans, and stock. Place the duck on top of the beans, cover, and place in oven. Bake for 2½ hours, checking every 30 minutes to make sure the beans are moist and adding more stock as necessary. Uncover, add salt and pepper to taste, and bake another 30 minutes, uncovered.★

To serve, remove the duck to a platter. Toss the beans with the grated orange zest and serve in a bowl.

★Can be made to this point up to 1 day in advance and refrigerated.

LAMB WITH PASTA E FAGIOLI   SERVES 6 TO 8

Pasta e Fagioli is a traditional Italian dish of pasta and beans. We don't usually think of combining two starches in the same dish, but it can be very successful if we choose ingredients for their textures. Of course this is not the usual dish found in Italian restaurants, where it is served as a first course. This version is intended as a main course.

6   tablespoons virgin olive oil
2   pounds boneless lamb stew meat
1   celery stalk, finely minced (about ½ cup)
1   small carrot, finely minced (about ½ cup)
1   tablespoon finely minced garlic
6   cups veal or lamb stock (page 259) or chicken stock (page 258)
     or canned low-sodium chicken broth
¾   cup dried *flageolet* beans or red kidney beans
4   sprigs fresh oregano or marjoram *or* 1 tablespoon dried
4   plum tomatoes (about ½ pound)
¾   cup uncooked elbow macaroni

Garnish:

½   cup grated Parmesan or Romano cheese
1   small onion, finely minced (about ¼ cup)
     freshly ground pepper
     virgin olive oil

In a Dutch oven or heavy 3-quart pot heat 2 tablespoons of the olive oil over high heat, add the lamb in batches, and brown well on all sides. Do not crowd the pot or the meat will steam rather than brown. Remove and reserve as pieces brown. Discard fat. Preheat oven to 350°.

Reduce heat to low and add the celery, carrot, and garlic. Cook, stirring, 1 minute. Return the meat to the pot. Add the stock and beans. Bring to a boil, add the marjoram or oregano, cover, and bake 1½ hours or until the lamb is cooked and the beans are tender.

Meanwhile, using a small paring knife, cut off tip and stem of each tomato. Remove the seeds and core, leaving only firm, outer pulp. Slit one side of the tomato and lay the tomato flat on work surface. Cut into ¼-inch lengthwise strips, pile up strips, and cut across into ¼-inch pieces. Reserve on a plate.

Add the macaroni to the casserole, replace in oven, and cook, covered, 20 minutes or until pasta is tender. Remove the fresh herb sprigs and add the tomatoes. Transfer to a large tureen or divide among individual soup bowls. Offer grated cheese, minced onion, fresh pepper, and olive oil as garnishes at the table. A perfectly simple green salad is all that is needed with this dish to make your guests very, very happy.

PASTA

When you use ingredients appropriately, you are much less likely to be disappointed. Don't expect pasta to have an exciting flavor—it's not even meant to combine with the other flavors of a dish. Pasta is a neutral ground, a vehicle for presenting other ingredients. Even a flavored pasta such as a vibrantly colored saffron pasta, pink beet pasta, or green herb pasta may titillate the imagination and the eye but doesn't really tantalize our taste buds. We love pasta because of its charming texture—it should be slightly chewy and contrast with the other ingredients in a dish.

GOAT CHEESE LASAGNE WITH EGGPLANT   SERVES 6 TO 8

This dish is a cross between eggplant *parmigiana* and *lasagne*—two of the most popular dishes imaginable. This *lasagne* is strongly flavored and will surprise people who expect the usual humdrum version.

We must use a strong goat cheese here as a catalyst flavor around which all the others revolve. Aromatic rosemary, tart yogurt, sweetly acid tomatoes, musty, bitter eggplant, and biting garlic all contribute to the fresh character of this dish.

⅓   cup kosher salt
2   medium eggplants, or about 2 pounds, unpeeled and cut cross-
     wise into ¼-inch slices
½   pound *lasagne* noodles
¼   cup virgin olive oil
1   pound fresh strong goat cheese, crumbled or thinly sliced
1   teaspoon finely minced fresh rosemary leaves *or* ½ teaspoon
     dried
10   overripe plum tomatoes (about 1¼ pounds)
1   cup dry white wine
1   tablespoon minced garlic
1½ cups plain yogurt

Lightly sprinkle kosher salt on the eggplant slices, layer them in a bowl, and nest another bowl on top of the slices. To weigh them down, a large heavy can from the supermarket or a brick from the garden works well. After 20 minutes, drain the liquid from the eggplant and pat dry.

Meanwhile, cook the *lasagne* noodles in salted boiling water for 5 minutes. They will be underdone. Reserve in a bowl of cold water to keep them from drying out.

In a large skillet over medium heat, heat 1 tablespoon of the oil and sauté the eggplant 1 minute on each side, until tender. Reserve the slices on paper towels as they are done. Repeat with more oil and the rest of the eggplant, making sure to reserve 2 tablespoons oil to grease the baking dish.

Preheat oven to 350°. Oil a 9-inch by 13-inch baking dish with the remaining oil. Layer the noodles, eggplant slices, cheese, and rosemary. Repeat, finishing with a layer of cheese. Cover with foil and place in the oven until bubbling, about 25 minutes.

While the *lasagne* is baking, prepare the sauce. Combine the tomatoes, white wine, and garlic in a medium saucepan. Bring to a boil, reduce the heat, cover, and simmer 20 minutes or until the tomatoes are falling apart. Remove to a food processor or blender and puree. Pass the tomatoes through a strainer to remove seeds and skins. Return the puree to the saucepan and continue to simmer, uncovered, until the mixture has reduced to a sauce consistency, about 15 minutes.★ Remove tomato puree from heat and whisk in the yogurt. Do not reheat or the sauce will separate. This sauce should be warm but not hot.

When the *lasagne* is done, remove from oven, pour half the sauce over, and serve. Pass the remaining sauce at the table.

★Can be prepared to this point up to 1 day in advance and refrigerated.

VEGETABLE FETTUCCINE   SERVES 5 TO 6

I don't like the implication that vegetables are fresh and exciting only in springtime, so I don't call this dish *pasta primavera.* It's always springtime *someplace,* and if you want a good vegetable assortment for this pasta dish, all you have to do is go to a good produce market.

A combination of green vegetables and root vegetables works best in this pasta, but the prime consideration is to choose vegetables carefully, achieving a satisfying blend of flavor and remembering that the marriage of garlic, Parmesan cheese, olive oil, and nutmeg forms a salty, cheesy background that makes the vegetable flavors seem more alive.

2	tablespoons salt
¾	cup virgin olive oil
½	cup pine nuts
6	ounces snow peas, cut into ⅛-inch julienne
6	ounces broccoli florets (about ⅔ cup packed)
1	medium carrot, about 6 ounces, cut into ⅛-inch julienne
1	medium zucchini, about 8 ounces, cut into ⅛-inch julienne
2	tablespoons finely minced garlic
2	tablespoons finely minced shallots
1	cup whipping cream
½	teaspoon freshly grated nutmeg
10	ounces *fettuccine* noodles, preferably fresh
⅔	cup grated Parmesan cheese
	salt and freshly ground pepper to taste

Fill a large pot with water and bring to a boil, covered, over high heat. Add the salt.

Place a large skillet or saucepan on the stove and heat the olive oil over medium heat. Add the pine nuts and cook until they start to turn golden, about 1 minute. Add the snow peas, broccoli, carrot, and zucchini and cook 1 minute, tossing. If you're using dried, boxed pasta, add it now to the boiling salted water. Cook 7 to 10 minutes, depending on its quality and shape.

Meanwhile, add the garlic, shallots, cream, and nutmeg to the skillet and cook, tossing, 4 to 5 minutes. The cream will reduce and combine with the olive oil. If you're using fresh pasta, add it to the boiling water now. It will take only 3 to 4 minutes to cook.

When the pasta is cooked but still *al dente* firm, drain and place in a large mixing bowl. Remove the vegetables from heat and add the cheese. Add to the pasta and toss well. Taste for salt and pepper. Mound *fettuccine* and vegetables on a serving platter. Offer additional grated cheese to your guests.

SOPHISTICATED MACARONI AND CHEESE   SERVES 4 TO 6

Remember boxed macaroni and cheese? If you do, I assure you that it is more wonderful as a memory than a reality and you would be disappointed with it today. I have tried to rehabilitate a childhood memory by revising it according to my adult tastes. So this is not at all a child's dish—the flavors are too intense.

Pasta and potatoes may seem like carbohydrate overkill, but these textures are great together. Garlic tames the cheese sauce— the strong raclette and Gruyère combination—a good example of how we can juxtapose two strong flavors so that they diminish each other.

½	pound russet potatoes
½	pound uncooked elbow macaroni
6	tablespoons virgin olive oil
¼	cup pine nuts
2	tablespoons finely minced garlic
1	cup whipping cream
1	cup milk
¼	pound raclette cheese, grated
¼	pound Gruyère cheese, grated

Peel the potatoes and cut into ¼-inch dice. Reserve in a bowl of cold water.

Bring a large pot of salted water to a boil on the stove, add the macaroni, and cook 5 minutes. Drain the potatoes and add to the macaroni. Cook 1 minute. Drain well and toss with 2 tablespoons of the olive oil to keep from sticking together. Reserve in a large mixing bowl. Preheat oven to 375°.

Combine the remaining olive oil and pine nuts in a medium skillet or saucepan and cook over medium heat, about 3 minutes.

Add the garlic and cream, raise the heat, bring to a boil, and continue boiling until the cream and olive oil combine, about 1 minute.

Add the cream mixture, milk, and half of each cheese to the macaroni and potatoes. Mix well. Place in a 9-inch by 13-inch baking dish and sprinkle with the remaining cheese. Place in oven, uncovered, for 20 minutes, or until mixture is bubbling and the top is golden brown. Serve this directly from the baking dish with a green salad or sliced tomatoes vinaigrette. It also makes a good buffet item or side dish.

QUICK STEWS

■●▲

Stew is both a method of cooking and a style of presentation. Although stews cook "by themselves," they are always better when tended with a careful eye, something that we don't always have time to do. The dishes in this chapter are not true stews. They are very similar to the sautéed recipes found in other chapters, but their presentation is different. Most of these "stews" are recipes that you can make on a moment's notice, a useful way of cooking for those who like stews but don't always have long hours to spend with them.

The secret to a good traditional stew is the long, slow cooking that develops flavor. Since the stews presented here cook quickly, there is no such development of flavor. We use a different strategy: bold ingredients that become tender very quickly. Because the time spent in the kitchen is minimal (indeed that is the *raison d'être* for these stews), it is essential to have all your ingredients ready and in place before beginning to cook.

STEAK, BROCCOLI, AND
GREEN PEPPERCORN STEW

SERVES 3 TO 4

This stew version of the familiar *steak au poivre vert* is a perfect example of food being appropriate to its setting. Although this dish is familiar home cooking in France, it lies in the domain of restaurant cooking in America. By presenting this dish as a stew instead of as a more-important-seeming steak, you avoid comparison to restaurant cooking and make this dish an expression of yourself.

Green peppercorns are more than merely spicy hot, and in this sauce we want to highlight their other flavors, such as the metallic character, so we place them in a busy background of tarragon, mustard, and brandy. The peppery character of tarragon is overpowered by the stronger pepper of green peppercorns; but at the same time its aromatic anise flavor is highlighted by the mustard. Don't be heavy-handed with the brandy—it's there only to smooth out the boldness of the peppercorns, helping to calm this almost frantic combination of ingredients.

1	tablespoon salt
2	cups broccoli florets (about ¾ pound whole broccoli)
2	tablespoons salad oil
1½	pounds beef tenderloin or sirloin, cut into 16 equal pieces
2	tablespoons minced shallots
2	tablespoons brandy
¼	cup dry white wine
3	tablespoons Dijon mustard
2	tablespoons green peppercorns packed in water, drained
1¼	cups veal stock (page 259) or canned low-sodium beef broth
¼	cup whipping cream
2	tablespoons chopped fresh tarragon *or* 1 teaspoon dried
3	tablespoons unsalted butter

Fill a 3-quart pot with water, add salt, cover, and bring to a boil over high heat. Add broccoli, return to boil, and cook, uncovered, 1 minute. Immediately drain and plunge into ice water to stop the cooking. Drain after 2 minutes and reserve on paper towels.

Heat the oil in a large skillet over high heat and when almost smoking add the meat without crowding. Quickly brown on all sides. Remove to a plate. Discard the cooking fat and lower the heat to medium. Add the shallots and cook, stirring, 1 minute.

Add the brandy, white wine, mustard, and peppercorns. If using dried tarragon, add it now. Raise the heat to high and cook to burn off the alcohol, about 1 minute. Add the veal stock and reduce until liquid starts to thicken, about 2 minutes.* Add the cream and continue to reduce until the liquid is thick enough to coat the back of a spoon.

Re-place the steak and any juices that have collected on the plate. Add the broccoli and continue to cook for 2 minutes. Remove from heat, add the fresh tarragon, and whisk in the butter. Transfer to a heated platter or lidded casserole and serve with buttered noodles.

*Can be prepared to this point up to 2 hours in advance.

LAMB, LEEK, CELERIAC, AND ENDIVE STEW   SERVES 4

Each ingredient of a stew can have a bold presence if the elements are combined in the right way. Here we have a combination of opposite flavors. Earthy, sweet, leeks are layered with bitter endive and pungent celeriac. The taste of lamb contrasts with the other three stew ingredients and is intensified by garlic. Tarragon combines with the aromatic quality of the celeriac, forming a stronger celery element.

1	celeriac bulb (about 1 pound)
1	tablespoon fresh lemon juice
4	small leeks _or_ 2 large ones
4	small heads Belgian endive _or_ 2 large ones (about 14 to 16 ounces)
1	tablespoon salad oil
1½–1¾	pounds boneless lamb rack or loin meat, cut into 16 equal pieces
1½	cups chicken stock (page 258) or canned low-sodium chicken broth
2	tablespoons finely minced garlic
½	teaspoon salt
¼	teaspoon freshly ground pepper
1	tablespoon chopped fresh tarragon leaves _or_ 1 teaspoon dried
1	tablespoon unsalted butter

Peel the celeriac, cut into ½-inch dice, and toss with lemon juice to prevent discoloring. Trim the roots from the leeks and trim 1 inch off the green tops. If using large ones, halve them lengthwise. If using large Belgian endive, halve them lengthwise.

Heat the oil in a deep 12-inch saucepan over high heat. When oil is almost smoking, add the lamb, in batches if necessary, without crowding the skillet. Brown on all sides. Remove pieces as they are done and reserve on a plate (see note below).

Reduce heat to medium, add the celeriac, leeks, and endive, cover the pan, and cook 3 minutes. Uncover and add the stock, garlic, salt, and pepper. If using dried tarragon, add it now. Increase the heat, bring to a boil, and simmer, uncovered, until the liquid reduces and thickens enough to coat a spoon, about 10 minutes.* Add the lamb and any juices that have escaped from the meat. Continue to cook 2 to 3 minutes. Add the fresh tarragon. Remove from the heat and swirl in the butter. Remove the stew to a covered serving dish and serve with boiled potatoes.

Note: If you use a less tender cut of lamb, such as a center cut from the leg, do not remove from the pot after browning. Let it cook for the entire cooking time along with the vegetables and stock.

*Can be prepared to this point up to several hours in advance.

DEEP-DISH BEEF AND VEGETABLE PIE   SERVES 5 TO 6

Savory pies are stews baked in a crust. Since everyone loves pastry and gravy, you can't go wrong preparing this dish. It evokes memories of a past that almost no one ever really had but that we all like to think we did.

Although the flavors of this stew are fairly straightforward, it is important to understand the secret to their marriage. When reduced, red wine highlights the sweetness of root vegetables, and the tannin (that's what makes your tongue feel "dry" when you drink red wine) is the right background for aromatic herbs. The concentrated intensity of the wine and stock brings all the ingredients together.

½   cup (1 stick) unsalted butter
2   cups plus 2 tablespoons all-purpose flour
1   egg yolk
5   teaspoons ice water
2   pounds sirloin tips, cut into 18 equal pieces
2   tablespoons salad oil
1   small onion, roughly diced (about ¼ cup)
1   celery stalk, cut into 1-inch slices (about ½ cup)
1   small turnip, cut into 1-inch dice (about ¾ cup)
1   medium carrot, cut into ½-inch slices (about ¾ cup)
½   tablespoon finely minced garlic
¾   cup dry red wine
2   cups veal stock (page 259) or canned low-sodium beef broth
½   cup peas, fresh or frozen (defrosted)
½   teaspoon salt
1   teaspoon chopped fresh sage or ½ teaspoon dried
1   small egg, lightly beaten

Prepare the pastry: Cut the butter into ½-teaspoon pieces. Place 2 cups of the flour in a food processor, add the butter, and pulse lightly to form a grainy meal. Add the egg yolk and ice water and pulse until the dough begins to form a ball. Remove from food processor, wrap in plastic wrap, and let rest in the refrigerator for 30 minutes before using.

Place remaining 2 tablespoons flour on a plate. Dry meat with paper towels and dust lightly with flour, shaking off the excess. Heat the oil in a medium skillet over high heat until almost smoking. Add the meat in batches, without crowding, and brown very well on all sides. Remove pieces as they are done and reserve on a plate.

Discard the cooking fat and reduce heat to low. Add the onion, celery, turnip, and carrot. Cover and cook slowly for 10 minutes. Add the garlic and the wine, raise the heat, and cook, uncovered, until the wine has reduced to almost nothing. Add the stock and continue to cook over high heat until reduced by two thirds, about 10 minutes. Add the peas to the skillet and re-place the meat and any juices that have collected on the plate. Add salt and sage.*

Preheat oven to 375°. Roll out the pastry dough to ¼-inch

*Can be made to this point up to several hours in advance and refrigerated.

thickness. Transfer the stew to a 3-inch-deep 9-inch pie dish or baking dish and cover with the pastry topping. Poke a few holes in the top to allow steam to escape. Lightly brush with egg. Place in oven and bake until pastry is golden, about 30 minutes. Transfer from the oven directly to the table and serve.

DUCK BREAST AND PICKLED PUMPKIN WITH BLACK BEANS

SERVES 2 TO 4

(Allow 1 week advance preparation time)

Although this is a quick stew and requires very little cooking time, you need to have two prepared ingredients ready before beginning—pickled pumpkin and cooked black beans.

Sugar needs to cook with something vinegary to be successful in this context; when a savory preparation is sweet but without a contrasting flavor background, it always seems like cheap perfume—loud, indiscreet, and with no surprise after the initial encounter. Dark-meated fowl, such as duck, goose, and squab, always taste more intense when combined with perfumy spices and sweet flavors. Here breast of duck is juxtaposed with pickled pumpkin, a sweet and sour preparation spiced with cinnamon, clove, and coriander. Black beans supply a rich textural background for the other ingredients and especially diminish the pumpkin's vinegar.

1   cup pickled pumpkin (page 267)
½   cup dried black beans
2   4-pound ducks
1   tablespoon salad oil
3   tablespoons soy sauce
1   cup chicken stock (page 258) or canned low-sodium chicken broth
½   teaspoon ground coriander
¼   teaspoon ground cumin
1   cup whipping cream
2   cups tightly packed spinach leaves, washed and trimmed

At least 1 week ahead, make the pickled pumpkin (page 267).

On the day or night before you'll serve the dish, place black beans in a glass crock or plastic container, cover generously with water, and place in the refrigerator to soften for at least 6 hours and up to 12. Drain the beans, place in a medium pot, cover with water, place over medium heat, and cook, covered, for 45 minutes. Pour into a storage container and reserve.

Remove the breasts from the ducks using method two (page 175). Carefully remove the skin without tearing the meat and cut into ¼-inch strips. Cut the breasts into 1-inch pieces. Remove the legs from the carcass and reserve for another use.

Heat the oil in a heavy 12-inch skillet over medium heat, add the duck skins, and cook, stirring with a wooden spoon, until they turn a dark honey color and become crisp. Remove with a slotted spoon and drain on paper towels. Discard all but 1 tablespoon fat and re-place the skillet on the stove over high heat. Add the duck breasts and quickly sear on both sides. Remove from pan and discard the cooking fat. Return the duck breasts to the skillet and add the black beans, pickled pumpkin, soy sauce, stock, coriander, and cumin. Bring to a boil and cook until liquid reduces and begins to thicken, about 3 minutes.★

Add the cream and continue to cook over high heat until the liquid thickens enough to coat a spoon, about 5 minutes. Toss in the spinach, remove from heat, and mix. The spinach leaves should only wilt from the heat of the other ingredients, so toss them through just before serving. Serve the stew in a large casserole with the crispy duck skins sprinkled over the top as decoration.

★Can be prepared to this point up to 1 day in advance and refrigerated.

LOBSTER AND FINNAN HADDIE STEW   SERVES 6

Anyone can serve lobster and be impressive, mostly because of its expense; but to pair it with an unlikely partner, a working-class delight such as finnan haddie, is uncommonly democratic, not to mention tasty.

The famous New England seafood stews are all based on richly flavored yet thin-textured broths; the sole concession to culinary extravagance is the addition of a healthy nut of sweet butter at the end. Finnan haddie (smoked haddock) is smoky and medicinal and nearly overpowers the other flavors of the stew. Snow peas are essential to the balance of this dish because their distinctive aroma, in tandem with garlic and shallots, enhances the flavor of lobster.

1	quart fish stock (page 260)
1	2-pound live lobster
1	pound finnan haddie
12	very small new potatoes
2	tablespoons finely minced onion
3	tablespoons finely minced garlic
¼	teaspoon cayenne pepper
½	pound snow peas, ends trimmed, slivered tip to stem
2	cups milk
3	tablespoons unsalted butter at room temperature

Bring the fish stock to a boil in a 3-quart pot over high heat and add the lobster. Boil, covered, 8 to 10 minutes. Remove lobster (it should be undercooked) and separate the tail and claws from the body. Return the body to the pot. Add the finnan haddie, potatoes, onion, garlic, and cayenne to the fish stock, reduce heat to low, and simmer, covered, for 10 minutes.

Meanwhile, crack the lobster claws and remove the meat. Cut the underside of the tail and remove the tail meat from the shell. Dice the lobster meat into bite-size pieces and add to the soup. Add the trimmed snow peas and milk and cook 1 minute. Remove from heat, remove the lobster body and discard it.

Arrange the lobster, finnan haddie, potatoes, and snow peas in individual bowls. Place 1½ teaspoons of butter on each mound of seafood and pour the broth into the bowls in front of your guests.

SNAPPER AND OYSTER STEW
WITH LEEKS AND APPLES

Astringent flavors need to be kept separate from other elements, tastes, and textures when we want them to have a balanced place in a recipe. The crunch of raw apple, the spark of fresh tarragon leaves, and the crack of the tiny celery seeds allow these astringent ingredients to maintain a separate personality. And since they do not blend, they do not need to be present in large quantity.

A dried herb always blends with other flavors when it becomes reconstituted. If you cannot find fresh tarragon leaves for this recipe, substitute fresh basil, which is peppery and anise-flavored.

2	tablespoons unsalted butter
2	medium leeks, white part only, sliced diagonally into 1-inch rounds
4	cups fish stock (page 260)
12–16	very small new potatoes
1	medium green apple
1	tablespoon fresh lemon juice
4	whole 12- to 14-ounce red snappers, gutted and scaled (see note below)
24	oysters, shucked (about 2 cups)
2	cups milk
½	teaspoon celery seed
1	tablespoon chopped fresh tarragon (*not* dried)

Heat the butter in a 3-quart pot over low heat and cook the leeks 2 minutes. Add the fish stock and potatoes. Raise heat to high, cover, and cook 5 to 7 minutes, depending on the size of the potatoes. They should still be firm when poked with a fork.

Meanwhile, cut the apple, without peeling, into ¼-inch julienne sticks and toss in lemon juice to prevent discoloring. Reserve on a plate.

Add the red snappers to the boiling broth, reduce heat, and simmer until done, about 10 minutes. Add the oysters, any liquid they may have released, and the milk and bring back to the boil. Immediately remove from heat and add the celery seed and tarragon leaves.

Serve each fish in a large individual bowl with the potatoes. Spoon the oysters over and sprinkle with julienned apple sticks. Pour the broth over the snappers at the table.

Note: If another small fish, such as trout or Coho salmon, seems to be better quality when you go to the fish market, substitute it for snapper.

MEATS

■●▲

Meat holds the greatest challenge for the cook, both in developing recipes and in cooking them. Aside from delicately flavored veal, meat cannot be "dressed up" the way poultry and seafood can. Meats have a strong personality, and this sometimes makes them difficult to match with other foods. Next to making pastry, cooking meat is probably the most exacting kitchen technique of all. Knowing when (and how) to roast, braise, or sauté is essential to the success of any recipe, but especially when the main ingredient is meat. Different cuts require different methods. A tenderloin is treated differently from a rump roast. You cannot prepare quickly sautéed veal shanks, for example; they need patient braising.

METHODS OF COOKING MEATS

Pot-roasting and braising are moist heat methods of cooking. Stewing is similar to pot-roasting and braising but refers more to a serving style than a cooking method. Good candidates for pot-roasting and braising are cuts that need to cook for a long time to become tender, like top round, brisket and veal shanks. These meats are high in two proteins, gelatin and collagen, and also have a good amount of fat. Large, tender cuts like leg of lamb, rib roast, and sirloin strip don't need long cooking to become tender and are preferred on the rare side; but they, too, benefit from pot-roasting or braising, becoming more flavorful when cooked with liquid.

Pot-roast in a tightly lidded container with very little liquid. You can cook the meat on top of the stove if you need to, but the radiant heat of an oven gives better results. Pot-roasting is a method of slow cooking by steam, with vegetables added to the pot for flavor. I never sear a pot roast before cooking because the meat will slowly form a delicious "crust" on its own while it roasts.

Braised meat usually cooks in stock or wine, the liquid eventually becoming a sauce or gravy. Before you add liquid to a braise, sear the meat well; it should be very dark but will lighten somewhat as it cooks. Searing forms a crust around the meat, forcing the juices to the interior and changing the color and flavor of the resulting sauce. First we concentrate, then we extract flavor into the braising liquid through long cooking. White meats, such as veal, and leaner cuts of pork, such as chops, can benefit from braising in milk. This keeps the meat moist and greatly increases flavor.

Long, slow cooking causes all flavors to mellow and to blend harmoniously and is why some dishes—pot roasts, braises, and stews—always taste better the second day. Onions, carrots, and celery are important foundation flavors and should always be added to slowly cooked meats. They give a sweet, aromatic background to the ensemble.

The dry heat methods are roasting, barbecue, sautéing, and grilling.

Roasting is normally done in an oven where the meat is exposed to intense, dry, radiant heat, which causes a crust to form on the outside. All the juices remain inside; indeed, as a roast progresses from raw to well done, the juices of the meat are forced more and more to the interior of the meat. Let a roast "rest" for a bit—between 5 and 15 minutes, depending on its size—before carving. This allows the juices to "relax" so they won't run out of the meat the moment it's carved. Sometimes I sear meat quickly on the outside to hasten the formation of a crust, especially if I'm roasting a smaller cut of meat or if I want the meat rare. Otherwise, start cooking the roast in a 500° oven, turning the temperature down after a few minutes. A larger cut of meat always roasts more successfully than a smaller one because of the ratio of surface to interior meat.

Barbecue—roasting over an open fire—is a method good for both small and large cuts of meat. Because the heat of a grill is more direct than the heat of an oven, never place your meat over the hot coals. Arrange the coals around the perimeter of your grill, leaving an empty space underneath the meat. If your grill has a lid, or if you can improvise one with some foil or an inverted roasting pan, you will be able to capture the heat rising off the grill and thereby approximate a kind of radiant oven heat. You will also capture smoke that will add flavor to your barbecue dishes. Barbecue is most successful when it is done slowly.

Sautéing, another dry-heat method of cooking, is quick and generally used for small, tender cuts of meat. It's very important that the heat be conducted through the pan, with just a little butter or oil to prevent sticking and burning. Don't crowd the pan or you risk steaming the meat.

For similar reasons, you should *grill* directly over very hot coals, quickly forming a crust on the meat. Grilling is like sautéing without a pan, but you have to be more careful because the heat of a grill is not as easily controllable as that of a stove top. When your grill flames up, it imparts a taste to the meat unlike any other.

Meat that is roasted, grilled, or sautéed is often accompanied by a sauce or gravy that is prepared separately. This enables the cook to combine bold or contrasting ingredients. Quickly cooked foods and dishes whose ingredients cook separately are always brighter in flavor than slowly cooked foods.

The most difficult part of cooking meat is choosing the right cut and choosing the right way of cooking it. If you want a luscious grilled or sautéed steak, don't try to save money—you will have to buy an expensive New York, Spencer, porterhouse,

T-bone, Delmonico, or fillet. Likewise, don't expect to prepare a hearty stew with a *Chateaubriand*—it will be dry and tasteless. Don't expect to have pot roast at seven o'clock if you don't begin to cook it until six. Cooking meat is easy when you understand the different cuts of meat and respect the rules for cooking them.

BEEF DISHES

PICKLED POT ROAST WITH
CAPER AND HORSERADISH SAUCE   SERVES 6 TO 8

(Allow 4 to 10 days advance preparation time)

To enhance the flavor of a steak or another tender cut of meat, you can marinate it—but only for up to an hour or you risk drawing out the juices and breaking down tissue. Tough cuts of meat that need to cook for a long time can be "pickled"— marinated for a long time with vinegar and a choice of herbs and spices. For this recipe brisket is marinated for at least 4 days but can be left up to 10 days for a stronger vinegar flavor. If the meat is then rinsed, it will keep for another several days, because pickling is also a method of preserving.

When cooking with vinegar, always try to muffle its sourness with strong opposite flavors. Here salty capers and spicy horseradish soften the tart vinegar. Salt is sensed on the tip of the tongue, vinegar on the sides, and horseradish in the throat and especially the nose. Flavors that are so neatly arranged in the mouth are very easy to combine.

2	pounds beef brisket, boneless top round, or chuck roast
1	cup malt vinegar or sherry vinegar
6	tablespoons white horseradish, preferably freshly grated
½	teaspoon salt
3	tablespoons salad oil
2	medium onions, finely minced (about 1½ cups)
1	celery stalk, finely minced (about ½ cup)
1	small carrot, finely minced (about ½ cup)
1	cup veal stock (page 259) or canned low-sodium beef broth
4	tablespoons drained capers

At least 4 days before cooking, combine the meat, vinegar, 2 tablespoons of the horseradish, and the salt in an earthenware or glass crock. Cover and place in refrigerator, turning once a day, for at least 4 days and up to 10 days for a stronger pickled flavor. (To keep several more days before cooking, rinse the meat well, dry it, wrap securely in plastic wrap, and refrigerate.)

The day of serving, preheat oven to 325°. Remove the meat from marinade, pat dry, and discard marinade. In a large heavy roasting pan or Dutch oven heat the oil over high heat and sear the meat until very brown, about 7 minutes on each side. Remove the meat to a plate and pour off the fat. Reduce heat to medium, add the onion, celery, and carrot, and cook, stirring, 3 minutes, dissolving the residue on the bottom of the pan. Replace the meat and add the veal stock. Bring to a boil, cover tightly, and place in the oven for 1½ to 2 hours, turning every 30 minutes.*

When the meat is tender, almost to the point of falling apart, transfer the pan from the oven to the top of the stove. Remove the meat to a cutting board. Using a large spoon, degrease the liquid. Add remaining horseradish and the capers to the cooking liquid, bring to a boil over high heat, and reduce to a thin gravy consistency. Slice the meat (see note below) and arrange on a platter, pour some gravy over it, and serve the remainder in a sauceboat. Serve with buttered, parslied potatoes or noodles.

Note on slicing brisket of beef: A whole brisket will most likely consist of two sections of meat joined by a thin layer of fat. Cook the brisket whole, but before serving separate the two sections, trimming and discarding the interior fat. Each section of meat has a very obvious grain to it. Slice the meat against the grain, at a 45-degree angle to the cutting surface in order to obtain wider slices.

*Can be prepared to this point up to 2 days in advance and refrigerated.

SPICY SKIRT STEAK WITH CINNAMON   SERVES 2 TO 3

Skirt steak is much ignored in this country, probably because it is not buttery tender like a porterhouse or New York steak. Skirt steak has a strong, flavorful "meaty" character and, although not buttery, is quite tender when sliced correctly. It can be grilled or broiled rare or slowly overcooked until falling apart. The little bits of crumbly fat on the outside of a skirt steak bathe it in fat when it cooks, adding flavor.

The heat of serrano and jalapeño peppers is more prominent in the throat than on the tongue and they are not very aromatic. So we need a forward flavor, in this case cinnamon. This dish can be made as spicy as you like, and still the cinnamon will not be overwhelmed, because its scent is so strong.

1	1¼- to 1½-pound skirt steak or flank steak
½	teaspoon salt
2	tablespoons roughly chopped onion
2	ripe plum tomatoes, roughly chopped (about ¼ pound)
1	cup veal stock (page 259) or canned low-sodium beef broth
2	dried pasilla or ancho chile peppers *or* 2 teaspoons dried pasilla powder
2	jalapeño peppers *or* 1 serrano chile pepper, seeds removed
½	teaspoon ground cinnamon
2	tablespoons chopped cilantro

Pat the steak dry. Heat a heavy 12-inch skillet over high heat without oil and, when hot, add the meat. Sear well, about 2 minutes on each side. Preheat oven to 200°.

Add the salt, onion, tomato, stock, dried peppers, jalapeño peppers, and cinnamon. Cook 5 minutes for medium-rare steak, turning once. For more well-done steaks, reduce heat and cook longer. Remove steak to a platter and keep warm in oven while finishing the sauce.

Transfer contents of the skillet to a food processor or blender and puree until smooth. Strain through a sieve with large holes to remove seeds and skins. If the puree is too thin to make a sauce, return to skillet and cook over high heat, stirring, until it is reduced enough to coat the back of a spoon.

Remove steak from the oven and place on a cutting board. Thinly slice the steak, arrange on a warm serving platter, pour the sauce over, and sprinkle with chopped cilantro.

Note on slicing skirt steak: Skirt steak (beef diaphragm) and flank steak are striated muscles that are thin and stringy. Slice them thinly against the grain at a 45-degree angle to your cutting surface.

ROASTED SIRLOIN OF
BEEF WITH FIVE ONIONS   SERVES 4 TO 6

Onions can be cooked differently to achieve different flavors. A slight cooking in a liquid makes them less intense. A long, slow cooking brings out a surprising sweetness. This recipe uses five variations on the taste of onion and also contrasts raw and cooked onion flavors.

1	tablespoon salad oil
1	2½- to 3-pounds New York sirloin
1	teaspoon salt
	freshly ground pepper to taste
4	tablespoons unsalted butter
1	medium leek, white part only, finely sliced
1	small yellow onion, finely diced (about ½ cup)
1½	cups veal stock (page 259) or canned low-sodium beef broth
24	chives, finely minced
4	scallions, finely minced
½	small red onion, finely diced (about ½ cup)

Preheat oven to 425°. Heat the oil in a 12-inch ovenproof skillet or small roasting pan over high heat. When the oil is very hot, sear the meat very well on both sides. Sprinkle with salt and pepper and place in the oven. Roast 30 to 40 minutes for rare to medium-rare, turning once.

Meanwhile, melt 1 tablespoon of the butter in a 1-quart saucepan over low heat, add the leek and yellow onion, and cook gently, without letting them color, for 8 minutes. Add the veal stock, raise the heat to high, and cook until liquid reduces and thickens enough to coat the back of a spoon. Remove from heat and whisk in the remaining butter.

Remove steak from oven when cooked to desired doneness and let rest on a carving board for 5 minutes before carving. Slice the steak against the grain into ½-inch slices, arrange on a platter, and spoon the sauce over it. Garnish with the chives, scallions, and red onion.

SAUTÉED FILLETS OF BEEF
WITH GARLIC AND CILANTRO   SERVES 4

The sauce for this steak is made *à la minute*. In a restaurant, that means "made to order"; at home it means "at the last moment." Since you are preparing this sauce at the last minute, take the opportunity to taste it before adding garlic and cilantro, trying to imagine these two flavors on the canvas of tequila, mustard, and shallots. This is a good way to begin training your palate: try to understand what the background is like before adding the foreground.

1	tablespoon salad oil
4	7-ounce *tournedos* of beef tenderloin
½	teaspoon salt
2	tablespoons finely minced shallots
½	cup tequila
2	tablespoons finely minced garlic
1	tablespoon Dijon mustard
1	cup veal stock (page 259) or canned low-sodium beef broth
2	tablespoons fresh lime juice
2	tablespoons unsalted butter
2	tablespoons chopped cilantro

Preheat oven to 200°. Heat the oil in a heavy 12-inch skillet over high heat. When skillet is hot, add the beef and sear 2 minutes on each side. Sprinkle with salt and continue to cook 2 to 3 minutes for rare or medium-rare, turning once. If you prefer meat medium to well done, lower the heat to medium and continue to cook. When the steaks are done, remove to a platter and keep warm in the oven while you make the sauce.

Reduce heat to medium, discard fat in skillet, and add the shallots. Cook 1 minute, stirring to scrape up any residue on the bottom of the pan. Add the tequila, garlic, and mustard and cook 1 minute more. Add the veal stock and lime juice, increase heat to high, and reduce liquid by half or until thick enough to coat the back of a spoon. Remove from heat, whisk in the butter, and add the cilantro.

Remove steaks from the oven and add to the sauce any juices that have escaped from the meat. Arrange on a platter and pour the sauce over the steaks.

BROCHETTES OF PEPPERED BEEF
WITH SWEET AND SOUR PEPPERCORNS   SERVES 4 TO 6

Brochettes are another insanely popular way of presenting food. When you can think of no other way of pleasing people, and if the cooking method is appropriate, give them a charming meal-on-a-stick. Whether it's the heel of a rye bread or the end cut of a roast beef, people love crust, and when ingredients are cut into cubes, there is a more pleasing ratio of crusty outside to juicy inside.

When using sugar in a savory context, always combine it with vinegar to make a more interesting sweet flavor than sugar alone.

1½–2 pounds sirloin or tenderloin, cut into 12–16 equal cubes
3   tablespoons whole black pepper, coarsely crushed
½   cup white wine vinegar
3   tablespoons sugar
½   teaspoon salt, or to taste
2   tablespoons green peppercorns in water, drained
1   tablespoon unsalted butter
1   tablespoon chopped fresh tarragon leaves or 1 teaspoon dried
2   tablespoons salad oil

Divide the sirloin cubes among four to six skewers and roll the brochettes in the crushed black pepper, pressing hard so that the pepper adheres to the meat. Reserve on a plate in the refrigerator for up to 30 minutes. Light a charcoal or gas grill or your broiler.

Combine vinegar, sugar, and ½ teaspoon salt in a small saucepan and cook over medium heat until the liquid becomes a light syrup, about 8 minutes. Add the green peppercorns. If using dried tarragon, add it now. Reduce heat to low and continue to cook another 2 to 3 minutes. Remove from heat, swirl in butter, and add the fresh tarragon and more salt if desired. Remove to a sauceboat and cool to room temperature.

Lightly brush the brochettes with oil and place on the grill once the coals have burned down and are covered with white ash. Grill to desired doneness, turning once. Serve brochettes on a platter and pass the green peppercorn syrup separately.

LAMB DISHES

BRAISED LAMB SHOULDER WITH BLUE
CHEESE, JALAPEÑOS, AND PORT   SERVES 6 TO 8

This is a truly magical combination of flavor and aroma. Port wine and a blue-veined cheese, sweet and salty ingredients, cancel each other and create a balanced ensemble. My friend Madeleine Kamman likes beef better with blue cheese than lamb because she finds it more harmonious. I prefer it with lamb because it is less harmonious. When we say that certain elements marry well together, we must not be so naive as to fail to recognize that there are many different kinds of marriages. In this marriage, the partners fight. When adapted to a quickly cooked dish, this combination is much bolder.

1	3½- to 4-pound boneless spring lamb shoulder
5	tablespoons unsalted butter
½	pound Roquefort, Stilton, or blue cheese, crumbled
2	fresh jalapeño peppers, seeded and finely minced
½	cup port wine
1	cup veal stock (page 259) or canned low-sodium beef broth

Trim excess fat and any gristle from the shoulder. In a small pan over low heat melt 4 tablespoons of the butter and pour it into a small dish or cup and set aside. Preheat oven to 325°.

Place lamb, fat side down, on work surface and spread half the blue cheese on the inside of the meat. Sprinkle with the jalapeño peppers, then roll and tie the roast with string in several places. Brush with clarified butter, place in a Dutch oven with a tight lid, and place in the oven for 1¼ hours. Baste frequently with remaining butter. Increase the oven temperature to 425°, uncover, and continue to cook 15 to 20 minutes to brown.

Remove the meat to a platter. Place the pot over high heat and cook for 2 minutes. This step separates the pan juices from the fat. Using a spoon, remove as much fat as possible. Add the port and boil 1 minute. Add the stock and reduce until liquid starts to thicken. Remove from heat and add remaining blue cheese. Whisk in the remaining butter.

Untie the lamb, carve into slices, arrange on a platter, and spoon the sauce over it. The plainer the vegetable accompaniment, the better. This is a powerful dish, and you don't want to overwhelm your guests with too many other things. Serve a robust red wine—a California Merlot such as Stag's Leap or a Rhone wine such as Côte de Roti.

RACK OF LAMB WITH CLOVE
GRAVY AND CANDIED SHALLOTS   SERVES 4

When clove is in the presence of something sweet, it reminds me of spice cake. When it's used in a savory context, I usually think of pâté. Red wine tempers this impression and changes the way we taste clove, masking it and making it seem sweeter. When you know that one flavor is going to predominate, as clove does here, it's never a good idea to use it alone.

2	7- to 8-rib racks of lamb (about 1¾ pounds each)
2	tablespoons sugar
3	tablespoons unsalted butter
¾	cup water
½	pound shallots
½	teaspoon salt
½	cup dry red wine
1	cup veal stock (page 259) or canned low-sodium beef broth
1	teaspoon ground cloves

Trim the fat from between the ribs and trim excess covering of fat from meat, leaving only a thin layer. Peel the shallots and cut an X in the root tips. Preheat oven to 425°.

Combine the sugar, 1 tablespoon of the butter, the water, and the shallots in a 12-inch saucepan or pot. Bring to a boil over high heat, reduce heat to medium, and simmer, uncovered, until all the water has evaporated and a glaze forms on the shallots. Continue to cook, stirring or tossing, as the glaze caramelizes, turning a dark golden color, another 2 to 3 minutes.★

Heat a small roasting pan over high heat on top of the stove,

★Shallots can be prepared up to 1 day in advance and refrigerated.

add the lamb, meat side down, and sear quickly without oil. Turn lamb meat side up in roasting pan, sprinkle with salt, and place in oven. Cook 20 to 25 minutes for medium-rare.

When the lamb is cooked to desired doneness, remove to a platter to "rest" for 5 minutes before serving. Pour off any grease in the roasting pan and place on the stove top. Add the red wine and cook over high heat, stirring to dissolve any residue in the bottom of the roasting pan. Add the veal stock and the cloves and cook until liquid thickens and looks saucelike.

Slice the racks of lamb into chops and arrange on a platter. Place the glazed shallots on the lamb and pour the gravy over the top.

PAN-ROASTED LAMB CHOPS
WITH CRACKED PEPPER AND TARRAGON   SERVES 3 TO 4

Most recipes direct the cook to pour off any fat or oil in a pan before adding a liquid. Adding citrus juice to an oil and stock mixture will cause an emulsion to form when the liquid is reduced. The resulting sauce is concentrated, and a spoonful or two is sufficient.

4	tablespoons coarsely crushed black pepper
12	loin lamb chops
1	tablespoon olive oil
½	teaspoon salt
½	cup veal stock (page 259) or canned low-sodium beef broth
¼	cup fresh lime juice
1	tablespoon unsalted butter
1	lime, grated zest only
1	tablespoon chopped fresh tarragon *or* 1 teaspoon dried

Place pepper on a plate and press the lamb chops firmly into the pepper so that it adheres to the meat. Preheat oven to 200°.

Heat oil in 2 large sauté pans over high heat and when very hot add the chops and sear quickly on both sides. Sprinkle with salt. Reduce heat to medium. Do not degrease the pan. Add the stock and lime juice and continue to cook until the chops reach desired doneness, about 2 minutes for medium-rare. Remove chops to a plate and keep warm in oven.

If using dried tarragon, add it to the liquid now. Continue to cook until liquid reduces to a shiny glaze. Remove from heat and whisk in the butter. Add the grated lime zest and fresh tarragon. Remove chops from oven to a warm serving platter. Add any lamb juices to the sauce. Spoon the sauce over the chops and serve.

VEAL DISHES

ROAST VEAL CHOPS WITH
MUSTARD AND CUCUMBER   SERVES 4

Mustard as an accompaniment to veal is not unusual, but the addition of cucumber lightens this combination and makes it a more "modern" dish. Mustard should be spicy and is always salty. Indeed, all condiments contain salt to balance either spice or vinegar. Cucumber is cleansing and aromatic and cuts through mustard.

½   European cucumber
2   tablespoons Dijon mustard
1½ cups veal stock (page 259) or canned low-sodium beef broth
1   tablespoon salad oil
4   veal loin chops (about 2 pounds total weight)
¼   teaspoon salt
    freshly ground pepper to taste
1   tablespoon unsalted butter

Peel the cucumber and halve it lengthwise; scoop out and reserve the seeds. Cut the pulp into ¼-inch by 2-inch julienne strips. Preheat oven to 425°. In a small saucepan combine the cucumber seeds, mustard, and veal stock. Place over medium heat and cook until the liquid thickens enough to coat a wooden spoon.

Meanwhile, heat the oil in a 12-inch skillet over high heat until nearly smoking and brown the veal chops well on both sides. Sprinkle with salt and pepper. Tilt the skillet to remove cooking fat and place in oven 12 to 15 minutes.

When liquid is reduced, remove the saucepan from the heat and whisk in the butter. Strain the sauce into a sauceboat, discarding the seeds. Remove chops from the oven onto a serving platter. Pour over the sauce and garnish each chop with the julienne strips of cucumber.

SAUTÉED VEAL CUTLETS WITH APPLE CIDER   SERVES 4

When salty anchovies cancel sweetness, their fish flavor goes mysteriously undetected.

Ask your butcher for veal *scaloppine* cut from the leg and insist on pieces that are free of muscle separations. If you don't succeed, try using end pieces from the tenderloin.

2   tablespoons olive oil
1½   pounds veal *scaloppine,* thinly sliced and lightly pounded
¾   cup unfiltered apple cider
2   tablespoons fresh lemon juice
1   tablespoon finely minced garlic
4   anchovy fillets, chopped
2   tablespoons chopped parsley

Heat the oil in a large skillet over medium heat. Pat the veal dry, add the cutlets to the skillet, in batches if necessary, and sauté 1 minute. Turn the cutlets and add the apple cider, lemon juice, minced garlic, and chopped anchovy. Increase the heat to high and cook until the cider reduces and forms a syrupy glaze on the veal. Remove from heat and add the chopped parsley. Arrange the veal cutlets on a platter and scrape the glaze over them.

BRAISED VEAL BREAST
WITH TAMALE STUFFING   SERVES 4

Do not use a brisket of veal for this dish. It's the wrong shape for rolling and takes too long to cook before becoming tender. Use the other cut from the breast, simply labeled "boneless breast."

¼   recipe tamale mix (page 234)
2   1¼-pound pieces boneless veal breast, trimmed of gristle and fat
½   teaspoon salt
2   tablespoons salad oil
I   medium onion, finely diced (about ¾ cup)
I   celery stalk, finely diced (about ½ cup)
I   small carrot, finely diced (about ½ cup)
2   cups milk
I   tablespoon tomato paste
½   cup tequila

Prepare the tamale mix (page 234). Lay the boneless breast flat, skin side down, sprinkle with salt, and spread with ½-inch layer of uncooked tamale mixture. Roll the meat up jelly-roll fashion and wrap tightly in a double layer of cheesecloth. Secure with string in several places.

Preheat oven to 350°. Place a heavy casserole or baking pan on the stove, add oil, and heat over medium heat. When the oil is very hot, add the meat and sear on all sides. Add the onion, celery, and carrot and cook, stirring, for 5 minutes. Add the milk, then the tomato paste, and bring to a boil, stirring. Transfer to the oven and cook, uncovered, until tender, about 1½ hours. Turn every 20 minutes. The milk should have mostly evaporated by the time the meat is cooked.*

Remove the meat to a cutting board and place the casserole on top of the stove. Add the tequila and bring to a boil, stirring. Let cook 1 minute. Untie the meat and carefully unwrap it. Cut into 1-inch-thick slices, arrange on a serving platter, and strain the cooking liquids over the meat.

*Can be prepared to this point several hours in advance. Do not refrigerate or the tamale mix will become tough.

BARBECUED SWEETBREADS AND
PEPPERS WITH WHITE VINEGAR SAUCE   SERVES 4 TO 6

Almost all recipes for sweetbreads ask the cook to blanch them and press them under weights. Then you're meant to clean them and proceed to cook them. I don't like this method—the finished product has none of the character of sweetbreads. They become a vehicle for a sauce and a garnish. Sweetbreads have a delicate flavor and texture that should be respected by the cooking method. When sweetbreads cook slowly, over the indirect heat of a grill, their texture becomes creamy and their flavor is improved by the smoke. Spread the coals around the perimeter of the grill, place the sweetbreads in the center, and improvise a loose-fitting cover to catch the smoke.

The sweet roasted peppers are a good foil for the woody charcoal flavor of any grilled or barbecued meat or fish. Vinegar sauces add a lift, or highlight, to both flavors and aromas. Clove is our secret. Masked by the vinegar, it still manages to sweeten the smoked aroma of grilled food.

4–6 large red peppers
1½–2 pounds veal sweetbreads
1   tablespoon salad oil
½   teaspoon salt
     freshly ground black pepper
¼   cup dry white wine
¼   cup white wine vinegar
¼   cup chicken stock (page 258) or canned low-sodium chicken broth
⅛   teaspoon ground cloves
2   tablespoons finely minced shallots
½   teaspoon finely minced garlic
4   tablespoons unsalted butter

Light a charcoal grill and let the coals burn down until completely covered with white ash. Place the peppers over the hottest part of the grill and cook until skin is completely blackened. Repeat on all sides. Transfer them to a small paper bag, twist the top closed, and let peppers steam for 5 minutes. Rearrange the coals so that they form a hollow circle around the perimeter of the grill or are piled to one side of it.

Meanwhile, remove any hard fat or cartilage and rub the

sweetbreads with oil. Place on the grill so that they are not directly over the coals. Sprinkle with salt and pepper. Place the lid on the grill, if it has one, or improvise a covering with foil so that the sweetbreads simultaneously smoke and grill. Grill for 20 minutes, turn, and continue to grill 20 to 30 minutes.

In a saucepan over high heat combine the wine, vinegar, stock, cloves, shallots, and garlic and reduce by three quarters or until nearly dry. Remove from heat and whisk in the butter. Reserve in a warm place.

While the sweetbreads are grilling, remove the peppers from the paper bag and place under running cold water, rubbing to remove their skins. Remove stem and seeds and discard. Reserve peppers on a plate.

When the sweetbreads are just about done, re-place peppers on grill to reheat. Arrange sweetbreads, surrounded by the peppers, on a platter and spoon the sauce over them.

SAUTÉED CALF'S LIVER WITH DRUNKEN PRUNES
SERVES 4

(Allow 1 to 2 weeks advance preparation time for prunes)

Since liver cooks quickly, there is no time for it to form any sort of seared crust, so we help it along by dusting with flour.

The taste of liver is strong, dark, and rich and is enhanced by prunes. The heavily spirited sauce combined with the liver and prunes reminds me of an oak-paneled library.

24	pitted prunes
½	cup Southern Comfort
8	thin slices calf's liver (about 14–18 ounces)
3	tablespoons flour
½	teaspoon salt
	freshly ground pepper to taste
3	tablespoons salad oil
½	cup veal stock (page 259) or canned low-sodium beef broth
2	tablespoons unsalted butter

At least 1 week (preferably 2) prior to making this dish, combine prunes and Southern Comfort in a glass jar. Cover tightly and leave in a dark place.

Ten minutes before serving, dust the liver with flour, shaking off excess. Sprinkle with salt and a few grinds of a pepper mill. Preheat oven to 200°.

Heat 1 tablespoon of the oil in a 12-inch sauté pan over medium heat. When hot, add 3 slices liver without crowding skillet. Cook 1 minute on each side for medium-rare or until liver reaches desired doneness. (Undercook the liver as it will continue to cook, slightly, in the warm oven while you finish the recipe.) Remove to a platter and keep warm in the oven while you sauté the other batches.

When all the liver is cooked, discard cooking fat and add the stock, prunes, and 3 tablespoons of their Southern Comfort marinade. Increase heat to high and cook until the liquids thicken and become saucelike. Remove from heat and whisk in butter. Transfer liver to a serving platter. Spoon the sauce and prunes over the liver and serve. I don't believe in eating liver without an accompaniment of mashed potatoes.

Note: Make a large batch of drunken prunes. They will keep for about a year and only get better with age. Use them as an accompaniment for a roast pork loin or improvise a perfectly wonderful vanilla ice cream parfait.

PORK DISHES

PORK POT ROAST WITH
ROSEMARY AND PORT   SERVES 4 TO 6

White meats are usually drier and therefore less successfully pot-roasted than red meats unless they are barded with fat, a tedious procedure. But pork butt has a good pork flavor and enough fat so that it stays moist when pot-roasted.

Rosemary is an oily herb and when used liberally gives a bitter taste to a dish. Port is sweet and rich and contrasts with the chemical undertaste of rosemary. There are two rosemary tastes here; I layer the mellow flavor of long-cooked rosemary with the rosemary that is added just before serving. The cooked rosemary lingers in the background and the fresh rosemary jumps out.

2   tablespoons salad oil
2   pounds boneless pork butt
1   medium onion, finely minced (about ¾ cup)
1   celery stalk, finely diced (about ½ cup)
1   large carrot, finely diced (about 1 cup)
1   cup chicken stock (page 258) or canned low-sodium chicken
     broth
2   cups port wine
2   tablespoons chopped fresh rosemary (not dried)
½   teaspoon salt
2   tablespoons unsalted butter

Preheat oven to 325°. Heat the oil in a heavy pot or Dutch oven over high heat and sear the pork on all sides, browning well. Remove the roast and discard the remaining fat.

Reduce the heat to low, add the onion, celery, and carrot, and cook, stirring, for 1 minute. Re-place the roast, moisten with the stock and port, and add half the rosemary and the salt. Cover tightly and place in the oven for 1¼ hours, turning the roast every 20 minutes.★

Remove the meat to a cutting board. On top of the stove, cook the liquid in the pot over high heat until it starts to thicken but has not yet reached a saucelike consistency. Remove from the heat and whisk in the butter. Strain the liquid into a gravy boat and add the remaining rosemary. Slice the meat and arrange on a platter. Pass the sauce separately.

★Can be prepared to this point up to 2 days in advance and refrigerated.

ROAST PORK LOIN GLAZED
WITH HONEY AND CORIANDER   SERVES 4 TO 6

The sweet and salt of honey and soy combine to form a background for the forward aroma of coriander. When I want coriander as the primary flavor of a dish, I secretly support it with a discreet amount of curry and cumin.

2	tablespoons salad oil
1	3-pound pork loin, chine bone removed
¼	teaspoon salt
½	teaspoon freshly ground pepper
1	medium onion, finely minced (about ¾ cup)
1	celery stalk, finely diced (about ½ cup)
1	medium carrot, finely diced (about ¾ cup)
½	cup honey
¼	cup soy sauce
½	teaspoon ground cumin
½	teaspoon curry powder (page 264)
2	tablespoons ground coriander
1	tablespoon all-purpose flour
1	cup chicken stock (page 258) or canned low-sodium chicken broth

Preheat oven to 450°. On top of the stove heat the oil in a 9-inch by 12-inch roasting pan over high heat and sear the pork loin on all sides, giving it a golden color. Sprinkle with salt and pepper, add the onion, celery, and carrot, and place, uncovered, in the oven. Reduce heat to 350° and roast for 20 minutes.

In a small bowl combine the honey, soy sauce, cumin, curry powder, and 1 tablespoon of the coriander. After the pork has cooked for 20 minutes, use a brush to coat it with the honey/soy mixture. Continue to roast for an additional hour, basting every 20 minutes. The honey/soy mixture will become very brown in the roasting pan. If it seems to be too burnt, add a tablespoon or two of water. Remove from oven and turn the oven off. Remove pork from pan. If serving immediately, keep pork warm on a platter in the still-warm oven; otherwise, cover roast with foil and keep at room temperature for up to 2 hours.

Transfer roasting pan to the top of the stove over low heat. Sprinkle flour over the vegetables, mixing. Mix chicken stock with any remaining honey mixture and add to the pan. Add the other tablespoon of coriander. Increase heat to medium and cook for 2 to 3 minutes or until liquid is thick and gravylike. Cut the loin into individual chops, arrange on a serving platter, and strain the sauce over the chops.

PAN-SMOTHERED PORK CHOPS
WITH CLOVE AND ORANGE   SERVES 4

Most American pork tends to be dry and tough and, in general, the larger cuts give more successful results because long cooking breaks down the muscle fiber. Smaller pieces of pork can be cooked in milk, greatly improving their texture and tenderizing them. Milk does not form a rich or creamy sauce, and when it curdles during the cooking, don't worry that you have done something wrong, you haven't.

Garlic is very important to the success of clove in a savory context, ensuring that it doesn't overpower other ingredients.

2   ripe plum tomatoes (¼ pound)
1   small onion, finely diced (about ¼ cup)
1   teaspoon ground cloves
1   tablespoon finely minced garlic
4   thick-cut loin pork chops
3   tablespoons all-purpose flour
2   tablespoons salad oil
2   cups milk
2   tablespoons white wine vinegar
1   orange, grated zest only

In a food processor pulse together the tomatoes, onion, cloves, and garlic. Or finely chop by hand. Pat the pork chops dry and dust on both sides with flour, shaking off the excess. Preheat oven to 200°.

Heat the oil in a heavy 12-inch skillet over high heat, add the chops, and lightly brown on both sides, about 6 minutes. Tilt skillet to discard remaining oil. Reduce heat to medium and add the tomato mixture and the milk. Let cook, uncovered, about 6 minutes. Turn the chops and cook 4 minutes more.

Remove the chops to a plate and keep warm in the oven.

Increase heat to high, add the vinegar and orange zest to the cooking puree, and cook 1 minute. Arrange the chops on a serving platter and strain the sauce over the chops, pushing the puree ingredients in the sieve with a wooden spoon to extract as much of their liquid as possible.

GRILLED BABY BACK RIBS WITH STAR ANISE   SERVES 4

Ribs are always more succulent when they are braised, then left to chill overnight before grilling. If you cannot find true baby back ribs, each slab weighing 14 to 16 ounces, then prepare this recipe using heavier ones. The result is equally delicious, but the cooking time needs to be increased slightly. If you'd like to substitute beef ribs, either long or short, the same method of cooking applies.

4   14- to 16-ounce slabs baby back ribs
6   star anise, crushed
2   tablespoons chopped fresh tarragon leaves *or* 1 tablespoon dried
3   tablespoons minced garlic
¼   cup Dijon mustard
¼   cup rice vinegar
1   cup chicken stock (page 258) or canned low-sodium chicken broth
2   tablespoons sugar

The day before or at least 12 hours before grilling, preheat oven to 375°. Place ribs in one layer in baking dish. Combine all other ingredients, mixing well, and pour this marinade over the ribs. Cover and place in oven for 40 minutes, turning after 20 minutes. Remove from oven, cool, cover, and refrigerate overnight.

The next day, light a gas or charcoal grill. Remove ribs from marinade. Strain marinade into a small bowl, discarding star anise and whatever bits of meat are left in liquid from the braising. Place the ribs on a hot grill. (A charcoal grill is ready when the coals are completely covered with white ash.) Grill ribs 15 minutes on each side, basting frequently with the marinade. Present the ribs on a platter and serve any remaining marinade as a dipping sauce on the side.

BAKED HAM WITH
SORREL VINEGAR GLAZE   SERVES 14 TO 18

You will probably prepare this recipe only for an occasion, either a holiday meal or an important buffet. Be assured that this is a festive dish—as good, perhaps, as your favorite ham.

I boil cured hams to get out some of the salt before baking, then I try to combine sweet, sour, and spicy ingredients to diminish the remaining saltiness and highlight the natural pork flavor. Sorrel, balsamic vinegar, and brown sugar are the sweet and sour ingredients in this recipe. Mustard powder is a spicier cooking ingredient than prepared mustard.

1	14- to 16-pound cured ham, bone in
1½	cups balsamic vinegar
2	cups chicken stock (page 258) or canned low-sodium chicken broth
½	cup dark brown sugar
2	tablespoons dry mustard
¼	cup fresh lemon juice
2	bunches fresh sorrel (about 4 to 5 ounces), leaves only, chopped, or ½ cup jarred sorrel

Place the ham in a 16-quart stockpot or very large kettle and cover completely with cold water. Bring to a boil, reduce the heat to low, and let simmer, covered, for 2 hours.

Meanwhile, combine vinegar, 1 cup of the chicken stock, the brown sugar, and the mustard in a small pot, bring to a boil over medium heat, and cook until liquid becomes a syrupy glaze.

Preheat oven to 350°. Remove the ham from the water and trim all covering skin and fat. Place in a large roasting pan and spoon or brush some of the glaze over it. Place in oven and bake, uncovered, for 1 hour, basting every 15 minutes with more glaze. Transfer ham to a platter and keep ham warm in turned-off oven.★

Place the roasting pan on the stove top. Add the remaining cup of chicken stock, the lemon juice, and any remaining glaze. Cook over high heat, scraping up and dissolving any brown bits in the roasting pan. If using sorrel in a jar, add it now. Using a rubber spatula, scrape this gravy into a large sauceboat and add the chopped fresh sorrel. Carve the ham at the table and pass the sauce separately.

★Can be prepared to this point a few hours in advance and kept, covered, at room temperature.

POULTRY

■ ● ▲

My favorite thing about birds is their skin. Animals—cows and sheep, for example—don't have skins; they have hides. Pigs have skin, but the butcher usually removes it and it's hard to find pork with crackling. Fish have skins, but with the exception of the scaleless ones, such as catfish, fish skins are not very interesting. Skin separates poultry from everything else that we cook. In the culinary world a roast chicken is perhaps most similar to a baked potato. Skin on poultry acts like a natural roasting bag, sealing in flavor and moisture. When the cooked skin of a bird becomes glazed and crusty, it is heavenly; when it stays soft, it is unctuous and comforting; and like virtually all good things in life, it is considered unhealthy for you.

Birds render their fat very easily, an important factor in how they cook. Ducks and geese have a thick layer of fat between their skin and flesh, much of which is rendered during cooking.

(Don't throw it out; it's great to cook with—for both sautéing and deep-frying.) Chickens don't have an important layer of fat, nor do turkeys, squabs, or quail; but there is enough fat in all birds to bathe their flesh as they cook. A properly cooked bird will be succulent and moist, even if it is a little overdone. (I disagree with the current fad of cooking chicken only until it's pink next to the bone, and I'm really tired of rare duck breasts. So many cooks take the soul out of food in the name of what's trendy, inventive, and even—supposedly—healthy.)

Fowl and game always taste like what they eat. Game birds that forage in the forests have the flavor of the berries, nuts, seeds, and grasses that they find. With the exception of squab, a red-meated fowl, I never buy commercially raised game birds because they are fed like chickens. Farm-raised pheasant, guinea hen, even quail, taste like bad chicken—dry, never succulent. (I don't even consider Cornish hens to be game birds.) Finding a tasty chicken has even become a problem; chickens are the tomatoes of the animal kingdom. I go to a natural-food store for my chicken. The poultry have been better fed, spared hormones and chemicals, and still taste like chicken; better yet, they may have roamed the barnyard and done their share of scratching. Buy only fresh, not frozen, ducks and avoid all game birds other than fresh squab unless you know who shot it.

ON COOKING BIRDS

It was just a few years ago that I finally understood the charm of boiled chicken. When I was younger, the skin of a boiled chicken seemed rubbery to me, and the bird was always dripping with some unappealing gelatinous "stuff." An appreciation of boiled chicken—or, rather, poached chicken—is either an acquired taste, a sign of impending middle age, or both.

Boiling or poaching transfers heat through a surrounding liquid to a solid in order to cook that solid. In cooking parlance *boiling* usually refers to cooking something rapidly in salted water and *poaching* to cooking something gently in a flavored water. It is always better to poach in a stock and then, perhaps, to turn that stock into a sauce. Boiling in salted water is almost never appropriate for animal protein, with the exception of lobsters.

When you poach something and your primary intention is

to flavor the liquid, always start with a cold liquid. Begin a chicken soup, for instance, with cold water. When stock bones and vegetables are moistened with cold water, the flavors will be drawn out of the stock ingredients as the water comes to a boil. If you want the central ingredient to *keep* its flavor, then begin the cooking in boiling liquid. This procedure seals the outside in the same way that putting the food into a hot pan or very hot oven does. The poached chicken recipes in this chapter ask you to put the chicken into a boiling stock because we want the chicken to retain its flavor.

I include fricassees, *blanquettes,* stews, and French *poêles* in the category of braising. Braising birds allows us to produce a boldly flavored sauce or accompaniment while accomplishing an exchange of flavor among all the elements of the braise. The recipe directions sometimes ask you to brown the skin of the bird, sometimes not. One method is not superior to the other; it is a decision that has to do with the nature of the dish.

Birds sauté nicely because their skin becomes crisp as they are bathed by the oil or fat used to sauté. Sautéing is a quick method of cooking that depends on fat for the transfer of heat from the pan to the bird. It is appropriate only for smaller pieces of meat—obviously, you would not sauté a whole turkey or goose.

I always batter or dredge any birds that I fry. Batter or dredging flour isolates the poultry from the oil, making the outside even crisper and keeping all the moisture and flavor inside. Battering or dredging in effect gives poultry another skin. Remember always to fry in hot (375°) oil, for both pan-frying and deep-frying. Often people prefer pan-frying at home because you need only a 2-inch depth of fat. In either case, don't crowd the pan or fryer or your birds won't turn golden and crispy.

Poultry is a grill favorite, I think, because birds take on a smoky flavor and because people like things crisp, almost burnt on the outside but still moist on the inside, and grilled chicken produces just that result. Smaller pieces of poultry or *paillards* are best for grilling. A *paillard* is a thin slab of poultry, meat, or fish. Some people call them *cutlets,* and I suppose they are the same thing, but I always think of cutlets as being breaded. Cutlets make me think of restaurants that buy prepared food that they recook, whereas *paillards* conjure an image of an outside grill on the Italian Riviera. *Paillards* are quick and easy to grill and benefit greatly from being marinated. Small pieces of meat that cook very quickly don't have time to develop any nuance of flavor. If they aren't marinated, they always taste too pure, and the impression is that we are eating austere food.

TWO METHODS OF CUTTING UP POULTRY FOR COOKING

Method One—for mostly boneless meat: First remove the legs by pulling them away from the body and cutting through the skin between the breast and thigh. Pull the legs back until the joint snaps. Turn the bird on its breast and cut the leg from the carcass, being careful to leave the "oyster" attached to the thigh. The "oyster" is a small disk-shaped piece of meat found in the small of the back at the intersection of the thigh and backbone.

Slice the meat on the skinless side of the thigh, exposing the bone. Scrape the meat completely off the bone, pull the bone backward, and snap it out of the joint. You now have a boneless thigh attached to the drumstick. Lay the leg flat; using a large chef's knife, cut off the stubby foot end of the drumstick.

To remove the breasts, cut along the breastbone to free the cutlet. Cut through the shoulder joint—next to the neck cavity— to free the cutlet from the carcass. Remember to keep your knife pointed as much as possible toward the bone, not toward the flesh. When the breast is removed, lay it flat on the cutting surface and chop through the wing midway between the first joint and the breast.

Method Two—for 8 pieces with bones: Insert a large chef's knife into the cavity of the bird and completely cut along one side of the backbone from neck to tail. Open up the bird and cut along other side of the backbone to remove it completely. Cut along the breastbone, dividing the bird in half. Separate legs from breasts by breaking the pelvic joint. Cut each leg into thigh and drumstick. Trim the lower carcass from the breasts. Cut off the wings. Cut each breast through the rib cage into two pieces.

GAME HENS WITH ROAST
GARLIC AND CANDIED ANISE

SERVES 4

This dish is a variation on the most popular menu item at Trumps—Sautéed Chicken, Roast Garlic, and Candied Lemon. That recipe has already appeared in various publications, but it's so beloved that some incarnation of it should be included in this book.

Here garlic is transformed—it becomes mildly sweet, nutty, and burnt. It's important to burn the garlic skins so that this flavor permeates the tart lemon in the sauce, the sweet candy of the anise, and of course the nutty, soft garlic. When garlic cooks in its skin, it becomes creamy and mild. Eat the garlic unceremoniously—pick up the whole cloves with your fingers and suck out the meat.

¼	cup virgin olive oil
2	medium garlic heads, separated into cloves, skins left intact
4	whole game hens, legs tied together
2	cups chicken stock (page 258) or canned low-sodium chicken broth
¼	cup fresh lemon juice
½	teaspoon salt
1	small bulb anise or fennel (about 6 ounces)
⅓	cup sugar
½	cup water
1	tablespoon chopped fresh tarragon (*not* dried)

Preheat oven to 425°. In a 12-inch ovenproof skillet, heat the olive oil over high heat, add garlic, and sauté until the skins are a dark golden color. Add the hens and brown on both sides. If hens do not all fit together, brown them in batches. If the garlic turns black, remove from skillet. When the hens are brown, re-place them along with the garlic in the skillet and without pouring off the cooking oil add the chicken stock and lemon juice. Sprinkle with salt, bring to a boil, and place, uncovered, in the oven for 30 minutes, turning once.

While the hens are cooking, prepare the anise or fennel bulb. Trim any discolored outer leaves. Cut the bulb in half from tip to root, then slice each half into ¼-inch cross sections. Place the anise in another skillet on the stove, more or less in one layer.

Add the sugar and water, bring to a boil over medium heat, and simmer gently until all the water is evaporated and the anise looks glazed and shiny. There will probably be a bit of syrupy liquid left in the pan. Add the chopped tarragon. Transfer anise and any glaze to a plate and set aside until hens are cooked.

Transfer the skillet with the hens to the stove top, place over high heat, and reduce the liquid on top of the stove until it has a shiny consistency. It will look more like a glaze than a sauce. Arrange the hens on a serving platter. Garnish with the candied anise and scrape the glaze and garlic over the top.

CHICKEN STEWED WITH FIG RATATOUILLE

SERVES 2 TO 4

Figs replace eggplant in this variation on a *Provençal* theme. Served hot or cold, this dish is a good summer idea. Dried figs are sweet and give only a slight impression of fresh fig taste. In the cooking they absorb the liquids of the other ingredients and take on their flavors.

4	plum tomatoes (about ½ pound)
2	tablespoons virgin olive oil
I	3- to 3½-pound fryer chicken, cut up using method one (page 175)
I	medium onion, finely diced (about ¾ cup)
I	large zucchini, sliced (about 2 cups)
12	dried figs
2	tablespoons finely minced garlic
½	teaspoon salt
	freshly ground pepper to taste
I	cup chicken stock (page 258) or canned low-sodium chicken broth
2	tablespoons finely chopped parsley
2	tablespoons unsalted butter

Using a small paring knife, cut off tip and stem of each tomato. Remove the seeds and core, leaving only firm, outer pulp. Slit one side of the tomato and lay the tomato flat on work surface. Cut lengthwise into ¼-inch strips, pile up strips, and cut across into ¼-inch pieces. Reserve on a small plate.

Heat the oil in a 12-inch ovenproof skillet over high heat,

add the chicken, and sauté until the skin is very dark brown. Remove to a plate and reserve. Add the onion to the skillet and cook, stirring, until softened. Remove with a spoon and reserve. Repeat with the zucchini. Discard the cooking fat and re-place the onion and zucchini. Add the figs and the garlic and re-place the chicken in the skillet.

Preheat the oven to 425°. Add the chicken thighs and stock to the skillet and bring to a boil over high heat. Sprinkle with salt and add pepper to taste. Place, uncovered, in the oven for 20 minutes. Add the breasts and cook another 10 minutes. Transfer skillet to top of the stove and cook over medium heat until the contents fall apart and become a compote. Remove chicken from skillet and reserve on a plate. Remove skillet from heat, add the tomatoes and parsley, and swirl in the butter. Arrange the *ratatouille* on a serving platter and place the chicken on top. Serve a nicely chilled French Tavel or California white Zinfandel wine.

Note: If you're serving this dish chilled, substitute virgin olive oil for the butter at the end of the recipe.

CHICKEN BRAISED WITH CINNAMON AND BASIL
SERVES 4

Many hybrid herbs have recently become available—lemon thyme and pineapple sage come immediately to mind. When a purveyor insisted that I sample cinnamon basil, my first reaction was "Only in California—designer herbs." I shouldn't have been so mistrustful. Most of these hybrids are quite magical. The combination of cinnamon and basil in this chicken recipe is a result of that first tasting.

Cinnamon highlights the peppery quality of basil, but the two also combine to form a new flavor. Our simulated hybrid flavor is more convincing when layered over a foundation of tomato paste, onions, and sherry vinegar.

2   tablespoons salad oil
1   3- to 3½-pound fryer chicken, cut up using method one (page 175)
1   tablespoon finely minced onion
3   tablespoons sherry vinegar
1   teaspoon tomato paste
1   cup chicken stock (page 258) or canned low-sodium chicken broth
½   teaspoon salt
¼   teaspoon freshly ground pepper
1   cinnamon stick *or* 1 teaspoon ground cinnamon (see note below)
4   tablespoons finely chopped fresh basil, leaves only (*not* dried; see note below)
3   tablespoons unsalted butter

Heat the oil in a 12-inch ovenproof skillet over high heat. Add the chicken and brown well. At this point the chicken should be darker than what you want as its finished color. Remove and reserve on a plate. Preheat oven to 425°.

Discard the cooking fat in the skillet, add onion, vinegar, tomato paste, chicken stock, salt, pepper, and cinnamon. Bring to a boil. Re-place the chicken thighs and transfer the skillet, uncovered, to the oven. Cook for 20 minutes, add the breasts, and continue to cook another 12 to 15 minutes. Remove skillet from oven and remove chicken to a plate.

Re-place skillet on the stove top over high heat and reduce the cooking liquid until it becomes shiny and somewhat thickened. Remove from the heat, add the basil, and swirl in the butter. Arrange the chicken on a serving platter and strain the sauce over it.

Note: If you use fresh cinnamon basil, omit the cinnamon and ordinary basil and add ¼ cup tightly packed, finely chopped leaves when you would add the ordinary basil.

BLANQUETTE OF CHICKEN
AND ROASTED PEPPERS

SERVES 3 TO 4

When ingredients cook in cream, the resulting dish requires carefully flavoring to retain a bright taste. In this recipe shallots, garlic, coriander, and cumin make a background to prime the palate so that the roasted peppers and chicken stay interesting.

4	green peppers
4	tablespoons unsalted butter
1	3- to 3½-pound fryer chicken, cut up using method one (page 175)
1	cup chicken stock (page 258) or canned low-sodium chicken broth
1	tablespoon ground coriander
½	teaspoon ground cumin
1	teaspoon finely minced garlic
2	tablespoons finely minced shallots
½	teaspoon salt
¼	teaspoon freshly ground pepper
1	cup whipping cream

Place the peppers directly on a high flame on the stove top or place under a preheated broiler. Roast until skin is completely blackened on all sides. Transfer them as they are done to a small paper bag, twist the top closed, and let them steam for 5 minutes to loosen the skins.

Meanwhile, heat 2 tablespoons of the butter in a Dutch oven over low heat. Add the chicken pieces and cook without browning, about 7 minutes. Preheat the oven to 375°.

Remove chicken from the pot and discard the cooking fat. Re-place chicken thighs and add the stock. Bring to a boil and add the coriander, cumin, garlic, shallots, salt, pepper, and cream. Place, uncovered, in the oven for 15 minutes. Add the breasts and continue to cook another 15 minutes.

Meanwhile, remove the peppers from the paper bag and place under running cold water, rubbing to remove their skins. Remove stems and seeds and discard.

Transfer the pot from the oven to the top of the stove. Remove chicken to a plate. Add the peppers. Cook over high heat, reducing the liquid until it begins to thicken and become saucelike. Re-place the chicken and swirl in remaining butter. Transfer everything to a large serving bowl. Accompany with plain rice or buttered noodles.

CHICKEN AND ARTICHOKES
IN ARUGULA CREAM   SERVES 3 TO 4

I	lemon
4	large artichokes
2	tablespoons olive oil
I	3- to 3½-pound fryer chicken, cut up using method two (page 175)
½	teaspoon salt
½	teaspoon freshly ground pepper
I	cup chicken stock (page 258) or canned low-sodium chicken broth
2	tablespoons finely minced garlic
3	tablespoons finely minced shallots
I	cup whipping cream
I	bunch arugula or watercress (about 2 ounces)
2	tablespoons unsalted butter

Cut lemon in half for rubbing the cut surfaces of the artichokes as you work. Trim ½ inch from the tops of the artichokes. Using scissors or a small knife, cut off the spiked ends of all artichoke leaves. Cut off the stems. Cut the artichokes into quarters and cut out the hairy chokes and small inner leaves.

Preheat oven to 425°. Heat the oil in a 12-inch ovenproof skillet or a baking dish over medium heat. When hot, add the chicken and sauté until the skin is a light golden color. Sprinkle with salt and pepper. Remove the breasts and set aside on a plate. Add the chicken stock and bring to a boil. Add the artichokes, garlic, and shallots and place, uncovered, in the oven for 15 minutes. Add the cream and the chicken breasts and return to the oven for another 10 minutes. Turn off the oven.

Transfer skillet to the top of the stove. Remove chicken breasts to plate and keep warm, covered, in turned-off oven. Over high heat, reduce the liquid in the skillet until it has a shiny consistency and a saucelike texture. Remove chicken thighs and artichokes to the plate with the breasts. Use a rubber scraper to transfer skillet ingredients to a blender or food processor. Add the arugula or watercress and puree until smooth. Add the butter and blend until incorporated. Arrange the chicken and the artichokes on a serving platter and spoon the pureed arugula over. Accompany with savory rice pudding (page 228).

MUSTARD-POACHED CAPON
WITH HORSERADISH SAUCE   SERVES 5 TO 6

We had a difficult time finding a capon to test this recipe and had to order it from a poultry shop. Capons, which are castrated roosters, have a stronger poultry character and a better texture for poaching than do chickens. If you have to place a special order for one, also ask for some chicken feet, which will greatly improve the sauce. If you can't get a capon, substitute the largest, oldest boiling hen that you can find.

Combinations of strong flavors, in this case mustard and horseradish, soften during long cooking and become part of the background of a dish. I add more mustard and horseradish at the end of the cooking so that flavors jump out at us.

The poaching broth is not reduced to a sauce consistency because I like the impression that strong flavors give when placed in a concentrated cream broth.

2	quarts chicken stock (page 258) or canned low-sodium chicken broth
1	medium carrot, roughly diced (about ¾ cup)
1	medium onion, roughly diced (about ¾ cup)
1	celery stalk, roughly diced (about ½ cup)
2	lemons, halved
½	cup Dijon mustard
5	tablespoons horseradish, preferably freshly grated
1	teaspoon salt
1	teaspoon whole black peppercorns
1	5- to 6-pound capon or large boiling chicken (pullet)
4	chicken feet (optional)
2	cups whipping cream
3	tablespoons unsalted butter

In an 8-quart stockpot or kettle combine stock, carrot, onion, celery, lemons, ¼ cup of the mustard, 3 tablespoons of the horseradish, salt, and peppercorns. Cover and bring to a boil. Add the capon, chicken feet, and enough water to cover completely. Bring back to a boil, reduce heat to low, and simmer 1 hour. When capon is done, the juices that run when a fork is pricked into the thigh will be clear. Preheat oven to 200°.

Remove capon to a platter, cover with a moist cloth, and reserve in the oven. Strain the poaching liquid into a storage container to remove the vegetables, lemons, and chicken feet. Measure 6 cups of the poaching liquid into a 2-quart saucepan, place over high heat, and reduce by one third. Add cream, remaining mustard, and remaining horseradish, and reduce again by one third. The liquid should have the consistency of a sauce that is much too thin. Remove from heat and whisk in the butter. Place the capon on a serving platter and spoon some of the cream broth over it. Carve the capon at the table and serve in soup bowls. Pass the cream broth on the side. Accompany with new potatoes in white wine (page 228).

GRILLED PAILLARDS OF TURKEY WITH
BURNT PEANUT BUTTER MARINADE   SERVES 4 TO 6

This marinade burns slightly on the grill and greatly increases the charm of the dish.

1	1½- to 2- pound boneless, skinless turkey breast
½	cup natural, smooth peanut butter
1	cup Madeira
1	tablespoon finely minced garlic
1	tablespoon finely minced shallots
1	tablespoon curry powder (page 264)
¼	teaspoon salt
½	teaspoon freshly ground black pepper
4–6	lemon wedges

Slice the turkey breast against the grain of the meat into 8 to 12 pieces. Place each piece between 2 pieces of wax paper and pound lightly to flatten using a mallet, a cleaver, or the side of a large chef's knife. Reserve on a plate.

At least 1 hour before grilling, combine the peanut butter, Madeira, garlic, shallots, curry, salt, and pepper and let the turkey marinate in this mixture for 1 hour.

Light a charcoal or gas grill. (When the coals are completely covered with white ash, the grill is ready.) Or preheat the broiler. Remove turkey from the marinade and place on grill. Cook 2 minutes on each side. Arrange *paillards* on a platter and garnish with lemon wedges.

HAM AND CHEESE FRIED CHICKEN
WITH MUSTARD GRAVY   SERVES 2 TO 4

Some combinations of ingredients are so satisfying that they don't need added flavors. Ham and cheese with mustard is an example. The inspiration for this recipe came from my craving for a ham and cheese sandwich, slathered with that unfashionable bright yellow mustard.

I think fried chicken should be completely boneless; I'm always frustrated when it has bones, especially rib bones, because then I don't get to eat all the crispy batter.

1	3- to 3½-pound fryer chicken with giblets
1	tablespoon unsalted butter
1	cup plus 1 tablespoon flour
1	cup chicken stock (page 258) or canned low-sodium chicken broth
½	cup whipping cream
2	tablespoons Dijon mustard
1	egg
1	10-ounce bottle pale beer
½	teaspoon salt
½	teaspoon freshly ground pepper
2	tablespoons dry mustard
4	thin slices country ham
½	pound Swiss cheese, grated
3	cups salad oil, or enough to fill skillet to a depth of 4 inches

First cut up the chicken using method one (page 175), but completely cut the wings from the breasts. After removing the thigh bones from the legs, slice the drumsticks open and remove the leg bones. Preheat oven to 425°.

Place gizzards, wings, necks, livers, and bones in a small baking dish and place in oven for 20 minutes. When brown, remove baking dish from oven and place on top of the stove over low heat. Add the butter and when it's melted add 1 tablespoon flour. Cook together, stirring, for 1 minute. Add the chicken stock, bring to a boil, and simmer, uncovered, until thick, about 10 minutes. Add the cream and Dijon mustard to the gravy and let cook until the gravy coats a spoon. Strain gravy through a strainer or sieve into a saucepan, discard bones and giblets, and reserve, covered, until the chicken is cooked.

Meanwhile, make the beer batter. Break the egg into a medium mixing bowl, sift 1 cup flour over it, mixing with a whisk and adding the beer a little at a time. Add salt and pepper, mix, and reserve, covered.

Using your fingers, lightly separate the skin from the meat of the chicken without detaching it. Rub this cavity with the dry mustard and stuff with ham and cheese.*

Heat a 4-inch depth of oil in a heavy, deep skillet to 375°. Preheat oven to 200°. Dip the pieces of chicken in the beer batter and place in hot oil, in batches if necessary to keep the skillet uncrowded. Fry 8 minutes, turn, and continue to fry 4 to 6 minutes or until golden brown and crisp. Remove pieces of chicken as they are done, drain on paper towels, and keep warm in the oven while the other pieces cook.

Heat the gravy, covered, over low heat and, when hot, transfer to a sauceboat. Arrange chicken on a serving platter and serve sauce on the side. Serve with your favorite mashed potatoes.

*Can be prepared to this point a couple of hours in advance and kept, covered, in the refrigerator.

GRILLED YOGURT CHICKEN   SERVES 3 TO 4

The yogurt marinade is meant to be a little tart so it will contrast nicely with the grilled flavor of the chicken. When grilling, consider the flavors of the grill—the burnt taste, the smoke—as additional ingredients.

1	cup plain yogurt
⅓	cup fresh lemon juice
½	teaspoon ground cloves
½	teaspoon salt
½	teaspoon freshly ground pepper
1	3- to 3½-pound fryer chicken, cut up using method two (page 175)
2	cups chicken stock (page 258) or canned low-sodium chicken broth
1	teaspoon finely chopped fresh rosemary or ½ teaspoon dried

At least 2 hours before grilling, combine yogurt, lemon juice, cloves, salt, and pepper in a 2-quart glass bowl and mix until smooth. Add the pieces of chicken, mix to cover with marinade, and refrigerate up to 6 hours.

Meanwhile, place stock in a medium saucepan over high heat. If you're using dried rosemary, add it now. Boil until reduced by two thirds and the liquid starts to thicken. Remove from heat and beat in the yogurt marinade. Add the fresh rosemary. Cover and reserve at room temperature for up to 2 hours.

Light a gas or charcoal grill (when the coals are completely covered with white ash, the grill is ready) or preheat a broiler. Remove the chicken from the marinade, scraping off excess. Reserve marinade and place chicken on grill. Grill 10 to 12 minutes on each side.

Five minutes before the chicken is ready to take off the grill, finish the sauce. Bring reduced chicken stock, covered, to a boil over medium heat. Immediately remove from heat and beat in the yogurt marinade. Transfer to a sauceboat. Do not reheat the sauce because it will break. This sauce is meant to be served warm, not hot. Remove the chicken from the grill and arrange on a platter. Serve the sauce on the side.

GINGER- AND GARLIC-GLAZED
DUCK WITH MINT SAUCE

SERVES 2 TO 3

When roasting fatty birds such as duck or goose, I find that a preliminary steaming or searing will open the pores of the skin so that the birds render more fat during roasting. Aside from cutting down on the fat, this procedure also improves the taste, bathing the flesh and crisping the skin.

The mint sauce for this duck, commonly paired with lamb, is classically English—an infusion of fresh mint in a mild vinegar. It's an appropriate accompaniment for any strong, red-fleshed meat or fowl because it cuts the gamy flavor. Candied ginger and garlic, indeed any sweet ingredient, go very well with duck, also cutting a gamy taste but highlighting the richness of the meat. The mint and vinegar excite the nose, while ginger and garlic overwhelm the mouth; this is a very satisfying dish altogether.

12	garlic cloves
3	ounces fresh gingerroot, peeled and cut into ½-inch pieces
⅓	cup sugar
½	cup water, or enough to cover garlic and ginger
2	tablespoons salad oil
1	4- to 4½-pound fresh duck
	salt and freshly ground pepper to taste
½	cup malt or cider vinegar
1	cup chicken or duck stock (page 258) or canned low-sodium chicken broth
3	tablespoons chopped fresh mint

Combine peeled garlic cloves, ginger, sugar, and water in a small saucepan over medium heat. Bring to a boil, reduce heat to low, and simmer, uncovered, until the water evaporates and has left a syrup around the ginger and garlic. Reserve in a small bowl.

Preheat oven to 325°. Pat the duck dry. Place a roasting pan on the stove top and heat the oil over medium heat. Add the duck and sear well on all sides, about 10 minutes total. Sprinkle with salt and pepper.

Remove duck and discard fat. Place the duck, breast side down, on a rack in the roasting pan and place in the oven for 1½ hours. Turn the duck on its back. Using a small brush, paint the skin with some of the syrup from the garlic and ginger. Repeat every 5 minutes and continue to roast for 45 minutes.

When the duck is done, remove to a platter. Place roasting pan on top of the stove over medium heat and cook 1 minute to separate pan drippings from fat. Pour off fat, reduce heat to low, and add the vinegar and stock to the pan. Using a wooden spoon, scrape up or dissolve residue that has collected on the bottom of the roasting pan. Pour this liquid into a sauceboat and add the chopped mint. Remove duck from the oven and place on a serving platter. Serve candied ginger and garlic as a condiment and encourage your guests to spread it on the duck. Serve the mint sauce on the side.

BRAISED DUCK WITH PARSNIPS AND APPLES
SERVES 2 TO 3

I'm very fond of braised or stewed duck, its flesh falling apart from two slow cookings. The skin adds a rich, gelatinous quality to the parsnip accompaniment as it crisps in the oven, while cleansing apple and tarragon insure that this dish will not leave us with a heavy, fatty feeling.

1	4- to 4½-pound fresh duck, cut up using method two (page 175)
1	tablespoon salt
12	whole cloves
2	garlic cloves
1	tablespoon whole coriander seed
1	medium onion, finely diced (about ¾ cup)
3	parsnips, peeled and diced into 1-inch pieces (about 2½ cups)
⅓	cup cider vinegar
1	cup chicken or duck stock (page 258) or canned low-sodium chicken broth
1	apple, peeled, cored, and minced
1	tablespoon chopped fresh tarragon (*not* dried)

Place duck in a 3-quart pot, cover with water, and add salt, cloves, peeled garlic cloves, and coriander. Bring to a boil on top of the stove over high heat. Reduce heat to low, cover, and simmer 1 hour. Remove duck and discard liquid.★

★Can be prepared to this point up to 2 days in advance and kept, covered, in the refrigerator.

Preheat oven to 375°. Combine onion, parsnips, vinegar, and stock in a medium baking dish or large ovenproof skillet. Add duck, breast side up. Place in oven and roast for 1 hour. Remove duck to a plate. Add apple and tarragon to the remaining ingredients and mix well. Pour onto a serving platter and arrange the duck on top.

SQUAB, CORNCAKES, AND RAPINI WITH RED WINE

SERVES 4

I use a robust wine for cooking, one that is high in tannin—a younger Burgundy rather than an older Bordeaux, for instance—because its flavor does not fall apart when reduced. Temper it with a hint of clove, which in this recipe also enhances the *rapini*. I keep instant coffee in my pantry for adding to red wine and other dark sauces. It adds a richness and is indiscernible as coffee. I think this is the only cooking secret I picked up from my mom, who makes a great pot roast.

2	cups water
½	teaspoon salt
6	tablespoons unsalted butter
½	cup yellow cornmeal
2	tablespoons olive oil
4	14- to 16-ounce squabs
1	cup hearty red wine
½	tablespoon finely minced garlic
½	tablespoon finely minced shallots
⅛	teaspoon ground cloves
⅛	teaspoon instant coffee
1	cup chicken stock (page 258) or canned low-sodium chicken broth
½	pound *rapini* (broccoli rabe or Italian broccoli), roughly chopped
¾	cup whipping cream

To make the corncakes: first, generously butter a 9-inch square pan. Combine water, salt, and 1 tablespoon of the butter in a 2-quart saucepan over high heat and bring to a boil. Slowly add cornmeal, stirring constantly. Cook until mixture bubbles, stirring constantly. Reduce heat to low and continue to stir until mixture is thick and begins to pull away from sides of pan, about 25 minutes. Pour into prepared pan, spreading evenly. Let cool completely.

Meanwhile, heat olive oil in a 12-inch skillet, add the squabs, and sauté on both sides, about 5 minutes total. Add the wine, garlic, shallots, cloves, and instant coffee and cook until reduced by one third. Add the chicken stock and *rapini* and cook until liquid thickens. Remove from heat.

When cornmeal is cool, remove from pan and cut into 12 to 16 cakes using a 2-inch round cookie cutter or cut into squares using a knife.*

Melt 2 tablespoons of the butter in a large skillet over medium heat and cook the corncakes until golden brown, turning once, about 8 minutes total. Meanwhile, add cream to the red wine sauce and squabs and return skillet to stove. Cook over high heat until cream reduces and becomes saucelike. Remove from heat and whisk in remaining 3 tablespoons butter. Arrange cakes on the center of a serving platter and surround with the squabs and *rapini*. Spoon the sauce over the squabs and serve.

*Squabs may be prepared to this point up to 1 hour in advance and kept, covered, at room temperature. Corncakes may be prepared up to 3 days in advance and kept, covered, in the refrigerator.

FOIE GRAS BRAISED IN GRAPEFRUIT JUICE   SERVES 2 TO 3

American *foie gras,* or fattened duck liver, is not as marbled with fat as its French cousin. Although this means to most lovers of *foie gras* that the American version is lacking in quality, it is better suited to a particular method that I have developed for cooking it. The fat released from the liver is emulsified by grapefruit juice and bathes the fattened liver as it cooks. A top-quality *foie* has a bit too much fat for this kind of cooking; indeed, you can economize by asking for a grade B *foie,* one that is a bit smaller.

You could probably stretch this recipe to make three servings, but I find that people who love *foie gras* can devour vast quantities of it. This is a dish to have *à deux*. Serve some warm toast to soak up the sauce and treat yourself to an expensive bottle of Sauterne.

1   14- to 17-ounce lobe fresh American *foie gras*
½   teaspoon salt
     freshly ground pepper to taste
1   cup chicken stock (page 258) or canned low-sodium chicken
     broth
2   tablespoons fresh lemon juice
1   cup fresh grapefruit juice
2   grapefruits, separated into sections, membrane removed
4   slices toast

Preheat oven to 375°. Place the *foie gras* in a ceramic baking dish, sprinkle with salt and pepper, cover, and place in oven for 20 minutes.

Meanwhile, combine the chicken stock, lemon juice, and grapefruit juice in a 2-quart heavy ovenproof saucepan. Bring to a boil over high heat and boil, uncovered, for 10 minutes.

Remove *foie* from the oven, pour off any rendered fat, and save for another use. Add the *foie gras* to the grapefruit juice mixture and transfer to the oven. Cook, uncovered, another 12 minutes. Remove the *foie gras* to a plate when it is soft to the touch and the juices run clear. Place the pan on top of the stove over high heat and cook, reducing, until the liquid becomes shiny and thick. Transfer the *foie gras* to a serving platter, pour the sauce over it, and garnish with grapefruit sections. Serve toast on the side.

FISH AND SEAFOOD

■ ● ▲

When people go out for dinner, usually they prefer to eat something they don't prepare at home. At Trumps I sell more fish than I do red meats, white meats, or poultry, so I conclude that people don't cook a lot of seafood for themselves. Happily for me, I like cooking fish and seafood—probably because I like eating it best of all.

If you're reluctant to cook fish at home, I can only guess that it is because you think you will ruin it. When it comes to cooking fish, quality is of paramount importance. Search out a good purveyor and buy what's freshest and in season. Take advantage of its new popularity to buy quality fish and seafood— even supermarkets now often have larger fish sections with a good variety of fresh items. Fresh fish is a newly discovered treat for many people, but rather than feeling intimidated by cooking it, experiment with it.

ON COOKING FISH

Baking Fish: Large, meaty fish can be braised, roasted, or baked in the oven, adding a little liquid, either stock or wine. The exterior flesh will have an interestingly different texture and flavor from the interior. Fish that bake well include whole salmon or whole carp, large halibut or snapper fillets, loins of swordfish, tuna, or monkfish, to name a few favorites. The smaller and more delicate fish—trout, for example—bake too quickly. These I prefer to sauté, grill, or fry, developing an outer crust to the flesh or perhaps a tasty, crispy skin.

Baking fish is probably the easiest method for the home cook. If the fish falls apart during cooking, it's not a disaster. If the finished dish sits in the oven because your guests are late, dinner will not be ruined. In those parts of the country where fresh fish is more difficult to obtain, baking is the method of choice since it can disguise the nature of frozen fish.

Poaching and Steaming Fish: The best fish for this method are the more delicate ones such as sole and trout; fillets or steaks of salmon, bass, snapper, and halibut are good cooked this way, too—and these are only the most common. I have a particular dislike for whole, poached salmon, a fashionable dish that I find less tasty than whole baked or braised salmon. I'm not fond of poached meaty fish such as swordfish and tuna, because they develop an unpleasantly grainy texture.

Poaching is usually the best method for fish to be served chilled. It should always be slightly undercooked so that its texture doesn't become chalky or dry. Remember that the fish will continue to cook slightly as it cools.

Poach the fish in fish stock and white wine, turning the poaching liquid into a sauce or serving the fish in its rich broth, a fish stew or *bouillabaisse.* Satisfactory results are also obtainable with a *court bouillon* (page 256), so if you don't have any fish stock in the house, don't despair.

Sautéing Fish: This technique requires more attention than any other method for cooking fish. Certain densely meated fish such as sturgeon and swordfish become dry or tough if cooked too long; delicate fish such as lemon sole, gray sole, and flounder will turn to mush if overcooked. If the fish you want to sauté or fry is too large, it will burn on the outside before it cooks on the inside. Success in sautéing fish depends on the size of the fish (or piece of fish) that you want to cook and the nature of the flesh. Fish that are appropriate for sautéing do not require long cooking. Thick, dense pieces of fish should be cut into thinner, smaller pieces before sautéing. Best for sautéing are fillets of fish such as whitefish, John Dory, turbot, catfish, red mullet, pompano, and grouper.

Sautéing conducts heat to the food through the medium of fat, not steam. When sautéing fish, it is important to develop a skin or crust to seal in the flavor and moisture. The fish must be patted dry and should also be dusted in flour or cornstarch to isolate the fish from the oil. It is particularly important not to crowd the skillet or sauté pan. Liquid will evaporate from the fish during cooking, and it must be permitted to escape quickly; crowding the pan will result in steaming the fish. Don't try to sauté defrosted fish; so much water remains inside that the fish will immediately fall apart. Baking or poaching defrosted fish will give much better results.

Frying Fish: The rules for sautéing fish apply equally to frying. Most generally, fish that is to be fried is either breaded, battered, or dredged, which makes cooking it easier than sautéing because its new crust helps keep it from falling apart. Fish, when fried properly, is very moist inside its crust. Deep-frying and pan-frying are very similar except for the volume of fat. If you don't want to deep-fry, pan-frying is as good a method. However, you cannot batter fish when you pan-fry; you are limited to dredging it in flour or cornstarch.

Grilling Fish: A clean, well-oiled, hot grill will ensure successful grilling. Place fish skin-side-up on the grill so that when you turn it, the serving side will be face up. The less you have to flip the fish, the easier it is to cook. If you are an inexperienced grill cook, develop confidence by grilling a meaty fish such as swordfish or tuna.

When I grill fillets of fish, small fish such as trout, or shellfish such as scallops and shrimps, I put them on the grill directly over the hot coals. Indirect grilling—I spread the coals around the perimeter of my grill and improvise a lid to collect the heat and smoke—allows grilling of larger whole fish such as salmon and catfish.

The flavor of burning wood and the charred marks of the hot grill give incredibly delicious flavor to all fish and seafood, but my favorite candidates for grilling are swordfish and scallops.

SCALLOPS SAUTÉED
WITH GINGER AND MINT

Ginger and mint are often combined in traditional Southeast Asian cooking. I'm very fond of the flavors of Southeast Asia, but I don't always want to prepare an ethnic dinner when I crave them. So I came up with this recipe as a way of using these ingredients outside their usual ethnic context.

4	tablespoons unsalted butter
2	medium carrots, peeled and finely grated or shredded (about 1½ cups)
1	tablespoon salad oil
1½–2	pounds small bay scallops (the size of a dime) or halved large sea scallops (the size of a half-dollar)
1	tablespoon finely minced shallots
½	cup dry white wine
1	tablespoon finely minced fresh ginger root
2	tablespoons chopped fresh mint
	salt and freshly ground pepper to taste

In a small pot or covered saucepan melt 2 tablespoons of the butter over low heat and add the carrots. Cover and cook slowly for about 15 minutes or until softened.

Meanwhile, heat the oil in a large skillet over high heat. Pat the scallops dry on a towel. When the skillet is very hot and the oil almost smoking, toss in the scallops, in batches if necessary, and cook for 30 seconds without stirring. Stir lightly with a wooden spoon and let cook 1 minute. Using a slotted spoon, remove the scallops from the pan and reserve on a plate. They should be only partially cooked. Discard the fat from the skillet.

Return the skillet to high heat, add the shallots and wine, then add the ginger. Cook until wine reduces by half. Meanwhile, the scallops will have released a small amount of liquid. Pour this into the pan, reduce heat to low, and cook until almost no liquid remains. Return the scallops to the pan, whisk in the remaining butter, and add the mint. Immediately remove from heat. Taste for salt and pepper. To serve, make a ring of carrots on a platter and mound the sauced scallops in the center.

Note: When sautéing or grilling scallops you want them to quickly take on a dark golden color—this browning is the result of caramelization, not burning. Quick cooking in a very hot, uncrowded pan, on a hot grill, or under a hot broiler close to the heat will not only bring out their sweetness but also keeps them from becoming stringy and tough. You won't find me steaming or poaching scallops—they simply can't compare with the sautéed or grilled ones. Grill larger sea scallops and sauté smaller bay scallops.

SCALLOPS WITH SAUTERNE, APPLES, AND TARRAGON
SERVES 4 TO 6

Use only a Sauterne or other late-harvest white wine such as Barsac for this dish. You can recognize them by their rich, amber color. Other sweet wines are merely sweet and have none of the musty, old character of even a poor-quality *botrytis* wine. Other sweet wines are best when combined with strong opposing ingredients such as cheese or pepper. This recipe depends on a clarity of delicate flavors: musty, sweet wine, astringent apple, and licorice tarragon.

1   tablespoon salad oil
1½–2 pounds small bay scallops (the size of a dime) or halved large sea scallops (the size of a half-dollar)
1   teaspoon finely minced shallots
½   cup Sauterne wine
6   tablespoons unsalted butter
1   green pippin apple, unpeeled and cut into julienne sticks
1   tablespoon chopped fresh tarragon *or* 1 teaspoon dried
     salt and freshly ground pepper to taste

Heat the oil in a large skillet over high heat. When the oil is almost smoking, toss in the scallops and cook for 30 seconds without stirring. Stir with a wooden spoon and let cook 1 minute. Using a slotted spoon, remove the scallops to a plate. They should be only partially cooked. Discard the fat from the skillet.

Return the skillet to high heat and add the shallots and Sauterne. If using dried tarragon, add it now. Let the Sauterne reduce by half. Meanwhile, the scallops will have released a certain amount of liquid. Pour this into the pan and reduce until almost dry.

Return the scallops to the pan and reduce the heat to low. Whisk in the butter and then add the apple and fresh tarragon. Taste for salt and pepper. Serve these scallops with simple accompaniments, such as new potatoes baked in their skins and sautéed spinach.

SCALLOPS SAUTÉED WITH PINE NUTS AND DRIED TOMATOES

SERVES 4

Dried fruits and vegetables have a particular kind of character, a reminder that they were once sweet and aromatic. This dish would be just as successful with an equal amount of dried lily blossoms (found in Asian markets) or dried hibiscus flowers (found in South American markets), and if you can find these ingredients, experiment with them; you will not be disappointed.

1	tablespoon salad oil
1½	pounds small bay scallops (the size of a dime) or halved large sea scallops (the size of a half-dollar)
4	tablespoons pine nuts
1	tablespoon finely minced shallots
1	teaspoon finely minced garlic
½	cup dry white wine
2	tablespoons fresh lemon juice
½	cup dried tomatoes, drained and patted dry if packed in oil
6	tablespoons unsalted butter
2	tablespoons finely chopped parsley
	salt and pepper to taste

Heat the oil in a large skillet over high heat. When the oil is almost smoking, toss in the scallops and pine nuts and cook for 30 seconds without stirring. Stir with a wooden spoon and let cook 1 minute. Using a slotted spoon, remove the scallops to a plate. They should be only partially cooked. Discard the fat from the skillet.

Return the skillet to high heat and add the shallots, garlic, wine, lemon juice, and dried tomatoes. Boil, reducing wine by half. Meanwhile, the scallops will have released a certain amount of liquid. Pour this into the pan and reduce until thick. Return the scallops and pine nuts to the pan. Reduce the heat to low, whisk in the butter, add salt and pepper, then the chopped parsley. Pour onto a serving platter. Baked potatoes are perfect with these scallops, but don't serve them with sour cream, which will interfere with the sauce.

SOFT-SHELL CRABS SAUTÉED WITH ORANGE   SERVES 4

Soft-shell crabs are blue crabs that have molted their shells and have not yet grown new ones. They are in season from the end of May through the middle of September, a sure sign of summer the way daffodils are a sign of spring. Soft-shell crabs have a sweet, creamy meat and should be cooked quickly so that their "skins" become crisp before the meat is overcooked. Prepare them simply; all they need is a little butter and a little tartness, supplied here by orange juice.

8–12 medium soft-shell crabs
3   tablespoons all-purpose flour
2   tablespoons salad oil
3   tablespoons unsalted butter
4   tablespoons fresh orange juice
½   teaspoon salt
1   tablespoon chopped parsley
     freshly ground pepper to taste

To clean the crabs, lift up each flap from the underside and remove the white, spongy gills. Remove the tail flap and discard. Rinse under cold water and dry well on towels. Dust with flour, shaking off excess. Preheat oven to 200°.

In a large skillet heat the oil over high heat until almost smoking. Add the crabs, underside up, and cook 1 minute. Turn them and continue to cook for 2 minutes. Remove from the skillet and keep warm on a plate in the oven. Wipe the skillet clean with a paper towel and re-place on stove top over medium heat. Add the butter. As it heats, it will foam. When the foam begins to subside, add the orange juice. The butter will turn a hazelnut color. Remove from heat and add the salt and parsley. Pour this butter over the crabs, give them a few turns of a pepper mill, and serve. When asparagus is in season—spring and summer—it's perfect with this dish.

MUSTARD-FRIED SHRIMPS
WITH TARRAGON BUTTER

SERVES 4

It's very often a good idea to divide flavors among the different elements of a dish. In this recipe I put mustard in the batter and flavor the butter sauce with tarragon. Each element has its own character, and the dish is more interesting than if all the elements tasted alike.

The ingredients of the tarragon butter must all be at room temperature—too warm and it will melt; too cold and it will separate.

1	cup fish stock (page 260) or ½ cup bottled clam juice
2	tablespoons Pernod
1	teaspoon celery seed
2	tablespoons chopped fresh tarragon or 1 tablespoon dried
6	tablespoons unsalted butter at room temperature
1	teaspoon finely minced garlic
4	tablespoons dry mustard powder
1	tablespoon mustard seed
¼	cup flour
¼	teaspoon salt
1	small egg
½	cup beer
24	jumbo shrimps (about 2 pounds)
2	tablespoons cornstarch
	salad oil for frying

To make the tarragon butter, combine the fish stock, Pernod, and celery seed in a small saucepan. If using dried tarragon, add it now. Cook over medium heat until the mixture is reduced by two thirds. Remove from heat and transfer to a small mixing bowl to cool to room temperature. Use a rubber scraper to transfer all the reduced liquid into a blender. Add the fresh tarragon and the butter cut into 1-inch pieces. Blend until smooth. Transfer to a small serving dish and reserve at room temperature.

To make the batter, combine the garlic, mustard, mustard seed, the flour, and the salt in a mixing bowl. Add the egg and beat until smooth. Add the beer and stir to combine.

Peel the shrimps, leaving tails on, and devein. Dry each shrimp and dust with cornstarch, shaking off the excess. Preheat oven to 200°.

Heat 2 inches of oil in a skillet, wok, or sauté pan to 375° over medium heat on top of the stove. Holding the shrimps by their tails, dip them into the batter, let the excess drip off, and fry them in batches 1½ to 2 minutes, until dark golden. Do not crowd the pan. Remove from oil as they are done and drain on paper towels. Keep shrimps warm in the oven while frying the rest.

Mound the fried shrimps into a serving bowl lined with a cloth napkin. Serve the butter in another bowl. Fried potatoes of any shape are wonderful with this dish; serve other vegetables as a separate course.

Note on frying: If you don't have a frying thermometer, test the oil temperature by dropping a little batter into it. It should immediately bubble; if not, the oil is not hot enough.

BAKED SALMON STUFFED WITH CABBAGE, CHESTNUTS, AND BACON   SERVES 4 TO 6

In this recipe salmon is treated almost as if it were meat. In fact, I devised this dish when a food writer asked me to provide an alternative Thanksgiving menu for a column she was writing.

32   chestnuts
½   pound slab bacon, cut into ½-inch cubes
2   small red cabbages, finely shredded (about 4 cups)
1   5-pound whole salmon
½   teaspoon freshly ground pepper
2   cups dry white wine
10   tablespoons (1¼ sticks) unsalted butter
4   tablespoons finely minced shallots
1   cup white vinegar
¼   teaspoon salt

Preheat oven to 350°. Using a small knife, make a slit in each chestnut and spread them on a cookie sheet in the oven for

30 to 35 minutes. Remove from oven and, when they are cool enough to handle, peel them.

Place the bacon in a large skillet over medium heat and cook, stirring, about 5 minutes. Add the cabbages, cover, and cook 6 to 7 minutes or until well wilted. Remove from heat, add the chestnuts, and transfer to a bowl. Sprinkle the cavity of the salmon with pepper and stuff with the cabbage mixture.★

Place the salmon in a roasting pan and add 1 cup of the wine and 2 tablespoons of the butter. Place in oven, uncovered, for 20 minutes. Turn salmon over and cook 15 to 20 minutes or until just barely cooked at the bone.

While the salmon is baking, prepare the sauce. In a small saucepan over medium heat combine shallots, remaining wine, vinegar, and salt. Cook until the mixture is almost dry. Remove from heat and whisk in remaining butter.

Arrange the salmon on a large serving platter and offer the sauce on the side. True to our American custom of putting too many different things on the same plate, serve this dish with many different vegetables and don't worry about things going together. The dish will be more festive—and it's a good excuse to break the rules.

★Can be prepared to this point several hours in advance and refrigerated.

BAKED SALMON ON WILD RICE
PANCAKES WITH TWO PUREES

SERVES 4

Many of my favorite recipes are for a complete, or composed, plate such as this one.

8   wild rice pancakes (page 92)
1½ pounds mushrooms
2   tablespoons minced shallots
¾   teaspoon salt
1   cup dry white wine
1½ teaspoons finely minced garlic
2   cups fish stock (page 260)
1   cup whipping cream
1   bunch arugula or watercress, long stems removed (about 2 ounces)
4   7-ounce salmon steaks or fillets
1   tablespoon melted unsalted butter
2   tablespoons unsalted butter

Preheat oven to 200° and keep the wild rice pancakes warm in the oven while preparing the rest of the recipe.

Place mushrooms, shallots, and ¼ teaspoon of the salt in a food processor and puree until smooth. Scrape this mixture into a medium saucepan over medium heat and cook, uncovered, stirring, until the moisture has evaporated and the mixture is dry. Remove from the heat and reserve in the oven. Preheat the broiler. Butter a 9-inch square baking dish.

While mushroom mixture is cooking, combine the wine, garlic, and ¼ teaspoon of the salt in another medium saucepan over medium heat. Cook, uncovered, until reduced by half. Add the fish stock and reduce again until the mixture starts to thicken. Add cream and reduce until sauce will coat the back of a spoon. Scrape into a food processor or blender, add the arugula or watercress, and blend until smooth. Re-place in saucepan.

Place the salmon in the baking dish and coat the surface with melted butter. Sprinkle with remaining ¼ teaspoon of salt and place under broiler for 5 minutes. Re-place arugula puree over medium heat on top of the stove and whisk in 2 tablespoons butter.

To serve, place a wild rice pancake on a plate and put a dollop of mushroom puree next to it. Lay a piece of salmon on top between the pancake and the mushrooms and spoon some arugula sauce over the top.

SAUTÉED CATFISH
WITH GRAPEFRUIT
SERVES 4

Although it's now being raised on farms, the marvelous-tasting catfish has not managed to shed its reputation of being a dirty river-bottom fish. Catfish sautés easily without falling apart or becoming mushy, and the fillets have no bones. Like all river fish, catfish has a sweet-flavored meat, not at all "fishy." I like fruity accompaniments with it, like grapefruit juice, or salty ones. The reduced juice is concentrated and intense—thickly sweet and cleansingly acidic—the kind of ingredient that makes it successful as a one-flavor dish.

2	large grapefruits
1	cup fresh grapefruit juice
7	tablespoons unsalted butter
4	6- to 8-ounce catfish fillets
	salt and freshly ground pepper
4	tablespoons flour
1	teaspoon salad oil

Using a zester or small knife, remove the grapefruit zest (just the yellow skin) without any of the white membrane. Chop finely and place in a small saucepan. Remove the bitter white pulp from the grapefruits and discard. Separate the grapefruit sections, remove the membranes, and reserve sections on a plate, adding any juice to the saucepan. Add the grapefruit juice to the saucepan, place over medium heat on top of the stove, and cook, reducing the liquid by half. Remove from heat and whisk in 6 tablespoons of the butter.

Meanwhile, pat the catfish fillets dry on towels, sprinkle with salt and pepper, and dust with flour, shaking off the excess.

Mix the oil and the remaining tablespoon of butter and divide between 2 12-inch sauté pans or skillets over medium heat. Add the catfish and cook 3 to 4 minutes per side, until nicely golden. Transfer fish to a platter, spoon over the grapefruit butter, and garnish with grapefruit sections.

PAN-FRIED CATFISH WITH
CHINESE BLACK BEANS   SERVES 4

Use whole catfish in this recipe; the skin is delectable. Since catfish have no scales, the skin becomes almost like a "crackling" when fried or grilled. Or prepare this recipe with catfish fillets, but decrease the cooking time of the fish accordingly.

The taste of Chinese fermented beans is pervasive and overpowering and reduces the other flavors in the sauce to accents. If you cannot find the right black beans, don't substitute another bean. The recipe will work without the beans, although the accent flavors—sherry, garlic, and ginger—will then become the focus.

¼   cup fermented Chinese black beans
¼   cup dry sherry
1   cup fish stock (page 260)
2   tablespoons finely minced garlic
2   tablespoons finely minced fresh gingerroot *or* 1 tablespoon ground
½   cup whipping cream
4   tablespoons unsalted butter
4   small catfish, about 14–16 ounces each, *or* 4 catfish fillets, 6–8 ounces each (see note below)
½   cup cornstarch
     salad oil for frying, enough to fill a large skillet to a depth of 1½ inches
½   bunch cilantro (about 1 ounce), bottom stems trimmed (for garnish)

Soak the black beans in water for 15 minutes. Drain and discard water. In a 1-quart saucepan combine the black beans with the sherry and cook for 2 minutes over high heat. Add fish stock, garlic, and ginger and cook for another 5 minutes, reducing by one third. Transfer the mixture to a blender or food processor and puree until smooth. Pass the puree through a strainer to remove the bean skins and re-place in the saucepan.

Re-place the saucepan on stove over medium heat, add cream, and cook until the mixture reduces and is thick enough to coat the back of a spoon. Remove from heat and whisk in the butter. Reserve in the covered saucepan.

Dry the catfish on towels and dredge lightly in cornstarch, shaking off the excess. Preheat oven to 350°. Place a large cast-iron skillet over medium heat and add oil to a depth of 1½ inches. Heat oil to 375° and add the catfish without crowding, in batches if necessary. Fry until nicely golden on all sides, about 8 minutes. Remove to paper towels, pat dry, and place in a large baking dish as they are done.★ Place catfish in the oven and bake for 8 to 10 minutes to finish cooking.

To serve, pour half the sauce into a warm serving platter and place the catfish on top. Decorate with cilantro sprigs and serve the remaining sauce on the side. Accompany with quickly sautéed, colorful vegetables such as red pepper, corn, and broccoli.

Note: When oil is hot enough to cook in, it will bubble vigorously when you add anything—a cube of bread, a bit of batter—to it. As you add food to the bubbling oil, the temperature will drop. If oil cools too much during the cooking, the bubbling will stop. Raise the heat until the oil bubbles again, or the food will absorb the oil.

Fillets of catfish will require only about 4 to 5 minutes frying in 1 inch of oil. They require no additional cooking time in the oven—and unfortunately you can't prepare them in advance.

★Can be prepared to this point up to 1 hour in advance. When preparing this dish in advance, do not finish the sauce with butter. Reserve unbuttered sauce in the saucepan, covered. Reheat over medium heat, remove from heat, and whisk in butter just before serving.

RARE TUNA WITH MINT, DILL, AND CILANTRO PESTO

SERVES 4

When completely cooked, tuna becomes dry and is only good for tuna salad. If the idea of rare or even medium-rare fish upsets you, then choose another fish for this recipe. Sole, monkfish, and halibut are a few fish that can be well cooked with decent results.

In this variation on a traditional basil pesto, three strong herbs—mint, dill, and cilantro—marry to form a new flavor.

2	tablespoons pine nuts
1	tablespoon finely minced garlic
4	anchovy fillets
¼	cup plus 1 tablespoon salad oil
4	tablespoons coarsely chopped fresh dill
2	tablespoons coarsely chopped fresh mint leaves
4	tablespoons coarsely chopped cilantro
4	7-ounce tuna fillets
4	lemon crowns

To make the pesto, combine pine nuts, garlic, and anchovies in a blender or food processor and puree until chunky. With the motor running, slowly add ¼ cup of the oil. Turn off motor. You will have a slightly lumpy paste. Add the dill, mint, and cilantro and pulse until blended.

Brush the tuna lightly with 1 tablespoon oil. Heat a large heavy skillet over high heat. When smoking, add the tuna and sear 1 to 2 minutes on each side, depending on the thickness of the fillets. To serve, cut each piece of tuna in half diagonally to emphasize the color of the interior meat. Arrange on a platter, place a generous dollop of pesto on each serving, and decorate the platter with lemon crowns.

MONKFISH ROASTED IN RED WINE WITH DRIED APRICOTS

SERVES 4 TO 6

The French often refer to monkfish (also known as angler or *lotte*) as *homard des pauvres* because the meaty texture of this humble fish resembles that of lobster. Roasting is a particularly successful way of preparing monkfish. Cook the tail whole—that's the only part that we eat—and then slice it for serving.

When we roast fish, we achieve a strong flavor by searing it in oil before placing it in the oven. This forms an outer crust on the fish that keeps the interior flesh moist and tasty, allowing us to choose bold flavor accompaniments. This cooking method is particularly appropriate for large pieces of densely meaty fish.

Red wine, when reduced, makes your mouth pucker. This changes the sweetness of the dried apricots so they do not seem trite. The red wine sauce is the first thing tasted, with the apricots supplying a surprising finish.

This red wine and apricot accompaniment is also delicious with freshwater fish, such as carp, or a strong-flavored, oily fish such as bluefish or mackerel.

1¾	pounds monkfish tails, either small individual tails or 2 large
¼	cup all-purpose flour
2	tablespoons salad oil
1	cup dry red wine
½	cup fish stock (page 260)
1	cup dried apricots (about 6 ounces)
	salt and freshly ground pepper to taste
2	tablespoons unsalted butter

Preheat the oven to 375°. Pat the monkfish dry on towels. Dust in flour, shaking off the excess. Heat the oil in a 12-inch ovenproof skillet or roasting pan over medium heat, add the monkfish, and brown on all sides. Remove to a plate and discard oil. Add the wine and stock to the skillet and bring to a boil. Re-place monkfish in the skillet, add the apricots, and sprinkle with salt and pepper. Place, uncovered, in the oven and cook 10 minutes for small tails, longer for larger ones. When done, transfer skillet to the stove top and remove the fish to a carving board. Cook the liquid in the roasting pan over high heat, stirring, until it thickens slightly. Remove from heat and whisk in the butter.

Cut the monkfish into ½-inch slices, arrange on a serving platter, and spoon sauce over. Fish cooked in red wine should be served with red wine. I suggest a young, light, fruity red such as Beaujolais.

BROILED RED SNAPPER WITH
SUN-DRIED AND FRESH TOMATOES

SERVES 4

On our Atlantic and Gulf coasts we find true snapper, but on the Pacific Coast we find only its poor relation, a rock fish perversely called snapper. True red snapper is a delicately flavored and finely textured fish that must be treated discreetly. Rock fish has a more pronounced fish flavor, is flaky, and tends to fall apart easily—don't use it for this dish.

The juxtaposition of the sweet and acidic components of dried and fresh tomato, balsamic vinegar, and lemon juice diminish each other, resulting in a vibrant sauce but one that doesn't overpower the delicate flavor of snapper.

⅓	cup sun-dried tomatoes
3	tablespoons fresh lemon juice
3	tablespoons balsamic vinegar
4	ripe plum tomatoes (about ½ pound)
4	7-ounce Florida red snapper fillets
2	tablespoons olive oil
¼	teaspoon salt
	freshly ground pepper to taste
4	tablespoons unsalted butter
2	tablespoons chopped parsley

If you're using dried tomatoes packed in olive oil, drain, pat dry, and don't bother to soften them. For plain dried tomatoes, combine the lemon juice, balsamic vinegar, and dried tomatoes and let sit for 20 minutes to soften the tomatoes.

Using a small paring knife, cut off tip and stem of each fresh tomato. Remove the seeds and core, leaving only firm, outer pulp. Slit one side of the tomato and lay the tomato flat on work surface. Cut into ¼-inch strips, pile up strips, and cut into ¼-inch pieces. Preheat the broiler.

In a baking dish just large enough to hold the fish, combine fresh tomatoes, dried tomatoes, and lemon-vinegar mixture. Arrange snapper on top, brush with olive oil, and sprinkle with salt and pepper. Place under hot broiler for about 6 to 7 minutes. Remove the fish to a warm serving platter. Whisk the butter into the tomato mixture and mix in the parsley. Garnish the fish with generous dollops of tomato mixture. This is a light dish, and I would accompany it with a rich vegetable preparation, perhaps a *gratin*.

SAUTÉED HALIBUT WITH
SORREL ANCHOVY SAUCE   SERVES 4

Most mild fish, such as snapper and flounder, are easily over-powered by other flavors, but halibut mysteriously takes on a stronger personality in the presence of a strongly flavored accompaniment.

Garlic underscores sorrel, giving it a stronger presence. Because it is astringent and sour, sorrel cancels the salt of anchovy and cuts through its fish flavor. Garlic and lemon juice, the secrets that make halibut and sorrel stronger, should not be obvious in their own right.

I	tablespoon finely minced garlic
4	anchovy fillets
I	cup dry white wine
2	tablespoons fresh lemon juice
½	cup whipping cream
I	bunch sorrel, stems removed (about 2 ounces)
4	7-ounce halibut pieces
3	tablespoons all-purpose flour
I	tablespoon salad oil
2	tablespoons unsalted butter

In a 1-quart saucepan over high heat combine the garlic, anchovy fillets, white wine, and lemon juice and cook, reducing by one third. Add the cream, reduce the heat to medium, and continue to cook until the liquid starts to thicken, another 5 minutes. Scrape into a blender or food processor, add the sorrel, and puree until smooth. Re-place in saucepan.

Pat the halibut dry on towels. Dust with flour, shaking off the excess. Heat the oil and butter in a 12-inch skillet over medium heat and add the halibut. Sauté on both sides until golden, about 6 minutes per side. Arrange the halibut on a heated platter and nap with the reserved sauce.

HALIBUT POACHED IN
BEER WITH RED ONION SAUCE   SERVES 4

Fish that cook very quickly—those that are not too densely textured, such as halibut, sole, and salmon—can be ruined in the blink of an eye. But this calamity can be avoided, and their texture greatly improved, if they are left to "rest" in a hot liquid. In this recipe halibut cooks slowly in a hot liquid while the sauce is prepared.

1   small carrot, roughly diced (about ½ cup)
1   celery stalk, roughly diced (about ½ cup)
2   bay leaves
1   teaspoon whole black peppercorns
1   cup fish stock (page 260)
1   12-ounce bottle pale beer
4   7- to 8-ounce halibut steaks
1   small red onion, finely diced (about ⅔ cup)
6   tablespoons unsalted butter

In a saucepan large enough to hold the halibut steaks in one layer combine the carrot, celery, bay leaves, peppercorns, fish stock, and beer. Bring to a boil over high heat and add the halibut. Cover, reduce the heat to low, and let simmer 1 minute. Remove from heat.

To make the sauce, remove 1 cup of poaching liquid to a small saucepan. Re-cover the fish and allow to "rest" off the heat for 5 to 10 minutes, depending on the thickness of the steaks. Place the small saucepan over high heat and bring liquid to a boil. Reduce heat to medium and cook, uncovered, until reduced by two thirds and the liquid starts to thicken. Add the onion. Remove from heat and whisk in the butter.

Using a slotted spoon, remove halibut from the poaching liquid, draining well, and arrange on a warm platter. Serve the sauce on the side.

SEAFOOD AND SOUR CABBAGE WITH THREE-MUSTARD SAUCE

SERVES 8

(Allow 2 weeks advance preparation for sour cabbage)

I came upon this idea because I had a craving for an Alsatian *choucroute,* a dish of mixed cuts of fresh pork, ham, and sausage cooked with sauerkraut and served with mustard. I wanted a lighter version, so I made it with seafood. But seafood is too delicate a companion for most sauerkraut, so I made my own, using Napa cabbage.

Fish and seafood taste milder when accompanied by something sour or acidic. People who like lemon on their fish will especially like this pairing with sour cabbage. You can substitute commercial sauerkraut if you can't make your own. The result is excellent but different.

1	recipe sour cabbage (page 265) *or* 4 cups sauerkraut
4	mixed seafood sausages (page 106)
8	small new potatoes
3	pounds mixed boneless fish such as salmon, bass, angler, and halibut, cut into 16 equal pieces
8	large shrimps, peeled and deveined, tails left intact
16	clams
16	mussels
½	cup sour cabbage liquid
3	cups fish stock (page 260)
2	tablespoons finely minced shallots
1	cup dry white wine
1	tablespoon mustard seed
2	tablespoons Dijon mustard
2	tablespoons grainy mustard
10	tablespoons (1¼ sticks) unsalted butter

Two weeks before serving, make the sour cabbage (page 265). If you're using commercial sauerkraut, drain sauerkraut, rinse with cold water, place in a 1-quart container, cover with water, let soak for 1 hour, and drain well.

Prepare and poach seafood sausages (page 106). When cool, carefully remove and discard the sausage casings or plastic wrap.

Place new potatoes in a 1-quart pot, cover with water, place on the stove over high heat, bring to a boil, and cook until potatoes are tender. Drain potatoes and reserve on a plate.

Roll sour cabbage leaves up jellyroll fashion and cut at ¼-inch intervals into strips. The cabbage will partially unroll once you cut it. Place a bed of sour cabbage or sauerkraut in a medium casserole or baking dish and arrange the fish, shellfish, seafood sausage, and potatoes on top. Moisten with the sour cabbage liquid and 1 cup fish stock. (If using commercial sauerkraut, moisten only with stock.)★ Preheat oven to 375°. Cover casserole tightly and place in oven for 25 to 30 minutes.

Meanwhile, prepare the mustard sauce. Combine shallots and wine in a 1-quart saucepan over medium heat, bring to a boil, and cook until liquid reduces by half. Add remaining 2 cups stock and mustard seed and reduce again by half. Reduce heat to low, add the Dijon and grainy mustards, and combine well. Swirl in the butter.

Transfer baking dish from the oven to the table, uncover, and serve the mustard sauce on the side.

★Can be prepared to this point up to 1 day in advance and kept, covered, in the refrigerator.

SEAFOOD PEPPER POT   SERVES 10 TO 12

This fish stew is prepared in two stages. First make the soup for the stew, then make the stew. The soup requires long cooking to extract the seafood essence from the fish bones and provide a rich background for the stew ingredients. The soup may be made in advance and frozen for up to 3 months. It can be the base for many different stews, or it can be reduced and served as a hearty first course.

Soup:

5   pounds fish bones and scraps (see note below)
2   teaspoons olive oil
2   onions, peeled and sliced (about 1½ cups)
12   garlic cloves
16   plum tomatoes, preferably overripe (about 2 pounds)
16–20 jumbo shrimps (1¼ to 1¾ pounds)
1   tablespoon salt
1   tablespoon whole black peppercorns
4   bay leaves
4   sprigs fresh thyme *or* 1½ teaspoons dried
2   cups dry white wine
3   quarts cold water

Stew:

2   each medium red, yellow, and green peppers
8–12 new potatoes
3   pounds assorted fish; cut into 16 equal pieces
2   tablespoons freshly ground pepper

Garnish:

garlic mayonnaise (recipe follows)

Rinse the fish bones well and drain. Combine olive oil, onions, and peeled garlic cloves in an 8-quart stockpot or kettle over medium heat and cook, stirring, for 5 minutes. Add tomatoes and fish bones, reduce heat to low, and cook for 20 minutes. Meanwhile, peel and devein shrimps. Add the shells to the pot. Reserve the shrimps on a covered plate in the refrigerator. Add salt, peppercorns, bay leaves, and thyme. Add wine and water to the pot, raise heat, and bring to a boil. Reduce heat to medium and simmer, uncovered, for 3 hours.

Pass the broth through a large cone strainer, pounding the bones with a large wooden spoon to extract their juices and so that the little bits of fish will give texture to the soup. Only 9 to 10 cups of broth should remain. Remove and discard any fat from the surface.*

Meanwhile, preheat broiler. Place the peppers on an ungreased

*Can be made to this point several days in advance and refrigerated. Will keep frozen for up to 3 months.

baking sheet, place under the broiler, and cook until the skins blister, pop, and begin to burn. Turn to char on all sides. Alternately, place peppers directly over a high gas flame, turning to char on all sides. Transfer peppers to a brown paper bag, twist the top closed, and let them steam a few minutes. Remove from bag and place under cold running water, peeling and discarding burnt skin. Remove the stems and seeds and discard. Slice each pepper into 6 pieces tip to stem and reserve.*

Place the fish stew base in a 5-quart pot over high heat and bring to a boil. Add the new potatoes and continue to cook until half done, about 4 to 5 minutes. Add the shrimps and assorted fish, roasted peppers, and ground pepper. Lower heat and simmer until seafood is cooked, another 5 to 7 minutes.

To serve, remove the seafood from the pot and arrange on a large platter. Remove the potatoes and peppers to another serving platter. Serve the broth in a tureen or in individual soup bowls. Pass garlic mayonnaise on the side. Serve a simply dressed green salad and a lot of good French bread to complete the meal.

Note: The best bones to use are from nonoily fish, such as halibut, John Dory, sole, or flounder. Salmon bones give a bitter flavor to stocks. Swordfish bones give an unpleasantly fishy flavor. Shrimp shells and lobster carcasses are important additions to fish stew soup.

*Can be prepared to this point up to a couple of hours in advance.

GARLIC MAYONNAISE FOR HOT SOUPS   MAKES 2 CUPS

This mayonnaise does not revert to oil and egg when added to hot soup because the potato keeps it from separating. Called a *rouille* in French because of its rust color, this accompaniment should be spicy and extremely garlicky.

¼ pound potatoes (one small potato)
½ cup fish stew soup (see preceding recipe)
1½ teaspoons cayenne pepper
¼ teaspoon saffron threads
12 garlic cloves
2 egg yolks
½ teaspoon salt, or to taste
1½ cups virgin olive oil

Peel potato and cut into ½-inch pieces. Place in a small saucepan and add fish stew soup, cayenne pepper, saffron, and garlic. Bring to a boil over medium heat and cook, covered, until potato is cooked. Uncover and continue cooking until liquid reduces and potato chunks fall apart and look mushy. Remove from heat and allow to cool 5 minutes.

Transfer mixture to a blender or food processor, add the egg yolks and salt, and blend until smooth. Add the olive oil in a slow, steady stream until it is absorbed and the mixture has a mayonnaise consistency. Scrape into a small serving bowl. Garlic mayonnaise will keep, covered, in the refrigerator for up to 2 weeks. If it separates, let it warm to room temperature and add it in a slow, steady stream to another egg yolk. This mayonnaise is also a good dip for raw vegetables.

VEGETABLES AND
SIDE DISHES

■●▲

When choosing a vegetable accompaniment for a main course, think of your plate as a complete recipe with the meat, starch, and vegetable all being recipe ingredients. Carefully consider how different elements will go together; you don't want too many different flavors in too many things, and you probably don't want more than one sauce on your plate. If it's an important dish in its own right, you might consider serving the vegetable as a separate course and leaving the main course unaccompanied.

Obviously, vegetables can be very satisfying served plain, as accompaniments. But they can also be the focus of an entire meal, elaborate preparations that satisfy both a cook's need to create and a diner's need to eat.

ON COOKING VEGETABLES

Steaming or Boiling: Only young and tender vegetables should be boiled or steamed. Older vegetables have a high cellulose content and remain tough and stringy when boiled.

When steaming vegetables, make sure the steam can get to all vegetable surfaces. Green vegetables cannot be crowded or they will turn a brownish color. Others will become soggy. Vegetables must steam quickly.

When boiling, do not crowd the pot by cooking too many vegetables at one time. The water should return to a boil as quickly as possible after the addition of the vegetables. This rule holds true for all vegetables but is very important for keeping green vegetables a vibrant color. Vegetables taste more like their raw selves when they are steamed or boiled.

Sautéing: This is another way of breaking down the cellulose of the vegetable and allowing its water to be released. Vegetables high in cellulose and low in water content—such as broccoli, cauliflower, and carrots—should be blanched (boiled quickly until barely soft) before sautéing. Don't blanch softer vegetables like zucchini or eggplant. Sautéing is a dry-heat method of cooking, and the heat is transferred to the vegetable through the butter or oil that you use to sauté. Do not crowd the skillet or the escaping water will cause the vegetables to steam, not sauté. Sautéed vegetables taste more intense than boiled or steamed ones because they have lost some of the water that keeps them crisp.

Roasting: Vegetables that are high in starch or sugar are the best ones to roast—root vegetables such as celeriac, parsnips, rutabagas, beets, turnips, and carrots or tubers such as potatoes, yams, and Jerusalem artichokes. Peppers are roasted to make it easy to remove the skin and because they become sweeter. Roasted vegetables can be prepared separately or cooked in a pan with a roast at 375°. Lightly blanch the vegetable, toss with a little butter or oil, and put in the oven to roast. Roasting vegetables is a dry-heat method of cooking. Use common sense to know when the vegetables are done. If you are cooking vegetables with a roast, a little experience will enable you to time your roast and your vegetables so that they finish at the same time. Until you get your timing right you will have to remove either the vegetables if they are done first or the roast if it is done before the vegetables.

Braising and Gratinées: Braised vegetables cook with just a little liquid and butter. In the process they release a lot of their own juices, which are then reduced and concentrated. This is the best way of using all the flavors in vegetables that have a high water content—such as Belgian endive, celery, and fennel.

Gratinéed vegetables are first braised in cream and then finished, often under the broiler, by quickly melting butter and cheese over the top to brown them. Many different vegetables may be either braised or gratinéed. The most common are either leafy, turgid vegetables such as celery, endive, and lettuce or starchy ones such as turnips and potatoes. The starchy ones require more liquid during cooking than the leafy vegetables.

Glazing: To glaze a vegetable, cook it in water or stock with butter and sometimes a little sugar until the liquid is completely evaporated and forms a shiny coating. If you're using sugar, it can be left "blond," without color, or can be cooked "brunette," the caramelized sugar giving the vegetables a nice honey color. Glaze onions, carrots, turnips, Brussels sprouts, and other vegetables that are not too soft, sturdy enough not to fall apart, and small, in pieces no larger than a walnut.

ASPARAGUS IN ITS OWN JUICES   SERVES 4

In this recipe asparagus cooks in a little butter and water so that when the water has evaporated the asparagus will be bathed in its own juices. This method of cooking asparagus is more successful with large asparagus than with the pencil variety. Quick blanching is a better way of cooking thin asparagus spears, but the full flavor of large asparagus is not released unless it's cooked for a longer time. Crispier asparagus may be pretty to look at, but this method results in much tastier asparagus.

1 ½ pounds medium to large asparagus
2   tablespoons unsalted butter
½   teaspoon salt
     freshly ground pepper to taste

Cut off the tough bottom end of each asparagus and discard. Peel the stalks with a vegetable peeler. Place asparagus in a skillet or saucepan just large enough to hold them lying down and barely cover with cold water. Add butter and salt and bring to a boil, uncovered, over high heat. Stir the asparagus so they will cook evenly. The asparagus are done when the water has evaporated, leaving only the concentrated, buttery juice of the asparagus. Grind fresh pepper to taste over the asparagus and arrange on a vegetable platter.

BRAISED ARTICHOKES   SERVES 4

Artichokes taste more like themselves when they are cooked with garlic and lemon. If they are available, this recipe is good with very tiny artichokes that need only to have their very tops and first layer of outer leaves trimmed.

4	large artichokes or 12 tiny artichokes
1	lemon, halved
3	tablespoons virgin olive oil
2	tablespoons finely minced garlic
1	cup vegetable stock (page 257) or water
¼	cup fresh lemon juice
½	teaspoon salt

Trim the stems from the artichokes and cut off the tops. (If you're using tiny artichokes, trim the tops and remove the outer layer of leaves.) Using scissors, carefully cut off the spiked ends of the leaves. Quarter the artichokes and immediately rub all cut surfaces with lemon to keep them from turning black. Using a small paring knife, cut out the very center leaves and remove the fuzzy choke. Preheat oven to 375°.

Heat the olive oil in a 12-inch stainless steel skillet with a heat-resistant handle over medium heat on top of the stove. Add the artichokes, cut side down, and cook for 5 minutes. Add the garlic and cook 1 minute. Do not let the garlic brown. Add the vegetable stock or water, lemon juice, and salt. Bring to a boil, cover, and place in oven for 20 minutes.★

★Can be prepared to this point up to 1 day in advance and kept, covered, in the refrigerator.

Transfer the skillet to the top of the stove over high heat. Remove cover and boil, stirring, until liquid reduces and forms a glaze around the artichokes. Transfer artichokes to a serving bowl and spoon over the glaze. Serve immediately. Do not rewarm artichokes or the glaze will separate and look greasy.

GLAZED BRUSSELS SPROUTS   SERVES 3 TO 4

I generally prefer undercooked vegetables, but Brussels sprouts are really not very good cooked *al dente*. They seem gassy, and their full flavor is not released until they are tender. Brussels sprouts are a perfect size for glazing, cooking to the proper point without becoming soggy or bland-tasting.

1	pound Brussels sprouts
1½	cups chicken stock (page 258) or canned low-sodium chicken broth, or vegetable stock (page 257)
1	tablespoon unsalted butter
½	teaspoon salt
⅛	teaspoon pepper

Trim the outer leaves from the Brussels sprouts and cut an X in the root. Combine the Brussels sprouts, stock, butter, salt, and pepper in a saucepan or pot large enough to hold the Brussels sprouts—they can be crowded, but in one layer. If your pot is too large, add additional stock or water to cover the sprouts. Bring to a boil over medium heat and simmer about 20 minutes. As the liquid starts to become a reduced, shiny glaze, gently toss or stir the Brussels sprouts so they become coated on all sides. Transfer to a vegetable dish, scraping any glaze over them. If not serving immediately, rewarm sprouts in a covered dish in the oven before serving.

SUCCOTASH   SERVES 4

The combination that we know as succotash is pleasing because of the textures of corn and lima beans. I add red peppers both to improve the color and to sweeten the limas and corn.

1   cup fresh lima beans or frozen (defrosted) baby lima beans
1   cup fresh or frozen (defrosted) corn kernels
1   medium red pepper, seeded and diced (about ½ cup)
1   cup vegetable stock (page 257) or water
2   ounces salt pork, diced (about ⅓ cup), *or* 2 tablespoons unsalted
    butter
¼   teaspoon salt
    freshly ground pepper to taste

Combine all ingredients in a saucepan, bring to a boil, and simmer, covered, for 10 minutes. Uncover and cook, stirring, until all liquid is evaporated. If you have used it, remove and discard salt pork and pour succotash into a vegetable serving dish.

MIXED VEGETABLE GRILL   SERVES 4

Vegetables are great on the grill because they have the added flavor of char and smoke. This vegetable plate is pretty to look at and is certainly more interesting than the usual pile of steamed vegetables. In the grilling process the water in vegetables is partially eliminated, making their flavors more concentrated. Choose your vegetables carefully for appearance, ripeness, and freshness. Combine colors so there is vivid contrast. Time the cooking so that the vegetables requiring longer cooking have enough time before you add those that cook more quickly. Arrange the grilled vegetables on a large platter for dramatic visual effect.

As an accompaniment to a main dish I count about ½ pound of vegetables per person. But this is a terrific summer meal on its own, and for a generous serving I'd include 1½ pounds of vegetables, for example: ½ green pepper, ½ small onion, 4 mushrooms, ½ artichoke, ½ medium Belgian endive, 1 small Japanese eggplant, and 1 small ear of corn.

Artichokes and Other Vegetables That Need Blanching

Very small artichokes may be trimmed and grilled without being blanched or dechoked. Large artichokes must be blanched until half done, then grilled to finish cooking. It is easier to cut large artichokes in half and cut the choke out with a knife. Rub cut surfaces with lemon or place in acidulated water until ready to blanch. Place artichokes in boiling salted water to which a little lemon juice has been added and boil for 10 minutes. Paint them with a little olive oil and place cut side down on the grill for 10 minutes. Turn and grill on the leafy side for another 5 minutes. Other sturdy vegetables such as carrots, cauliflower, broccoli, and beets would not seem like good grill candidates; however, if you blanch them until they're half cooked, they'll grill successfully.

Belgian Endive and Other Leafy Vegetables

Leafy vegetables are best if first wilted in salted boiling water. Drain well on towels and rub with olive oil before grilling. This can be done hours in advance. Wilt whole heads of Boston lettuce for 2 minutes, then cut in half tip to root and drain on towels. Grill for 5 minutes. A small head of romaine requires 5 minutes of blanching and never really wilts. Cut in half from tip to root and grill 7 to 9 minutes. Belgian endive and radicchio should be cut in half from tip to root before blanching for 1 minute. Grill endive for 8 minutes, radicchio for about 5.

Squashes

Yellow squash or zucchini squash should be cut in half or quarters lengthwise, depending on their size. Place cut squash in a colander and sprinkle with coarse salt. Leave for 30 minutes. Rinse, pat dry, coat with a little olive oil, and place, cut side down, on grill for 4 or 5 minutes.

The pumpkinlike squashes such as acorn and butternut should be cut in half lengthwise and blanched in salted water for 5 minutes before oiling and grilling. Depending on their size, they can take anywhere from 5 to 12 minutes to become tender.

Eggplant

The small elongated variety, Japanese eggplant, should be left whole and grilled. The larger, more common variety should be sliced tip to stem in ¾-inch slices. Sprinkle with coarse salt and leave for 30 minutes. Rinse, oil, and grill for 2 minutes on each side.

Corn on the Cob

Use the freshest possible corn; the sugar should not have turned to starch. Soak the corn for 10 minutes in water to moisten the husk so it won't burn before the corn is done. Place the unhusked corn either directly in the coals or on the grill. The corn steams as it cooks, and the husks add a woody burnt flavor. If you're cooking directly on the coals, cook for 7 minutes, turn, and cook another 7 minutes. Increase cooking time to 12 minutes on each side if corn is on the grill rack.

Bell Peppers

Cut peppers in half or quarters, remove seeds, and rub with olive oil. Grill 3 minutes on the fleshy side, only 1 minute on the skin side. The peppers stay a little crunchy because there is so much water in the pulp. The skins will burn slightly, giving a pimiento taste to the peppers.

Onions and Garlic

Soak unpeeled onions, shallots, and garlic in water for 15 minutes, rub with olive oil, and grill them in their skins on a part of the grill that is not too hot. Large red and yellow onions should be cut in half tip to root and grilled, cut side down, for 15 to 20 minutes. Smaller white onions and shallots should be left whole and grilled for 10 to 15 minutes. A whole head of garlic will take anywhere from 20 to 30 minutes to grill and should be served whole, then separated into cloves by the guests.

Mushrooms

When it comes to grilling mushrooms, choose the largest ones you can find. Trim the stems so they lie flat on the grill and marinate in lemon juice and olive oil for 15 minutes before grilling. Shiitake and oyster mushrooms should have stems removed because they are stringy, tough, and bitter. Grill for 3 to 6 minutes on each side, depending on the size and type of mushroom. Fresh *cèpes—Boletus edulis—*are available in winter, and there is practically nothing in creation better than a fresh grilled *cèpe.* Even if you live in a part of the country where winters are cold, it's worth the trouble to get out the grill.

CREAMED ORANGE CARROTS WITH DILL   SERVES 4

A flavor twist makes this traditional vegetable recipe sparkle, yet not so much that it overpowers a main dish. Orange merges with carrots, making them sweeter. Dill is layered as a contrasting flavor, making the carrots more aromatic.

2   tablespoons unsalted butter
1½   pounds carrots, peeled and sliced into ¼-inch rounds (about 6 cups)
½   cup water or vegetable stock (page 257)
1   cup whipping cream
½   teaspoon salt
¼   teaspoon freshly ground white pepper
1   small orange, grated zest only (about ½ teaspoon)
1   tablespoon chopped fresh dill

Preheat oven to 375°. Melt butter in a large skillet over medium heat, add carrots, and cook, stirring, for 5 minutes. Add water, cream, salt, and pepper. Increase heat to high and cook, uncovered, for 5 minutes. Transfer contents of skillet to a 9-inch square baking dish and place in oven. Bake, uncovered, for 20 minutes or until tender but not falling apart. Remove from oven. Add the grated orange zest and the chopped dill and transfer to a warm serving dish.

CELERY BRAISED IN MINT JELLY

SERVES 4

Celery leaves become bitter when cooked. Remove as many as possible from the exterior stalks, but you will have to leave the small interior ones. A little bitterness is okay, given the sweetness of the mint jelly.

2	large celery heads (about 2½ pounds), leafy tops removed
1	tablespoon olive oil
2	tablespoons unsalted butter
½	teaspoon salt
½	cup vegetable stock (page 257) or water
2	tablespoons tarragon vinegar
3	tablespoons finely chopped fresh mint leaves
4	tablespoons sugar

Trim any brown parts from the heads of celery and discard any discolored or bruised outer stalks. Cut each head of celery in half lengthwise, making sure that the root tip holds the stalks together. Preheat oven to 375°.

Combine the oil and butter in a medium roasting pan or large ovenproof skillet. Place over medium heat and add the celery. Cook, turning once, until lightly golden on both sides, about 10 minutes. Sprinkle with salt. Add the vegetable stock, vinegar, mint, and sugar. Raise heat to high, bring to a boil, and transfer, uncovered, to the oven. Cook 10 minutes, turn the celery, and continue to cook another 10 to 15 minutes. When done the celery should be tender but not falling apart. Place on top of the stove and over medium heat boil any remaining liquid until it forms a glaze around the celery. Arrange on a vegetable platter and scrape any glaze over the top.

GRATIN OF TURNIPS AND BLUE CHEESE   SERVES 4 TO 5

Roquefort and other blue cheeses of course have a strong presence. We create a balance by masking the cheese flavor with anchovy and onion and highlighting the turnip aroma with pepper and nutmeg. This is a good teaching recipe because the flavors of the dish change as each new ingredient is added during cooking. Almost everyone is skeptical of this dish until they taste it. When I serve it without naming it, people always remark that these are the best potatoes they have ever eaten. But this dish prepared with potatoes will not give you as good a "potato" result as the turnips do.

4	medium turnips, peeled and sliced paper-thin (about 5 cups)
1	large yellow onion, peeled and finely sliced (about 1 cup)
4	tablespoons melted unsalted butter
½	cup whipping cream
4	anchovy fillets, finely chopped
¼	teaspoon freshly grated nutmeg
¼	teaspoon freshly ground pepper
½	cup crumbled Roquefort, Stilton, or other blue cheese

Preheat oven to 375°. Toss together the turnips and onion with the melted butter and place in a 9-inch square or round baking dish. Cover tightly and place in preheated oven for 30 minutes.

In a small pot over medium heat combine cream, anchovies, nutmeg, and pepper. Bring to a boil and let cook 1 minute.

Remove turnips from oven, remove cover, and pour the cream mixture over them. Sprinkle with Roquefort and return to oven. Let bake, uncovered, another 20 to 25 minutes.★ If the gratin is golden brown, it's ready to serve. If not, preheat broiler. Place gratin under hot broiler about 3 minutes to brown the top before serving.

★Can be prepared to this point a couple of hours in advance and kept, covered, at room temperature.

BRAISED BELGIAN ENDIVE
AND MUSHROOM GRATIN
SERVES 4

When we prepare *gratinéed* vegetables, our sense of smell and taste focus on the cheese. Belgian endive can be bitter, but when combined with cheese and cooked like this, the bitter edge is not noticeable. Mushrooms contrast with endive in this marriage of flavor and texture.

¼	pound cultivated mushrooms
2	large shallots
3	tablespoons unsalted butter
4	heads Belgian endive (about 1 to 1¼ pounds)
1	tablespoon olive oil
	salt and freshly ground pepper to taste
⅛	teaspoon freshly grated nutmeg
½	cup whipping cream
¼	pound grated Gruyère cheese

Wash the mushrooms to remove any sand. Peel the shallots and add to the mushrooms. Place in food processor and puree until smooth. Butter a 9-inch baking dish with 1 tablespoon of the butter. Preheat oven to 375°.

Trim any discolored outer leaves from the endive and cut them in half from tip to root. Combine the oil and remaining butter in a large skillet on the stove over medium heat and when hot add the endive and cook, turning once, until golden, about 10 minutes. Add the mushroom mixture and cook 15 minutes, stirring. The mushrooms will begin to lose their water. Transfer to the baking dish, laying the endive in a row and evenly spreading the mushrooms. Sprinkle with salt, pepper, and nutmeg and add the cream. Place in oven and cook, uncovered, for 20 minutes.★

Remove from oven and sprinkle with cheese. Place under broiler until the cheese starts to bubble and turn a golden brown. Serve directly from the oven.

★Can be prepared to this point a couple of hours in advance. Do not refrigerate or the *gratin* will dry out.

NEW POTATOES IN WHITE WINE

SERVES 4 TO 6

Vinegar changes the taste of potatoes and gives them more character, highlighting the earthy flavor. In this recipe we don't want the vinegar to be too strong, so it's diluted with white wine. Shallots and garlic sweeten vinegar and mask the wine aspect of the broth. Tarragon is easily added as an accent because the vinegar and wine background makes it stand out.

2	pounds small white new potatoes or small Finnish potatoes
2	cups dry white wine
½	cup white vinegar
2	tablespoons unsalted butter
1	teaspoon finely minced garlic
¼	cup finely minced shallots
1	teaspoon salt
½	teaspoon freshly ground pepper
1	tablespoon chopped fresh tarragon or 1 teaspoon dried
¼	cup chopped parsley

Rinse unpeeled potatoes under cold water, place in a 2-quart pot, and add the white wine, vinegar, butter, garlic, shallots, salt, and pepper. If using dried tarragon, add it now. Cover, bring to boil over high heat, reduce heat to low, and simmer until potatoes are tender, about 15 minutes. Preheat oven to 200°. Using a slotted spoon, remove potatoes to a serving platter and keep warm in the oven. Cook the vinegar mixture over high heat, reducing by one third. Add the fresh tarragon and chopped parsley. Remove potatoes from the oven and pour the liquid over them.

SAVORY RICE PUDDING

SERVES 6

Rice is naturally bland and a pudding with no additional flavors would be very boring indeed. Onion, celery, and mace provide an aromatic base for savory and thyme. By using these two similar herbs, we produce an effect that is more noticeable than if we had used only one of them in double quantity.

I	cup chicken stock (page 258), canned low-sodium chicken broth, or vegetable stock (page 257)
3	tablespoons unsalted butter
I	large onion, finely diced (about I cup)
2	celery stalks, finely sliced (about I cup)
I	tablespoon finely minced garlic
I	cup white rice, long-grain or basmati
I	teaspoon salt
¼	cup fresh bread crumbs
4	eggs
2	cups whipping cream
I	teaspoon chopped fresh thyme, leaves only *or* ½ teaspoon dried thyme
I	tablespoon chopped fresh savory, leaves only *or* ½ teaspoon dried savory
¼	teaspoon ground mace
½	teaspoon freshly ground pepper

Preheat oven to 375°. In a small pot bring the stock to a boil. In 1-quart pot with a heat-resistant handle melt 2 table-spoons of the butter over medium heat and add the onion, celery, and garlic. Cook without coloring for 5 minutes. Add the rice and mix to coat all grains with butter. Do not let the rice brown. Pour the boiling stock over the rice and add the salt. Cover and place in oven until rice has absorbed all liquid and is tender, about 12 minutes. Butter a 3-inch-deep, 11-inch round baking dish with remaining tablespoon of butter.

Remove rice from oven and transfer to a mixing bowl. Add the bread crumbs and mix. Let cool for 5 minutes before proceeding. Add the eggs, cream, thyme, savory, mace, and pepper, mix well, and scrape into baking dish. Place in oven and bake until mixture is set, about 25 minutes. Remove from oven, run a knife around the outside of the pudding, and turn onto a serving plate. This pudding can be made up to 2 days in advance, refrigerated, and easily rewarmed, covered, in a 350° oven for about 25 minutes.

GRATINÉED LEEK AND POTATO PUDDING   SERVES 6

Certain dishes should be on the heavy side, not delicate or airy. Leeks lighten the texture of this potato pudding without diminishing its rustic charm.

Leeks have an earthy taste, and when they are combined with potatoes, it is difficult to tell the two apart. This is particularly true if you are using freshly dug potatoes. The potatoes in the shops are usually months old, and much of their natural sugar has turned to starch. Nutmeg adds a highlight to both potatoes and leeks and changes the aroma of melted cheese by interfering with it.

2	large leeks
1	large russet potato
1	tablespoon fresh lemon juice
9	tablespoons (1 stick plus 1 tablespoon) unsalted butter
½	cup dry bread crumbs
3	eggs
1½	cups whipping cream
2	tablespoons white vinegar or white wine
⅛	teaspoon freshly grated nutmeg
1	teaspoon salt
¼	teaspoon freshly ground pepper
1	cup grated Swiss cheese

Remove the roots from the leeks and discard. Trim the green parts from the leeks and save for another use, in a stock or soup for example. Cut white parts of leeks into ¼-inch rounds and wash under cold water. You should have about 3 cups. Wash the unpeeled potato and grate by hand or in a food processor. If using a food processor, cut the potato into 1-inch chunks and pulse until coarsely grated. Combine potato and lemon juice in a mixing bowl. Preheat oven to 375°. Butter a 3-inch deep, 11-inch round baking dish with 1 tablespoon of the butter.

Melt the stick of butter in a medium skillet or sauté pan over medium heat. Add the leeks and cook, stirring, until well wilted, about 10 minutes. Add to the potatoes in the mixing bowl. Add the bread crumbs, eggs, cream, vinegar, nutmeg, salt, pepper, and ½ cup of the cheese. Mix well and scrape into baking dish.

Place in oven and bake, uncovered, until set, about 35 minutes. Preheat broiler.

Remove from oven, run a knife around the outside of the pudding, and turn onto an ovenproof plate. Sprinkle remaining cheese over the pudding and place under the broiler to brown. This pudding can be made up to 2 days in advance and refrigerated; rewarm in a 350° oven for 25 minutes.

WARM POTATO SALAD   MAKES 1 QUART, SERVES 6 TO 8

Vinegar is poured over warm potatoes to firm the flesh.

4	pounds large russet potatoes
¼	cup tarragon vinegar
¼	pound mushrooms
2	hard-cooked eggs, peeled and chopped
2	tablespoons grainy mustard
2	tablespoons sour cream
1	tablespoon chopped fresh tarragon leaves (*not* dried)
¼	cup virgin olive oil
¾	teaspoon salt
½	teaspoon freshly ground pepper

Scrub and peel the potatoes and cut into 2-inch pieces. Place in a medium pot, cover generously with salted water, bring to a boil over high heat, and cook until soft, about 7 minutes. Drain potatoes and place in a mixing bowl. Pour the vinegar over the potatoes, cover, and let sit for 5 minutes. Slice the mushrooms ¼-inch thick. Add mushrooms, hard-cooked eggs, mustard, sour cream, and tarragon to the potatoes and mix. Add olive oil, salt, and pepper and mix. Serve at room temperature.

CORN PUDDING   SERVES 6

Vegetable puddings are like custards because they are bound with cream and eggs. They're good vegetable accompaniments for main courses that are not too rich. Or make them quiche-style in a pastry crust and serve as a light lunch accompanied by a green salad.

3   tablespoons unsalted butter
½   medium onion, finely diced (about ½ cup)
2   cups corn kernels, fresh or frozen (defrosted)
½   cup yellow cornmeal
2   eggs
1½   cups whipping cream
⅛   teaspoon ground mace
¾   teaspoon salt
¼   teaspoon freshly ground pepper

In a 12-inch skillet melt 2 tablespoons of the butter over medium heat, add the onion, and cook without coloring for 5 minutes. Add the corn and continue to cook, stirring, for 5 minutes. Remove the corn and onion to a food processor and pulse to slightly break up the corn. Butter a 9-inch by 11-inch baking dish with remaining butter. Preheat oven to 350°.

Scrape corn mixture into a mixing bowl. Mix in the cornmeal, then the eggs, cream, mace, salt, and pepper, and mix well. Transfer mixture to the baking dish and bake, uncovered, until set, about 20 minutes. Remove from oven, run a knife around the outside of the pudding, and turn onto a serving plate. This pudding can be made up to 2 days in advance, refrigerated, and easily rewarmed, covered, in a 350° oven. Allow 25 minutes to rewarm.

DRIED-TOMATO NOODLE PUDDING   SERVES 6 TO 8

This noodle pudding is much better made with boxed egg noodles than with fresh pasta. It's good served at room temperature
on sliced, fresh tomatoes. This rendition of noodle pudding will
pleasantly surprise those who are accustomed to a sweet one.

I	cup sun-dried tomatoes
4	cups whipping cream
2	ounces egg noodles
2	tablespoons olive oil
8	eggs
½	teaspoon salt
	teaspoon freshly ground pepper
½	pound cheddar cheese, grated
½	pound mozzarella cheese, cut into ½-inch pieces

If the dried tomatoes are packed in oil, drain them and
pat dry on paper towels. If dried tomatoes are not packed in oil,
combine them with 1 cup of the cream and let stand to soften for
15 minutes. Drain tomatoes, reserving cream. Roughly chop
dried tomatoes and place in a medium mixing bowl.

Meanwhile, bring a pot of water to a boil on the stove over
high heat, add the egg noodles, and cook 4 minutes, keeping
them *al dente*. Drain, place in mixing bowl, and toss with 1
tablespoon of the olive oil. Grease an 8-inch by 10-inch baking
dish with remaining olive oil. Preheat oven to 325°.

In another bowl combine eggs, all the cream, salt, and
pepper and beat well. Add the cheddar and mozzarella cheeses to
the noodles and mix. Add the cream mixture and pour into
baking dish. Cover baking dish with aluminum foil, place in a
larger pan filled with boiling water, and place in oven until the
pudding is set, about 35 minutes. The pudding is done when it
has puffed slightly and a knife inserted in the center comes out
clean. Remove from water bath and let rest for 5 minutes before
serving.

TAMALES

MAKES 14 TO 16 TAMALES, SERVING 7 TO 8

Tamales are different throughout Latin America. Some are made with *masa harina,* a treated corn flour, some are full of fresh corn, and some are like *polenta* wrapped in a husk. I've had them wrapped in banana leaves, but the common wrapping is corn husks, either fresh or dried. They almost always have a center of either diced or shredded beef, chicken, or seafood.

Mine are not the usual tamales. I designed these to be as neutral as possible, with the flavor of *masa harina* being the focus. They can be eaten as a side dish with seafood, poultry, or meat; garnished, they can be a main dish. Prepare one of the recipes in the Pancake chapter, substituting tamales for pancakes, or try garnishing tamales with one of the quick stews.

28	large corn husks
¾	cup (1½ sticks) unsalted butter
3	cups fresh or frozen (defrosted) corn kernels
1	medium red pepper, seeded and roughly diced
1	medium green pepper, seeded and roughly diced
1	medium onion, roughly diced
1	cup *masa harina*
1	cup yellow cornmeal
1	tablespoon baking powder
1	teaspoon salt
½	teaspoon freshly ground pepper
1	cup water

Place corn husks in a large pot and cover with cold water. Let soak for 30 minutes before using.

Heat the butter in a large skillet over medium heat, add the corn, peppers, and onion, and cook, stirring, for 10 minutes. Transfer mixture to a food processor and pulse to break up the corn kernels. Scrape into a mixing bowl. Add the *masa harina,* cornmeal, baking powder, salt, and pepper. Mix well. Add the water and mix until incorporated.

Place two corn husks flat on a work surface, their widest ends overlapping. Place 1½ to 2 heaped tablespoons of tamale mixture on one husk, leaving the thin end free. Roll one husk around the mixture and fold over the thin end. Roll the second husk around the first one and fold over the thin end. Place, folded ends down, in a steaming basket with a flat bottom. Repeat with the rest of the husks, placing the tamales tightly together. It's this arrangement that keeps the wrappers closed during steaming. It's okay to layer the tamales if your steamer is too small to fit them in one layer.★

Steam over boiling water for 45 minutes, being careful that tamales do not touch water. Remove from the steam and let "rest" for at least 15 minutes before serving. The tamales will hold for a couple of hours before serving, but don't refrigerate them. Resteam tamales for 10 minutes before serving.

★Can be made to this point 1 day in advance and kept, covered, in the refrigerator before cooking.

CORN RISOTTO WITH OKRA
AND SHIITAKE MUSHROOMS

SERVES 4

I call this dish *risotto* (although there is no rice) because that's the source of its inspiration. I think it's important, when creating a dish and giving it a name, to let people understand how you arrived at the idea. The texture of the corn and reduced cream reminded me of a risotto I once had in Cremona. It was autumn and *porcini* mushrooms were in season. Something sparked my memory of this dish, but I was in California and it was summer, so I made the dish with corn and shiitake mushrooms.

½   cup (I stick) unsalted butter
3   cups fresh summer corn kernels (about 3 large summer corn cobs)
2   tablespoons finely minced shallots
I   cup vegetable stock (page 257), or chicken stock (page 258), or canned low-sodium chicken broth
I   cup whipping cream
½   cup grated Parmesan or *pecorino* Romano cheese
12   okra
12   medium shiitake mushroom caps
½   teaspoon salt
    freshly ground pepper to taste

Preheat the oven to 200°. Place half the butter in a medium saucepan over medium heat and when melted add the corn and shallots and cook 1 minute. Add half the stock, raise heat to high, and cook quickly until liquid is reduced. Add the cream and cook, reducing again until thick, approximately 7 minutes. Remove from heat and add the cheese. Transfer mixture to a blender or food processor and pulse to break up the corn kernels. Scrape corn onto a serving platter and keep warm in the oven.

Place remaining butter in another skillet over medium heat and when hot add okra and mushrooms and cook, stirring, for 3 minutes. Add the remaining stock and continue to cook until the stock reduces and thickens. Add salt and pepper. Remove corn from the oven and arrange sautéed mushrooms and okra and their juices on top.

DESSERTS

■ ● ▲

The common denominator of flavor in all desserts is, of course, sweetness. When people say they don't like sweet desserts, that doesn't mean that they don't want sugar; it means, I think, that they want a more complicated taste than *just* sugar.

Exactly what sugar does to taste is different in individual cases. Chocolate is unpalatable without sugar, though in small amounts, as a secret ingredient, it can be used as a savory to enrich meats and game. In a dessert context we want chocolate for its own taste, and for that we need sugar to help create the chocolate taste.

Sweet sensations can be combined with spicy sensations. In a savory context we can make things very spicy and then balance them with sweetness so that we can still taste accurately. In a sweet context spicy or peppery sensations add an element of surprise. Candied ginger is a good example—it's very spicy, but it's basically a sweet, not a savory confection.

Tart and acidic flavors function opposite sweet flavors. Sweetness is necessary in savory preparations to balance sour flavors. That's why a mixture of sugar and vinegar is so important to all sweet sauces for duck, for example. In a sweet preparation, a lemon custard for example, sweetness balances tartness and creates the lemon flavor.

Sugar and salt fight each other in such a way as to highlight each other. A little salt in a sweet confection makes it seem less one-dimensional. That's why a good butter pecan ice cream should be made with salted pecans.

By making desserts less sweet we can taste more of their other flavors. By adding other aspects to a sweet preparation we prevent it from becoming sickeningly sweet—it becomes more complicated and therefore more interesting.

BREAD AND BUTTER PUDDING
WITH DRUNKEN PRUNES   SERVES 5 TO 6

(Allow 2 weeks advance preparation for prunes)

Bread pudding should have a combination of textures—a creamy, custardy center and a crisp, crusty top. It should also have a flavor to complement its monochromatic vanilla flavor. So, most people add raisins. I find raisins too sweet and prefer my drunken prunes. They too are sweet but with a dark, alcoholic edge that surprises.

½	cup pitted prunes or raisins
¾	cup Southern Comfort
2	tablespoons unsalted butter, melted
2	cups good white or French bread, cut into 1-inch cubes
1	cup milk
1	cup whipping cream
1	vanilla bean, slit lengthwise
2	eggs
2	egg yolks
½	teaspoon salt
¼	cup sugar

Make the drunken prunes: At least 2 weeks prior to preparing the pudding, roughly dice the prunes, place in a jar, and pour Southern Comfort over them. Cover tightly and leave in a dark place. Drunken prunes (or any drunken dried fruit) will keep at least a year.

Preheat oven to 350°. Using 1 tablespoon of the melted butter, butter a 1½-quart baking dish and set aside.

In a mixing bowl toss the bread with the remaining butter, place in a small baking pan, and place in the oven to brown lightly. (If using stale bread, be careful not to burn it.) Remove bread from oven and set aside.

Meanwhile, in a small saucepan combine the milk, cream, and vanilla bean. Bring to a boil over high heat. As soon as the mixture starts to boil, remove from heat. Let sit for 15 minutes and then remove the vanilla bean. Scrape out the seeds of the bean and add to the cream mixture.

In a mixing bowl combine the eggs, yolks, salt, and sugar and whisk until smooth. Pour the cream mixture over the eggs and mix well.

Remove prunes from the Southern Comfort and place in another mixing bowl. Toss the prunes and bread together and place in buttered baking dish. Fill the baking dish with the cream and egg mixture. Place the baking dish in a boiling-water bath (*bain marie*). The water should come three quarters of the way up the sides of the dish. Place in preheated oven for 1 hour or until set. When done, the pudding will have puffed and a knife inserted into the center will come out clean. Remove from water bath and chill for 4 hours in the refrigerator before unmolding. If you prefer to serve this hot, let rest only until the pudding has unpuffed, but do not unmold it to serve.

LEMON AND ROSEMARY
STEAMED PUDDING

SERVES 6 TO 8

The balance between sweet sugar and tart lemon juice is what gives this pudding its strong character. The surprising addition of rosemary does not make this pudding at all savory. The rosemary becomes diminished as a flavor and more important as an aroma.

This pudding is quite dense and hearty. Covered, it rewarms easily in the oven.

13   tablespoons sweet butter (1½ sticks plus 1 tablespoon)
1   cup sugar
2   eggs
2½   cups dry bread crumbs
½   cup milk
1   teaspoon baking powder
1   lemon, grated zest only
2   tablespoons chopped fresh rosemary (*not* dried)
2   cups lemon custard (page 253)

Butter a pudding mold (or a 1-pound coffee can) with 1 tablespoon of the butter. Fill a 3-quart pot with water and bring to a boil over high heat.

In a mixer cream sugar and remaining butter together on medium speed. Add the eggs and mix to incorporate. Add bread crumbs, milk, baking powder, lemon zest, and rosemary and mix until smooth. Pour the batter into a mixing bowl and fold 1 cup of the lemon custard into the batter. Do not mix well. Pretend you are making a marble cake.

Pour the batter into the prepared pudding mold or coffee can. Do not fill more than three-quarters full. Cover tightly. Place in boiling water, reduce heat to low, and gently simmer for 2½ hours. Remove pudding from water and let cool for 10 minutes before unmolding. The pudding should be served warm or at room temperature with the remaining cup of lemon custard as accompaniment.

WHITE CHOCOLATE AND
RASPBERRY LAYER CAKE
SERVES 6

White chocolate tastes more like vanilla to me than chocolate, which is why I like it so well with raspberries. This cake must be refrigerated and then left to return to room temperature before serving.

Cake:

½   pound white chocolate
¾   cup unsalted butter (1½ sticks)
12   eggs
¼   pound sugar (½ cup)
½   cup all-purpose flour

Vanilla Buttercream:

1   cup vanilla sauce (page 252)
1   pound unsalted butter (4 sticks)
½   cup confectioners' sugar
2   pints fresh raspberries
1   cup berry sauce (page 251), made with raspberries

Make the cake: Preheat oven to 325°. Place white chocolate in the top of a double boiler and melt. Cut butter into 1-tablespoon pieces and place in the bowl of a mixer on medium speed. Slowly add chocolate, creaming until smooth, but don't let it get too soft. Add the eggs one at a time, beating until each one is incorporated. Add sugar. Turn the mixer to slow speed and add the flour. Do not overbeat at this point.

Line a 9-inch by 11-inch baking pan with parchment or wax paper. Lightly butter and flour the paper. Spread the cake batter evenly in the baking pan and bake 25 to 30 minutes or until puffed and golden. Let cool before turning out of baking sheet. Cake may be tightly wrapped and kept for up to 1 day before assembling.

Make the buttercream: Make certain that the vanilla sauce is at room temperature. Cut the butter into 1-tablespoon pieces and bring to room temperature before starting. In a mixer on medium speed cream the butter until smooth. Increase speed to high and add the sugar until incorporated and smooth. Slowly add the vanilla sauce with the mixer on high speed until it is incorporated. The mixture will look broken and grainy. Continue to beat until it becomes smooth, perhaps as long as 5 to 7 minutes. Scrape into a bowl and set aside. Keep the buttercream in a cool place for up to 2 hours or refrigerate. To use after refrigerating, let return to room temperature and remix until smooth in the mixer.

Assemble the cake: Turn the cake out of the baking pan and cut into 4 9-inch lengths. Spread a layer of buttercream ¼ inch thick on the first rectangle. Arrange raspberries on the buttercream. Place the second rectangle of cake on the raspberries and repeat with layer of buttercream and raspberries. Repeat with remaining 2 layers, but do not frost the top layer of the cake. Refrigerate for 30 minutes.

When the cake is firmly set, trim the sides so that the cake is uniformly even and smooth. Frost top and sides with the remaining buttercream. Refrigerate.

Remove the cake from the refrigerator 30 minutes before serving to let the buttercream soften. Serve with an accompaniment of raspberry sauce. This cake can be baked and assembled up to 2 days in advance. Wrapped and refrigerated, it does not get stale quickly.

MARGUERITE'S FLOURLESS CHOCOLATE CAKE   SERVES 5 TO 6

Cornstarch replaces flour in this cake and gives it the texture of a brownie. I've added a couple of unusual flavors. The cinnamon in the cake and the anise extract in the buttercream give the cake an almost indescribable taste. The cinnamon enriches the chocolate by merging with it. The anise extract adds an opposite sensation. If you cannot find anise extract, don't use the cinnamon. These two ingredients both need to be present to be interesting. The cake is delicious as ordinary chocolate cake.

Cake:

I	cup (2 sticks) plus I teaspoon unsalted butter, softened
½	pound bittersweet baking chocolate
4	eggs
½	pound (I cup) sugar
I ½	teaspoons ground cinnamon
⅓	cup (I ¾ ounces) sifted cornstarch

Chocolate Buttercream:

¼	pound bittersweet chocolate
½	pound unsalted butter
⅔	cup granulated sugar
⅓	cup water
4	egg yolks
I	teaspoon anise extract or Anisette

Make the cake: Preheat oven to 325°. Butter a 9-inch by 12-inch baking sheet with 1 teaspoon of the butter or line with parchment paper. Melt the chocolate in the top of a double boiler.

Place remaining butter in a mixer and cream until smooth. Slowly add the chocolate and mix on medium speed until smooth. Continue to beat, adding the eggs one at a time until incorporated. Add the sugar and cinnamon and continue to beat until smooth. Lower speed to low and add the cornstarch. At this point be careful not to overmix.

Scrape batter into the prepared baking pan to a depth of 1½ inches. Place pan on middle rack of oven and bake for 35 minutes. Remove from oven and let cool before removing from pan. Tightly wrapped, the cake may be kept for up to 2 days before assembling.

Make the buttercream: Place chocolate in the top of a double boiler and melt. Cut butter into 1-tablespoon pieces and set aside.

In a small pot combine the sugar and water and cook until the liquid reduces to ½ cup and becomes a syrup. Place the syrup in a mixer on medium-high speed and add the egg yolks, beating until the mixture has a heavy ribbon consistency. Add the butter piece by piece and continue to beat until the mixture is fluffy and smooth. (If the butter has gotten too warm, if it is no longer stiffly fluffy, refrigerate before using.) Slowly add the melted chocolate and anise extract and mix until smooth. Scrape into a bowl.

Assemble the cake: When the cake has cooled, turn it out onto a clean surface. Cut the cake into 4 9-inch lengths. The cake will be crumbly and difficult to handle. It can be pieced back together with buttercream as you assemble it, and once refrigerated, it is quite durable.

Lay one layer of cake on the table and spread with ½-inch thickness of buttercream. Place a second layer on the frosted first layer. Repeat with the remaining 2 layers but do not frost the top yet. Place the cake in the refrigerator to chill and become firm, about 25 minutes. Remove chilled cake from the refrigerator and trim the sides of the cake so that it has a uniformly even shape. Frost the sides and the top.

Keep the cake refrigerated until needed, but it must be left at room temperature to soften for 45 minutes before serving. May be kept in the refrigerator, tightly covered, for up to 1 week.

LEMON NUT CAKE

SERVES 8

The lightly salted nuts are an important foil to the sweetness of the lemon custard. This cake is dense, sweet, and tart, with a savory background.

13 tablespoons unsalted butter (1½ sticks plus 1 tablespoon)
1   cup sugar
5   eggs, separated
½   cup fresh bread crumbs
2½ cups chopped pistachios, blanched almonds, or pecans
½   teaspoon salt
4   cups lemon custard (page 253)

Preheat oven to 375°. Butter a deep 9-inch cake pan with 1 tablespoon of the butter and set aside. Combine remaining butter and sugar in a mixer and cream on medium speed until smooth. Add the egg yolks one at a time. When they are incorporated, add the bread crumbs. Add 2 cups of the chopped nuts and mix. Remove to a large mixing bowl and reserve.

Wash and completely dry the bowl of the mixer. Combine the salt and egg whites in the mixer and beat until stiff. Add one third of the egg whites to the nut batter and mix to soften the batter. Place the rest of the egg whites on the batter and gently fold together. Pour batter into prepared cake pan. Place on middle rack of preheated oven and bake for 30 minutes. When done, a wooden toothpick inserted into the cake should come out clean. Let cake cool before unmolding.

Cut the cake in half horizontally. Spread on a layer of lemon custard and re-form cake. Frost the entire outside with lemon custard and cover with remaining chopped nuts. Serve more lemon custard as an accompaniment.

PINEAPPLE UPSIDE-DOWN CAKE   SERVES 6

Upside-down cakes are charming because of their rustic austerity. To me they are like fancy coffee cakes, not at all rich, decadent desserts. Serve this one with ice cream. Madeira wine makes the cake more aromatic, and cornmeal adds an interesting texture.

⅔   cup sugar
¾   cup (1½ sticks) unsalted butter
1   teaspoon vanilla extract
¼   teaspoon ground mace
2   eggs
2   egg yolks
1½ cups milk
2   teaspoons baking powder
¼   teaspoon salt
1½ cups all-purpose flour
1   cup yellow cornmeal
⅓   cup Madeira
1   pound pineapple, cut into ½-inch slices, core removed (about ½ medium pineapple)
¾   cup dark brown sugar

In a mixer cream granulated sugar and 1 stick of the butter together on medium speed until smooth. Lower the speed and add the vanilla, mace, whole eggs, yolks, and milk. Mix until incorporated. Add the baking powder and salt, then the flour and cornmeal. Mix until fluffy. Transfer to a bowl and set aside.

Combine remaining ½ stick butter, the Madeira, and the pineapple in a heavy 10-inch ovenproof skillet over medium heat and cook 20 minutes. The pineapple will release a lot of liquid. Using a slotted spoon, remove the pineapple from the skillet and reserve. Continue cooking until reduced to almost a glaze. Add the brown sugar and cook until the sugar and butter mixture become smooth, about 2 minutes more. Preheat oven to 375°.

Re-place pineapple slices and arrange them nicely in the syrup. If they do not fit together attractively, you can cut them and arrange them in a pattern.

Pour the cake batter over the fruit and place on the middle rack of the preheated oven for 20 to 25 minutes. When done, a toothpick inserted into the cake will come out clean. Remove the cake from the skillet by turning it upside down over a large plate.

GINGERSNAP CHEESECAKE

SERVES 12

Crust:

4	tablespoons unsalted butter
⅔	cup sugar
I	egg
2	tablespoons molasses
½	teaspoon white vinegar
I	cup plus 2 tablespoons all-purpose flour
¼	teaspoon baking soda
2	teaspoons ground ginger
2	tablespoons finely chopped candied ginger
	pinch ground cloves
	pinch ground cinnamon

Cheesecake Filling:

1½	tablespoons unsalted butter
½	cup plus I tablespoon sugar
2	pounds cream cheese
4	eggs
⅓	cup sour cream
I	teaspoon vanilla extract
½	teaspoon ground ginger
3	tablespoons finely chopped candied ginger

Make the crust: In a mixer on medium speed, cream the butter and sugar until smooth. Add the egg, molasses, and vinegar and mix to incorporate. Turn the mixer to low and add the flour, baking soda, both gingers, cloves, and cinnamon. Scrape into bowl and set aside.*

Make the filling: Cream the butter in a mixer on medium speed, then add sugar and cream cheese together and beat until smooth. Add the eggs one at a time until incorporated. Add the sour cream, vanilla, and both gingers. Mix until smooth. Do not overmix or too much air will be whipped into the batter, making it more difficult to set when baked.

Assemble and bake the cheesecake: Preheat oven to 300°. Spread a ¼-inch layer of gingersnap crust batter on the bottom of a 10-inch round springform pan. Refrigerate for 15 minutes.

Scrape cheesecake batter into prepared pan and place on the middle rack in preheated oven for 45 minutes. The cheesecake will puff as it cooks. It's ready when the sides are set and the center jiggles slightly when shaken gently. The cheesecake will continue to set as it cools. An overdone cheesecake is dry; slightly undercooked, it stays creamy and moist. Let cheesecake cool to room temperature. Refrigerate for at least 6 hours before unmolding and serving.

*If you like, you can also use this mixture for gingersnap cookies: Place teaspoon dollops of dough on a buttered, floured cookie sheet and bake at 350° for 10 minutes.

GOAT CHEESE TORTE WITH
ALMONDS AND DRIED PEARS
SERVES 6 TO 8

I like the less sticky, more complex sweetness that honey gives to certain desserts. Sugar, being only sweet, is not flavorful enough to bring goat cheese into balance. The added flavor of honey is necessary here.

Pastry Crust:

4	tablespoons unsalted butter
¼	pound all-purpose flour
4	tablespoons sugar
¼	teaspoon salt
1	egg yolk
1	tablespoon ice water

Goat Cheese Filling:

1	11-ounce package fresh (not aged) goat cheese
2	tablespoons sugar
2	eggs
¼	cup honey
¼	teaspoon vanilla extract
½	cup sour cream
6	pieces dried pears, coarsely diced
½	cup sliced almonds

Make the crust: Cut the butter into ½-teaspoon pieces. Place flour in a food processor, add the butter, and pulse lightly to form a grainy meal. And sugar, salt, yolk, and water and pulse until it begins to form a ball. Remove from processor, wrap in plastic wrap, and let rest in the refrigerator for 30 minutes before using.

Make the filling: Cream the goat cheese and sugar together in a mixer on medium speed. Add the eggs, honey, and vanilla and mix to incorporate. Add the sour cream and pears and mix until smooth.

Assemble and bake the torte: Preheat oven to 375°. Roll the chilled pastry into a 12-inch circle about ¼ inch thick and line a 9-inch pie dish with it. Scrape the goat cheese filling into the pie dish and sprinkle with the sliced almonds. Place on the middle rack of the preheated oven and bake for 25 to 30 minutes. Remove from the oven and let cool before serving. This torte should be served either warm or at room temperature.

FRUIT DOUGHNUTS

SERVES 4 TO 5

Cinnamon and vanilla form the background flavors of these doughnut holes. The very slight taste of baking powder is a wonderful surprise, the way it is in a scone or soda biscuit. Serve these warm doughnuts with ice cream.

1	cooked baking potato, pulp only (about 1 cup)
¾	cup all-purpose flour
½	cup sugar
1	egg
2	tablespoons baking powder
⅓	cup buttermilk
½	teaspoon vanilla extract
½	teaspoon ground cinnamon
1¼	cups diced strawberries
⅓	cup chopped walnuts
4	cups salad oil
	ice cream (optional)
2	cups berry sauce (page 251)
2	tablespoons confectioners' sugar

Scoop out the pulp of a warm baked potato, place in a bowl, and mash well. Do not put in blender or food processor. Add flour, sugar, egg, and baking powder and mix. Gradually blend in buttermilk. Stir in the vanilla, cinnamon, strawberries, and walnuts.

Heat a 4-inch depth of oil in a fryer or deep heavy saucepan to 350°. Preheat oven to 200°. Drop heaped tablespoons of batter into hot oil. Do not crowd the pot. Fry in batches until browned and crispy. Test one by cutting in half to make sure that the inside is cooked. Using a slotted spoon, remove doughnuts as they are done, drain on paper towels, and keep warm in the oven until they are all cooked.

To serve, place a scoop of ice cream in a bowl, surround with a few doughnuts, and spoon some berry sauce over the ice cream. Sprinkle the doughnuts with confectioners' sugar.

PEARS POACHED IN RED
WINE WITH ROQUEFORT CREAM   SERVES 4

My favorite combination is a sweet taste with a pungent, acrid
aroma. This combination works because of the balance of sweet,
salty, and aromatic. Vanilla is the foundation, and it brings the
cheese flavor into harmony with the fruit. The sweetness of the
pears and the vanilla sauce oppose the saltiness of the Roquefort,
and the two cancel each other in an interesting and complex
manner.

4   hard, ripe pears such as Bosc
4   cups dry red wine
½   cup sugar
l   cup vanilla sauce (page 252)
¼   pound Roquefort cheese, crumbled

Peel the pears, halve them lengthwise, and remove the core.
Place cut side down in a large saucepan and add the red wine and
sugar. Bring to a boil over high heat, reduce heat to low, and
simmer, uncovered, for 20 minutes. Turn the pears over and
continue to cook until tender, 10 to 15 minutes.

Heat a double boiler. Remove pears from the wine and
refrigerate. Raise heat to medium and cook the poaching liquid
until it is reduced to about ¾ cup and is syrupy. Scrape into a
bowl, cover, and refrigerate.

Measure 1 cup of vanilla sauce into a mixing bowl. Place
cheese in the top of the double boiler to soften. When melted,
add this to the vanilla sauce and chill. Divide the Roquefort
cream among four dessert plates. Place a pear half on the cream
and spoon a little red wine syrup over each pear.

VANILLA ORANGES   SERVES 4

The vanilla perfume and the orange blossom water create a cleansing aroma that seems to cut the sugary syrup. Tahitian vanilla beans are best, if you can find them.

8   medium navel oranges
⅓   cup sugar
½   vanilla bean, slit lengthwise
1½   cups water
¼   teaspoon orange blossom water (optional)

Using a zester, remove the zest of 4 of the oranges and combine in a small pot with sugar, vanilla bean, and water. Bring to a boil and let cook until reduced to 1 cup of lightly syrupy liquid. Remove vanilla bean, scrape seeds into syrup, and discard bean. Pour into a medium serving bowl and chill.

Carefully remove the remaining peel, including the white pulp, from all the oranges and discard. Remove the orange sections, discarding membrane, and add to the vanilla syrup. Just before serving, add the orange blossom water and mix.

BERRY SAUCE   MAKES 2 TO 3 CUPS, DEPENDING ON THE BERRY
USED, SERVES 6 TO 9

Dessert sauces are good on ice cream; they also can be used to moisten sponge cake.

Berry sauces should be cooked very briefly or they will taste like preserves. It's essential that they retain their freshness and that sugar doesn't cover up their flavor or their perfume.

1   cup sugar
½   cup water
1   pound fresh raspberries, strawberries, blueberries, or blackberries

Combine sugar and water in a large heavy saucepan over high heat, bring to a boil, and cook 10 minutes. Add berries, bring back to the boil, and immediately remove from heat. Pour into a bowl and cool completely. When cool, transfer to a food processor and puree. Pass through a strainer to eliminate any seeds. Berry sauce will keep for up to 5 days in the refrigerator. Freeze for up to 3 months.

VANILLA SAUCE (CRÈME ANGLAISE)   MAKES 3 CUPS, SERVES 9

This versatile sauce is good with almost everything from chocolate cake to fresh berries. It can also be the basis for buttercreams and may be flavored with a few tablespoons of liqueur or other alcohol.

5   egg yolks
¼   cup sugar
l   cup whipping cream
l   cup milk
l   vanilla bean, slit lengthwise

Combine egg yolks and sugar in a medium mixing bowl. Using a wire whisk, beat together until the yolks turn from bright to pale yellow.

Combine the cream, milk, and vanilla bean in a medium pot over high heat. As soon as the mixture begins to boil, remove from heat and remove and discard vanilla bean. Slowly pour the scalded milk over the yolks, stirring.

Place mixture in a clean pot and over low heat cook the mixture until it begins to thicken. Stir continuously with a wooden spoon. When the mixture has the consistency to coat a spoon, immediately pour through a strainer into a glass or ceramic container. Continue to stir as the mixture cools, helping to stop the cooking process and allowing the heat to escape. Be very careful not to overcook or the yolks will curdle. The difference between properly cooked and curdled is a matter of only seconds. When cool, cover and place in refrigerator to chill. This sauce will keep for up to 5 days. It cannot be frozen.

LEMON CUSTARD

MAKES 1 QUART, ENOUGH TO
FILL 3 9-INCH PIE SHELLS

Although sugar makes tart things palatable, we don't want tart things to become sickeningly sweet. The right balance is essential for elegance of flavor.

5   eggs
5   egg yolks
2   cups sugar
1   cup fresh lemon juice
2   lemons, grated zest only
½   cup (1 stick) unsalted butter

Combine the eggs, egg yolks, and sugar in a mixing bowl and beat until smooth. Add the lemon juice and lemon zest and mix. Place the bowl over a pot of boiling water or in the top of a double boiler and stir vigorously with a wooden spoon until the mixture thickens. This mixture will not curdle, so don't worry about overcooking it a little. Remove the bowl from the boiling water and stir in the butter until melted. Refrigerated, this will keep for up to 3 months.

To make a lemon custard pie, fill a 9-inch baked pie shell and bake the custard for 15 minutes at 375°.

WALNUTS AND FRESH FIGS IN PERNOD SYRUP   SERVES 4

Walnuts can be bitter, and their bitterness is an important element in this dessert, the catalyst that changes the impression of the Pernod syrup. Here's a good example of how sugar can change the way a savory tastes. Although it's high in sugar content, Pernod doesn't *seem* sweet and is important in savory cooking. In a sweet context, it marries differently with other flavors.

1	cup Pernod
¼	cup water
⅓	cup sugar
1	cup walnuts
16–20	fresh Mission figs
4	scoops vanilla ice cream

Combine the Pernod, water, sugar, and walnuts in a medium pot. Bring to boil over medium heat and simmer until the liquid reduces and forms a medium-thick syrup. Add figs and continue to cook, stirring, for 1 minute. Pour into a bowl or container and refrigerate. Place a scoop of ice cream in each of four dessert bowls, add the figs, and spoon the walnuts and syrup over the top.

KITCHEN PANTRY

■●▲

STOCKS

It seems silly to be tied always to a menu or a shopping list when we want to cook. With a supply of prepared odds and ends in the refrigerator one can quickly shop for a main ingredient—a fresh fish or an aged steak—and toss together a seemingly complicated meal in a matter of moments. The greater my supply of interesting odds and ends the greater the possibilities of spontaneous invention.

Stocks are the basis of most soups and sauces. They are easy, although time-consuming, to make. Fortunately, they have a long shelf life when frozen. I find that I can improvise more freely when I have a supply of stock in the freezer because I can quickly make a sauce or soup. All food tastes better when the liquid used in cooking has flavor. The only things you really need water for are cooking pasta, boiling eggs, and steaming vegetables.

If you can't or won't make stocks, it's possible to compromise, using store-bought canned chicken broth as a basis for many preparations. To be successful, you must follow certain guidelines. First, use only low-sodium chicken broth. Low-sodium broth can be reduced without becoming oversalty. Also, read the list of ingredients on the back of low-sodium chicken broth and you will find that it contains nothing except chicken and water. The others contain a myriad of essences, extracts, and chemicals that perhaps make things easy for the manufacturer but will be of no advantage to you, the cook and consumer.

To make a mock veal stock, add some roasted veal bones to low-sodium chicken broth or save the bones from last night's steak and cook that in the broth. If you're preparing fish, cook 2 parts low-sodium chicken broth and one part white wine for 15 minutes and use either for poaching or as the basis of a sauce. The flavor of the fish will overpower any hint of chicken flavor.

COURT BOUILLON (FOR POACHING FISH)

MAKES APPROXIMATELY 2½ QUARTS

1	large onion, peeled and roughly diced (about one cup)
2	celery stalks, roughly diced (about 1 cup)
1	large carrot, roughly diced (about 1 cup)
1	tablespoon whole black peppercorns
2	bay leaves
1	sprig fresh thyme *or* 1 teaspoon dried
2	cups dry white wine
2	quarts water

Combine all ingredients except the water in a large saucepan. Bring to a boil over high heat and let boil 1 minute to rid the wine of its alcohol. Add the water, bring to boil, cover, and cook 10 minutes. Strain and reserve the liquid; discard the vegetables. *Court bouillon* may be used as a base for making fish stock.

VEGETABLE STOCK

MAKES 1 GALLON

Stocks that are based on fish, poultry, or meat are rich in flavor but depend on a strong vegetable element for a background of aroma and sweetness that enhances their flavor; in a vegetarian stock the background flavor becomes the focus. It's important to manipulate the combination of vegetables so that you have the right proportion of aromatics (celery, leeks, parsley, bay leaves) to sweetness (carrots, onions, parsnip, turnip, garlic). Don't bother to peel any vegetables except the onion.

1	tablespoon unsalted butter
2	medium onions, roughly diced (about 1½ cups)
1	medium carrot, diced or thinly sliced (about ¾ cup)
1	parsnip, roughly diced (about 1 cup)
1	turnip, roughly diced (about 1½ cups)
3	celery stalks, roughly diced (about 1½ cups)
1	large leek, roughly diced
4	garlic cloves, crushed
6	quarts cold water
1	bunch parsley, stems only (save leaves for another use)
4	bay leaves
1	sprig fresh thyme or ¼ teaspoon dried
1	teaspoon whole black peppercorns

Wash all the vegetables well. In a stockpot or large kettle, melt the butter over medium heat and add the onions. Cook, stirring, for 10 minutes. Add the carrot, parsnip, turnip, celery, leek, and garlic. Cook 15 minutes, stirring frequently so they do not burn, or until all the vegetables are tender. Add the cold water and increase heat to high. Add parsley, bay leaves, thyme, and peppercorns. Bring to a boil, reduce heat to low, and simmer, covered, for 1 hour. Strain the vegetables from the stock and discard them. Put the broth back in the pot over high heat and cook, uncovered, until reduced to 4 quarts. Freeze this stock for up to 3 months.

CHICKEN OR DUCK STOCK   MAKES 1 GALLON

To extract all the flavor from the bones, chicken and duck stocks
need to cook until the bones have a spongy appearance and can
be broken with a spoon. This will take 3 to 3½ hours, so I
suggest that you make as large a quantity as possible at one time
and freeze the stock in 1-pint containers or in ice cube trays. This
long cooking ensures a strong stock that will greatly improve the
many soups and sauces that are based on chicken stock. The
extraction of gelatin from the bones will also give a good jellied
consistency to any of these soups you'd like to serve chilled.
Because of the long cooking, and because we want the vegetables
to maintain their aromatic quality rather than their sweet quality,
it's not advisable to sweat the vegetables prior to moistening. A
well-flavored stock can also be achieved using the bones of a
cooked chicken—don't throw them out.

5   pounds chicken or duck carcasses and necks (feet, if your butcher
     has them, are great to add)
3   large onions, peeled and roughly chopped (about 3 cups)
4   celery stalks, roughly chopped, without leaves (about 2 cups)
4   medium carrots, roughly chopped (about 3 cups)
4   bay leaves
I   tablespoon whole peppercorns
I   bunch parsley, stems only (about ½ ounce)
2   sprigs fresh thyme or ½ teaspoon dried
6   quarts cold water

Place all ingredients in a stockpot or large kettle and cover
with the cold water. Cover and bring to a boil over high heat.
Reduce heat to low and simmer, uncovered, for 3 to 3½ hours.
Pass through a fine strainer. Remove chicken fat from surface.
Freeze in cup or pint containers for up to 3 months.

VEAL OR LAMB STOCK   MAKES 1 GALLON

The method for making a good veal or lamb stock is different from the others in that the bones are roasted in the oven until they are very dark, giving a rich flavor and color to the stock. The aromatic vegetables are also roasted, emphasizing their sweetness more than their aroma.

10 pounds veal bones
2   pounds onions, halved
1   pound carrots, coarsely chopped
4   celery stalks, chopped (about 2 cups)
1   cup dry white wine
2   gallons cold water
2   tablespoons tomato paste or 6 plum tomatoes (about ¾ pound) quartered
4   sprigs fresh thyme or 1½ teaspoons dried
1   teaspoon whole black peppercorns
4   bay leaves

Preheat oven to 350°. Place the bones on a large roasting pan and place in oven for 40 minutes. Turn after 20 minutes so bones brown evenly.

Meanwhile, place the onions, cut side down, over the open flame of a burner or directly on the coil of an electric range and let them burn, approximately 8 to 10 minutes.

When the bones are a dark golden color, add the carrots and celery and continue to roast for 10 minutes. Transfer contents of the roasting pan to a stockpot or large kettle on the stove top. Place roasting pan over medium heat on top of the stove and add the wine. Scrape up any residue on the bottom of the roasting pan as the wine bubbles. Pour this liquid into the stockpot and add the water. Add the onions, tomato paste, thyme, peppercorns, and bay leaves. Bring to a boil over high heat, reduce heat to low, and simmer, uncovered, for 6 hours, skimming from time to time. Pass through a fine strainer and discard all vegetables and bones. Freeze the stock in small containers for up to 3 months.

FISH STOCK

MAKES 1 GALLON

Because of the nature of fish bones, this preparation differs from that of other stocks. Long cooking is not needed to extract the flavors or the gelatin from the bones; indeed, a long cooking produces a bitter fish stock. Use bones from a lean fish such as halibut or any of the soles. Avoid fatty fish like salmon or whitefish. Since the cooking time is so short, sweat the aromatic vegetables before adding water in order to break down the cellulose, thereby allowing the aromas to develop quickly.

4	pounds fish bones (heads may be included but not organs)
1	tablespoon butter
1	pound onions, coarsely chopped
4	celery stalks, coarsely chopped, leaves discarded (about 2 cups)
½	pound carrots, coarsely chopped (about 2 cups)
1	cup white wine
1	gallon cold water
4	sprigs parsley
2	bay leaves
1	teaspoon whole black peppercorns

Place fish bones in a large pot and rinse with cold water to eliminate any blood. In a stockpot or large kettle melt the butter over medium heat and add the chopped onions, celery, and carrots. Cook, stirring, for 10 minutes without letting anything color. Add the drained fish bones to the pot and cook for 5 minutes more. Add the white wine and water, parsley, bay leaves, and peppercorns. Bring to a boil over high heat, lower heat and simmer, uncovered, for 20 minutes. Pass through a fine strainer and discard bones and vegetables. Frozen, this stock will keep for up to 3 months.

DIPS

SWEET PEA GUACAMOLE   SERVES 8

I served this dip at a press party for food writers, and a woman from El Paso told me that along the border between Texas and Mexico taco joints would cut their guacamole with peas when the price of avocados got too high. I think she was trying to insult me, but it doesn't matter because this guacamole, weird as it sounds, tastes good. It's quick and easy to make, so don't prepare it more than 12 hours in advance or the color will turn dull.

Unless you grow your own peas and can eat them straight from the garden, frozen ones work better because the color is more vibrant and the sugar in the peas has not been allowed to turn to starch. This sweet foundation is important for highlighting the dry perfume of cumin. The sweetness also opposes the tartness of the lime juice and the hotness of the jalapeño peppers. Cilantro is added to complete the disguise—these are peas in avocado clothing.

2	tablespoons virgin olive oil
2	tablespoons fresh lime juice
¼	bunch cilantro, trimmed of long stems
1	jalapeño pepper, seeded, or 2 serrano peppers, seeded
1	pound frozen (defrosted) peas
¼	teaspoon ground cumin
¾	teaspoon salt
¼	medium red onion, finely diced

Combine oil, lime juice, cilantro, and jalapeño in a blender or food processor and blend until cilantro and hot pepper are roughly pureed. Add peas, cumin, and salt and blend until smooth. There will still be some lumps, but this adds to the textural interest of the guacamole. Scrape into a mixing bowl and add the diced red onion. Serve as a dip with tortilla chips or potato chips. Or use to accompany tamales (page 234) or *arroz con pollo* (page 128).

EGGPLANT CAVIAR   MAKES 2 CUPS

The preponderance of eggplant seeds gives this puree its caviar texture; it tastes nothing like caviar. It can be served cold as a cocktail dip or hot as a tasty vegetable accompaniment. It's good with cold turkey or chicken in a sandwich, or serve it on toast topped with poached eggs. Add 2 beaten eggs and a cup of bread crumbs and use it as a stuffing or prepare eggplant pancakes (page 95).

2   medium eggplant
¼   cup olive oil
I   · tablespoon finely minced garlic
2   tablespoons finely minced shallots or onion
¼   teaspoon salt

Preheat oven to 375°. Place eggplant on a baking sheet and bake in oven until completely soft, about 25 to 35 minutes. The skins will burn and the eggplant will ooze slightly when done. Remove from oven and let eggplant cool until you can handle them comfortably.

Meanwhile, combine olive oil and garlic in a small pot over low heat on the stove and cook, stirring, for 5 minutes without coloring. Remove from heat and add the minced shallots.

When eggplant are cool enough to handle, peel them, cut off and discard the stems. Place eggplant pulp in a mixing bowl. Slowly add the olive oil mixture to the eggplant pulp, mashing well so that no lumps are left. Serve immediately as a vegetable or chill and use as a dip.

CONDIMENTS

MUSTARD SEED AND PAPAYA CHUTNEY   MAKES 1 QUART

Chutneys depend on a background of sweet and sour to give
backbone to the flavor of the fruit so that it isn't overwhelmed
by the flavors of the curry spices.

1½ cups white vinegar
½   cup water
¼   cup sugar
2   tablespoons mustard seed
3   ripe papayas, peeled, seeded, and roughly chopped
1   tablespoon curry powder (page 264)
½   medium red onion, finely diced (about ½ cup)

Combine vinegar, water, sugar, and mustard seed in a 1-quart
pot over medium heat. Bring to the boil and cook, reducing,
until the liquid starts to become syrupy. Add the papayas and the
curry powder. Cook an additional 2 minutes, stirring constantly.
Remove from heat and mix in the onion. Pack into a jar and
leave in the refrigerator for 1 week before using.

CURRY POWDER

MAKES ½ CUP

This confusing-to-the-palate mixture of spices can be adjusted endlessly, emphasizing different aspects of the curry, depending on its destined use. The following recipe is only a guide and need not be followed exactly.

½   teaspoon ground cloves
1½ teaspoons ground cinnamon
1   tablespoon fennel seed
1½ teaspoons dill seed *or* 1 tablespoon dried dill
1   tablespoon turmeric
1   tablespoon coriander seed
1–2 tablespoons cayenne pepper
½   teaspoon ground ginger
½   teaspoon ground saffron
½   teaspoon celery seed
1   tablespoon dried fenugreek (see note below)
1½ teaspoons dry mustard
1   teaspoon cumin seed
4   bay leaves

Combine all ingredients in a spice mill or electric coffee grinder and grind into a fine powder.

Note: Fenugreek is available at Middle Eastern and Indian markets or, surprisingly, at health food stores. There is no substitute, but if you can't find it, make the curry powder anyway—it will still be very interesting.

SOUR CABBAGE

Sour cabbage, or sauerkraut, is particularly easy to make, and you'll be surprised at the difference between the commercial product and your own fresh version. Homemade sauerkraut has a delicate balance of flavor and can be used with many foods that would not taste right with the supermarket variety. Use green cabbage or, for a more interesting variation, try fermenting Napa cabbage.

Once the fermentation process is complete, keep the sauerkraut in the refrigerator for up to 2 months.

1	medium head green cabbage *or* 2 small heads Napa cabbage
1/3	cup kosher salt
2	tablespoons sugar

For green cabbage, cut in half and cut out the central core. Sliver the leaves as finely as you can. For Napa cabbage, separate the head into leaves and sliver them from tip to root.

In a large mixing bowl toss the cabbage with the salt and sugar. Place cabbage in a large stainless steel, earthenware, glass, or plastic container. Cover with a plate, weight the plate with a brick or heavy can, and leave for 6 hours. The cabbage will wilt and compress. Remove the weight but not the plate and add enough cold water to cover cabbage by 1 inch. Cover the container with a cheesecloth and place in a warm, dark place to sour for 12 to 21 days. After about 4 days the cabbage will begin to smell like sauerkraut. As the fermentation progresses the smell becomes more pervasive. You should put the cabbage in a well-ventilated place because the gases released during the fermentation process are quite unappetizing. A garage might be ideal. The cabbage is ready when its flavor is as strong as you like.

Pack the sauerkraut tightly into jars and fill with the brine. Store in refrigerator for up to 3 months. The fermentation process stops in the absence of air or when the temperature is too cold.

DILL AND GARLIC PICKLES

MAKES 1 GALLON

Pickles need a complexity of flavor and aroma or they taste only of vinegar. Use herbs and spices that infuse well and don't disintegrate during the pickling process. Most commercial pickles are too salty and don't have enough herbs and spices to make them taste interesting.

5	pounds pickling cucumbers
1	bunch fresh dill, including flowers
1	quart white vinegar
2	cups water
1	teaspoon mustard seed
1	tablespoon ground turmeric
1	teaspoon coriander seed
½	teaspoon celery seed
1	tablespoon salt
2	garlic heads, crushed
1	teaspoon whole black peppercorns

Wash the cucumbers and place in a 4- or 5-quart plastic, glass, or ceramic container with a lid. Add the dill.

In a 2-quart pot combine the vinegar, water, and all other ingredients. Bring to a boil and let simmer 5 minutes. Pour this mixture over the cucumbers. If there is not enough liquid to cover, then top off with enough white vinegar to submerge the cucumbers. Let cool to room temperature. Cover and place in refrigerator for at least 2 weeks before using. If you like new pickles, then they will be ready after 1 week. These pickles are best after 2 months and will keep indefinitely if refrigerated.

SWEET AND SOUR WATERMELON RIND   MAKES 2 CUPS

2   cups unpeeled watermelon rind, cut into 1-inch cubes
½   cup sugar
1   cup white vinegar

Combine all ingredients in a 1-quart pot over high heat. Bring to a boil, reduce heat to low, and simmer, uncovered, for 15 minutes. Remove from heat and pour into a plastic, glass, or ceramic lidded container. Cover and place in refrigerator for 1 week before using. Will keep 6 months in the refrigerator.

PICKLED PUMPKIN   MAKES 1 QUART

During most of the year, when you cannot find pumpkin, substitute banana squash.

1   small pumpkin or banana squash (about 2 pounds)
2   cups white vinegar
1   cup water
½   cup sugar
¼   stick cinnamon *or* ½ teaspoon ground cinnamon
2   cloves *or* ¼ teaspoon ground cloves
1   tablespoon coriander seed *or* 1 teaspoon ground coriander
½   teaspoon salt

Using a vegetable peeler, peel the tough outer layer off the pumpkin and discard. Cut the pumpkin in half, scoop out the seeds, and reserve for another use, such as roasted pumpkin seeds. Dice the flesh into 1-inch cubes. Combine the pumpkin cubes with the remaining ingredients in a medium pot. Bring to a boil over high heat, reduce heat to low, and simmer, uncovered, for 5 minutes, or until the pumpkin is barely tender. Pack the pumpkin into a plastic, glass, or ceramic lidded container and pour enough liquid over to cover. Place in refrigerator for at least 1 week before using. Will keep for 6 months.

METRIC CONVERSION CHART

CONVERSIONS OF QUARTS TO LITERS

Quarts (qt)	Liters (L)
1 qt	1 L★
1½ qt	1½ L
2 qt	2 L
2½ qt	2½ L
3 qt	2¾ L
4 qt	3¾ L
5 qt	4¾ L
6 qt	5½ L
7 qt	6½ L
8 qt	7½ L
9 qt	8½ L
10 qt	9½ L

★Approximate. To convert quarts to liters, multiply number of quarts by 0.95.

CONVERSIONS OF OUNCES TO GRAMS

Ounces (oz)	Grams (g)
1 oz	30 g★
2 oz	60 g
3 oz	85 g
4 oz	115 g
5 oz	140 g
6 oz	180 g
7 oz	200 g
8 oz	225 g
9 oz	250 g
10 oz	285 g
11 oz	300 g
12 oz	340 g
13 oz	370 g
14 oz	400 g
15 oz	425 g
16 oz	450 g
20 oz	570 g
24 oz	680 g
28 oz	790 g
32 oz	900 g

★Approximate. To convert ounces to grams, multiply number of ounces by 28.35.

CONVERSIONS OF POUNDS TO GRAMS AND KILOGRAMS

Pounds (lb)	Grams (g); kilograms (kg)
1 lb	450 g★
1¼ lb	565 g
1½ lb	675 g
1¾ lb	800 g
2 lb	900 g
2½ lb	1,125 g; 1¼ kg
3 lb	1,350 g
3½ lb	1,500 g; 1½ kg
4 lb	1,800 g
4½ lb	2 kg
5 lb	2¼ kg
5½ lb	2½ kg
6 lb	2¾ kg
6½ lb	3 kg
7 lb	3¼ kg
7½ lb	3½ kg
8 lb	3¾ kg
9 lb	4 kg
10 lb	4½ kg

★Approximate. To convert pounds into kilograms, multiply number of pounds by 453.6

CONVERSIONS OF FAHRENHEIT TO CELSIUS

Fahrenheit	Celsius
170°F	77°C★
180°F	82°C
190°F	88°C
200°F	95°C
225°F	110°C
250°F	120°C
300°F	150°C
325°F	165°C
350°F	180°C
375°F	190°C
400°F	205°C
425°F	220°C
450°F	230°C
475°F	245°C
500°F	260°C
525°F	275°C
550°F	290°C

★Approximate. To convert Fahrenheit to Celsius, subtract 32, multiply by 5, then divide by 9.

CONVERSION OF INCHES TO CENTIMETERS

Inches (in)	Centimeters (cm)
¹⁄₁₆ in	¼ cm*
⅛ in	½ cm
½ in	1½ cm
¾ in	2 cm
1 in	2½ cm
1½ in	4 cm
2 in	5 cm
2½ in	6½ cm
3 in	8 cm
3½ in	9 cm
4 in	10 cm
4½ in	11½ cm
5 in	13 cm
5½ in	14 cm
6 in	15 cm
6½ in	16½ cm
7 in	18 cm
7½ in	19 cm
8 in	20 cm
8½ in	21½ cm
9 in	23 cm
9½ in	24 cm
10 in	25 cm
11 in	28 cm
12 in	30 cm
13 in	33 cm
14 in	35 cm
15 in	38 cm
16 in	41 cm
17 in	43 cm
18 in	46 cm
19 in	48 cm
20 in	51 cm
21 in	53 cm
22 in	56 cm
23 in	58 cm
24 in	61 cm
25 in	63½ cm
30 in	76 cm
35 in	89 cm
40 in	102 cm
45 in	114 cm
50 in	127 cm

*Approximate. To convert inches to centimeters, multiply number of inches by 2.54.

INDEX

■ ● ▲